THE ⌐

DIVE
GUIDE

BRITISH
COLUMBIA

Nigei Island

Port Hardy

Seymour Channel
Quadra Island
Cortes Island
Campbell River
Courtenay
Comox
Comox Valley
Texada Island
Sechelt Inlet
Cumberland
Denman Island
Gambier Island
Hornby Island
Howe Sound
VANCOUVER
ISLAND
Nanaimo
Vancouver
Steveston

Barkley Sound
Thetis Island
San Juan Islands
Guemes Island
Sidney
Bellingham
Neah Bay
Sekiu
Victoria
Anacortes
Oak Harbor
Strait of Juan de Fuca
Lopez Island
Camano Island
Hat Island
Port Angeles
Port Townsend
Everett
Langley
Mukilteo
Whidbey Island
Edmonds
Hood Canal
Seattle
Hoodsport
Bremerton
Lake Washington
PACIFIC
OCEAN
Gig Harbor
Olympia
South Puget Sound
Tacoma
Vashon Island

WASHINGTON

Garibaldi
Depoe Bay

Newport

OREGON

Coos Bay

THE NORTHWEST
DIVE GUIDE

A Scuba Handbook for BC, Washington & Oregon

MIKE HUGHES

HARBOUR PUBLISHING

Harbour Publishing Co. Ltd.
P.O. Box 219, Madeira Park, BC, V0N 2H0
www.harbourpublishing.com

Cover photograph assemblage: kelp by Bernard P. Hanby and diver by Mike
Hughes. All interior photography by the author except where noted. Additional
photo credits: title page (old growth kelp), contents p. 6 (strawberry anenome) and
contents p. 7 (pink soft coral) by Bernard P. Hanby.
Edited by Betty Keller
Map by Roger Handling, Terra Firma Digital Arts
Printed on 10% PCW recycled stock using soy-based ink
Printed and bound in Canada

Caution: Every effort has been made to ensure the reader's awareness of the hazards
and level of expertise involved in the activities in this book, but your own safety
is ultimately up to you. The author and publisher take no responsibility for loss or
injury incurred by anyone using this book.

THE CANADA COUNCIL | LE CONSEIL DES ARTS
FOR THE ARTS | DU CANADA
SINCE 1957 | DEPUIS 1957

BRITISH
COLUMBIA
ARTS COUNCIL
Supported by the Province of British Columbia

Harbour Publishing acknowledges financial support from the Government of
Canada through the Book Publishing Industry Development Program and the
Canada Council for the Arts, and from the Province of British Columbia through
the BC Arts Council and the Book Publishing Tax Credit.

Library and Archives Canada Cataloguing in Publication

Hughes, Mike, 1956–
    The Northwest dive guide : a scuba handbook for B.C., Washington and
Oregon / Mike Hughes.

Includes index.
ISBN 978-1-55017-476-2

    1. Scuba diving—Northwest Coast of North America—Guidebooks.
2. Northwest Coast of North America—Description and travel. I. Title.
GV838.673.P32H83 2009   917.9504'44   C2009-900851-3

This book is dedicated to my wife,
Kristina Grace Hughes

CONTENTS

DIVING GEAR 72

DIVE DESTINATIONS

INTRODUCTION

The main purpose of this book is to get you excited about diving the cold yet beautifully bodacious waters of the Pacific Northwest, but my ultimate goal is that you will enjoy the scuba diving here so much that you'll share your experiences with your friends and neighbors and get them interested in scuba diving too. This said, however, *The Northwest Dive Guide* is also designed to fill the position of your own private master scuba dive instructor and Northwest diving tour guide. The book is divided into three major sections— Diver Training, Diving Gear and Dive Destinations—and is for all levels of divers who wish to extend their exploration of this watery planet we ironically call Earth.

Reading this book will give you an overview of the 350-plus dive sites in British Columbia, Washington State, Oregon, Idaho and Montana. If I don't mention all the sites, it's only a question of time and future editions. While reading an article about Comox or Victoria will give you basic information on a few of the 120-plus dive sites around Vancouver Island, a more precise book such as Betty Pratt-Johnson's *151 Dives in the Protected Waters of British Columbia & Washington State* (Adventure Publishing, 2007) will give you details about particular sites. Where this present book excels, however, is in informing you about dive resorts located near specific dive sites and the dive charters that service those areas. Not only will you meet the local operators and learn about the local dive resorts, but more importantly you will also get a feel for what to expect before you even start your next great dive adventure.

Cold-water diving is more gear-intensive than warm-water

diving, but extremely rewarding in terms of the abundance of wild-life and the panoramic beauty of their habitat above and below the waterline. I have, therefore, added training tips and mentioned dive gear that will make almost every future dive more enjoyable. Sometimes it's hard to separate the training from the gear involved, or the location from the training or gear involved, so some crossover categories will naturally occur.

And if you want a better idea of what you'll see when you dive the Pacific Northwest, pick up a fish identification book such as *Whelks to Whales* by Rick M. Harbo (Harbour, 2000), *Marine Life of the Pacific Northwest* by Andy Lamb and Bernard P. Hanby (Harbour, 2005) or *Coastal Fishes of the Pacific Northwest* by Andy Lamb with photos by Phil Edgell (Harbour, 1986; 8th printing 2008) and read about harbor seals, giant octopuses, gray whales and ultimately, as many have said, one of the best diving regions in the world.

Wolf-eels are typically very shy, but very photogenic.

ACKNOWLEDGEMENTS

I'll take this opportunity to thank a few people who have helped me reach this point in my dive career. I'd like to thank my brother Patrick Hughes for forcing me to take scuba diving lessons while we were living in Hawaii some 30 years ago. I'd like to thank my wife for putting up with my writing addiction and give a special thanks to Rick Stratton, president, CEO, publisher, editor-in-chief and fellow writer of *Northwest Dive News*, for so many article ideas, so many scuba dive-related things to learn and experience and so many deadlines to meet.

A special thanks also goes to: my first PADI open-water instructor in Hawaii, Carol Burger, in 1980; my advanced open-water instructor, Dave Peterson, in 1997 (yeah, it took 17 years and 500 dives to get my advanced diver card!); my divemaster instructor, Joe Brigham; my PADI course director, John Merrill, in 1998; my IANTD advanced Nitrox instructor, Don Kinney, in 2002; John Jensen for all his instruction on working with students and making me become a better dive instructor; and Ron Akeson, who taught me so much about tech diving, gas blending, regulator repair and diving in general. And thanks to all my other fellow dive instructors and divemasters, including but not limited to Tim Lade, Steve Lodge, Mike and Dolly Salvadore, Jerry Effenberger and to fellow master instructor and dive buddy Fred Doner.

Lastly, a special thanks to my editor, Betty Keller, who took some 105 articles and pieced them together into a cohesive, readable and interesting format, not to mention all the work she had to do with my spelling and grammar errors. And thank you to the entire team at Harbour Publishing.

Unless specifically mentioned, all photos were taken by me or one of the many thousands of dive buddies or spectators that I handed my camera to on split-second notice.

A special thanks goes to Andy Lamb and Bernie Hanby for reviewing the marine life content and to Bernie Hanby for contributing many artistically outstanding photos.

Puget Sound king crabs have short legs, but they have big and heavily armoured claws. LOU COX

DIVER TRAINING

The $99 Dive Course

It's hard to believe that it's been over 25 years since I first signed up for a dive class. My brother dragged me out of my downtown Honolulu apartment because he needed a dive buddy and because he wanted to do something more strenuous than sit on a sandy beach all day and gawk at the strangely adorned and continuous procession of tourists. The course fee of just $99 helped persuade me to join my brother and sign up for a two-week open-water dive course.

So how is it that during the last 25 years, when the price of gasoline, ski lift tickets and houses has tripled or quadrupled, you can still find promotional sales for beginning dive courses for as little as $99? How can any dive shop offer such a low-priced deal and still make enough profit to survive? As much as $50 of that fee goes straight to the dive instructor—approximately $25 for all the pool sessions and $25 for all the open-water dives. If you divide this amount by the number of students and the number of hours needed to fulfill the core requirements, you will quickly see that there are better ways to make money. However, there are few better ways to obtain the satisfaction an instructor receives by introducing others to the amazing world beneath the waves. The dive shop is left with just $49 to cover rental gear, air fills, pool fees and repairs on equipment. In fact, that amount doesn't even cover the cost of the shop staff assembling gear prior to the students' first pool session. What the $99 course fee does is bring new students into the dive shop where hopefully they will purchase masks, snorkels, fins, gloves and booties, along with a course book and materials. Of course, if the students purchase this equipment on-line or borrow from friends, the course could be a big bust for the dive shop.

As an instructor, I prefer my students to purchase from the dive shop for my own selfish reasons. First, on-line items may have strange clips and unfamiliar straps, and it will take extra time to deal with such isolated oddities. Fins purchased on-line may be cheap, but they may work like plywood in the water and lead to charley horses and leg cramps. It's hard to keep students together when one of them is floundering in the water due to inadequate gear.

Second, when a student is wearing used gear from a friend or relative, no matter how small the class there just isn't time to deal with 10-year-old fin straps waiting to break the minute he steps into the water or to struggle with a World War II dive mask that leaks like a sprinkler system. An old high-volume mask means the student

The *Juan de Fuca Warrior* departs almost daily from Ogden Point to Race Rocks.

will have to work harder to clear his mask, and an old snorkel that doesn't swivel out of the way or clear like the new semi-dry or dry snorkels means the student will have to fight with it every time he switches to his regulator. As an instructor, I want the beginning class to go as smoothly as possible and leave students with a positive experience. If they are wearing new gear or rental gear from the dive shop, I will be able to concentrate on teaching the benefits of selected dive gear rather than convincing students that even duct tape isn't going to fix their problems or that perhaps they should reschedule their dive course for some time after a suitable burial of their prehistoric rubberized artifacts.

Is the $99 course a good deal for everyone? Not necessarily. A $250 course that includes training in a drysuit may be the better option in the long run. Most Northwest divers who remain active with the sport eventually become drysuit divers, so being trained initially in a drysuit puts a student on the fast track for a lifelong passion for cold-water diving. Like most drysuit owners in the Northwest, I do own a wetsuit, and I diligently think about using it every time I go to Hawaii. Here at home, though, it's just nice to know that you could be wearing a tuxedo under your drysuit, and you would not only keep it dry until you walked out of the water and into the shoreline restaurant, but you would be warm the whole time too.

Say that you opted for an introductory dive course plus books for $150, then took a drysuit specialty course for $100 to $200. Being initially trained in a drysuit for $250 won't get you an extra drysuit specialty insignia or chevron unless you do more dives and pay more, but it does give you more training time both in the pool and open water. This is actually fun and the skills don't take that long to master. Oh, and did I mention that after training in a drysuit you'll be able to rent drysuits wherever available? Not all dive shops rent or train in drysuits, of course, so this option may not be available in your area and you might have to consider a dive course in Bellingham or south of Seattle.

To my mind, probably one of the greatest benefits of low-cost beginner dive courses or the special $99 dive course is the immediate appeal to people who are sitting on the fence and not sure if scuba diving is a sport they really want to explore. But at $99 it's worth the price to see if discovering the water world is for you. My brother used the low introductory price to get me off the beach and into the water, and in turn, I've spent half my life trying to get other people wet. Now I'm in favor of anything that will act as a catalyst to get people motivated to explore our watery planet. With some of the best diving in the world in our own backyard, we owe it to all our friends and family to try and get them wet too.

Your local dive shop may not become rich by offering such low-margin introductory courses, but they could bring in new divers, lifelong customers, future dive instructors and dive shop owners. . . and so the circle of adventure continues.

A Briefing for New and Returning Divers

If you're a brand new diver, new to the area, ready to get back into the water after a long dry spell or just want to have access to more dive buddies, dive sites and an endless supply of dive activities, then here is a list of things to do so you just can't miss.

Dive clubs

These are the best places to meet fellow diving enthusiasts. Depending on the size of the membership and the activities provided, for a small fee (usually less than $50) you'll get access to dive buddies and dive activities year-round. Don't let the size of the membership sway you, either. Small dive clubs can be just as active as some of the larger clubs and may give an added "family feel" to the experience. Also, don't limit yourself to one or two clubs if your diving needs are not being met. You might need three to four clubs-worth of activities to meet your personal aquatic addiction.

Most dive clubs have at least one club-sponsored dive a month, and their yearly calendar of events is either snail-mailed or emailed out to all members. The club itself typically meets once a month at a local dive shop, restaurant or tavern. The group may have elected officers and run a very organized meeting according to Robert's Rules of Order with guest speakers, slide shows and more, or it could consist of a bunch of laid-back divers who just get together to plan the next group dive. And then there are clubs whose organizational set-up falls somewhere between these two realms of nitrogenic bliss. Individual members may lead or host additional weekly or monthly dive excursions. Still other members may just post a name and number and the days they are free to go diving, such as "every Wednesday evening" or "Call anytime."

Dive clubs may have access to exclusive sites too. Some have cultivated arrangements to dive certain restricted areas where they procure or harvest sea creatures for aquariums or academic institutions. They may also be involved in semi-annual cleanup work around piers and other public locations usually closed to water activities. If you don't mind picking up old bottles and a little trash, you could dive some very interesting locations.

Periodicals

Each month the "Club Meetings and Activities" section of *North-west Dive News* displays a list of activities sponsored by dive shops, clubs and charter operations, as well as a plethora of meetings where groups discuss and plan for their next local dive or next year's great tropical adventure. You don't have to be a club member to go on every outing. In fact, most clubs will invite you to come along just

Right in front of the Red Lion Hotel in Port Angeles is a great beach and popular training area for new divers.

to see if you might like to join. So whether you see a club-sponsored event in *Northwest Dive News* or discover an activity on-line on a club or shop web site, just call them up and ask if you can come.

Dives sponsored by manufacturers are advertised in *Northwest Dive News, PADI Sport Diver, Scuba Diver* and other magazines. The annual DUI Dog Day Rally held nationwide is a good example. In Washington it's held at Owen Beach, Point Defiance Park in Tacoma and in Oregon at Newport.

The annual treasure hunt and scuba show sponsored by *Northwest Dive News* is another place to find a buddy, talk to dive industry representatives, possibly find some treasure and have fun. Some dive shops also sponsor annual events like underwater pumpkin-carving contests. Check the fliers displayed in dive shops, dive shop blackboards citing current events and local web sites.

Charters

If you are on a limited time schedule you may want to try dive charter operations or resorts. Their web sites generally have a monthly calendar of activities that will often point out the days they are scheduled to go out, as well as the names of dive groups they are taking out on a particular day and a dive group contact phone number. You can then contact either the group or the boat charter directly to see if any spots on the boat are still available. Keep in mind that most boats cater to advanced certified divers who are comfortable with local currents and conditions. South Puget Sound diving conditions are typically milder than north Sound areas except for destinations such as the Tacoma Narrows, but you'll have to dive the north end past the San Juan Islands to see all the varieties of creatures and underwater beauty the great Puget Sound truly has to offer. A bit of caution, though: once you've been exposed to the luxury and ease of boat diving, you may find it difficult to make a shore entry ever again.

Classes

One of the best ways to meet other divers is to take a continuing education course from your local dive shop. Not only do you gain knowledge and experience, but you will also have fun and meet fellow divers with similar interests in the sport. If you take an advanced class or equivalent course, you could be buddied up with several different divers over the duration of the dive portion of the course. If you meet a student you would like to dive with in the future, just trade business cards or put a phone number on the back of a dive slate. If you don't meet anyone you care to contact for a future dive, then sign up for a specialty course you would really like to try—underwater photography, deep diving, wreck diving, night diving or search and recovery. Haven't met enough contacts yet? Then enroll in a divemaster course. You will meet a pool full of potential future dive buddies every time a new open-water course begins. Be careful, however, as becoming a divemaster leads down the road to becoming a dive instructor, and once you become an instructor, you'll be too busy teaching and coordinating local and long-distance dive excursions to find the time for spur-of-the-moment fun dives without checking your monthly planner.

With local dive sites mere minutes away and Canadian waters just a few hours away, it's safe to say that Northwest divers have got it made. Just follow the four simple steps outlined above, add water and the rest is just a matter of time. Great dives!

Upgrade Your Skills

The best way to improve your diving skills is by diving, so you owe it to yourself to continue to upgrade your skills. You'll become a better and safer diver and more knowledgeable about dive gear and diving activities in general. If you just got an open-water certification card, I recommend that you sign up for the advanced certification course or something similar right away. If you wait a couple of months before you feel you are ready, chances are you will feel intimidated and never get around to it. The instructor will streamline your diving skills and give you pointers that will last you the rest of your dive career. An advanced diver course typically goes over fundamentals such as navigation, deep diving and at least three selected skill areas. The course is designed buffet style: you can sample different diving activities and later come back and take specialty courses that are designed around what you learned and what you found that really interests you. Dive clubs recommend all their members upgrade to rescue diver status or similar programs. At this level, not only are you confident about your own diving skills, but you can also be a great asset and help out other divers as well.

If you've been diving tropical waters or are unfamiliar with the local Northwest dive sites, upgrading your skills will help you to meet the people of your local dive shop as well as fellow students who may become future dive buddies. Through the courses you may discover new dive sites such as night diving in the Bruce Higgins Underwater Trails, deep diving off Mukilteo or wreck diving in British Columbia. You will also learn to use new gear such as drysuits, cameras, lift bags and reels.

Some perks that dive shops offer students when they upgrade to divemaster status and help out with new open-water students may include free air, storewide discounts and special dive activities. I used to go to Canada three times a year with fellow instructors and divemasters. The trips were all arranged by word of mouth and they filled up within a week. When you have the chance to dive with people you really respect and like working with, the diving doesn't get any better.

Another excellent opportunity to upgrade your dive skills may be presented by foreign travel without a buddy. A friend of mine

A thorough pre-dive briefing makes every dive comfortable, fun, safe and easy.

went to Vietnam and took a specialty dive course in nudibranchs. It's not that she was nuts about snails without shells, but by taking the course she was directed to all the cool local dive spots and learned a lot of new things from her overqualified dive buddy/instructor. Another of my friends did the same thing when he went to Florida. He wanted to check out the caves so he upgraded to a cavern diver in the process. The combinations of upgrading skills and travel destinations are endless. Currently, besides dozens of other popular dive course specialties, I'm the only instructor in the Northwest that I know of who is sanctioned to teach a marine reserve specialty course. My former instructor taught underwater sign language. It might be interesting for you to see what other courses your local dive instructors teach.

Finally, upgrading your skills can become an enjoyable lifelong process. Right now I'm a master instructor with a degree in marine biology, and I'm just finishing up a Nitrox gas blender course. I've got my eyes set on three other technical diving courses that I would love to complete within the next year or so. It seems the more you learn about our oceans and the world of diving, the more you want to know. Some say diving is like starting out by flying a kite and ending up a commercial airline pilot. You can take a few recreational dive courses to build up your skills and confidence, and the next thing you know you are a technical diver ready to descend on the *Titanic*. Well, maybe not quite that deep or technical, but you get the drift.

Some things to think about when upgrading:

1. When taking a dive course over a single weekend, you will need to calculate travel time and distance to dive sites.
2. Some courses require pre-qualifications or prior self-study.
3. Some courses may require you to provide dive lights, glow sticks, pony bottles or cool dive gear that you may carry around with you for the rest of your future dive adventures.
4. Upgrading may cause fatigue on Sunday nights due to dive group activities, fun and excitement.
5. The desire to wear a mask and snorkel may become addictive.

Enjoy your next upgrade course.

The Rescue/Stress Diver Upgrade

There comes a point in every diver's life when he really feels comfortable with his dive equipment and most diving conditions. To get to this point he may have taken an advanced diver course and gathered a few extra dives along the way or he may have logged hundreds of dives around the world. The next step in his continuing education is a course that puts other people's needs first. And I say "people's needs" rather than "diver's needs" because most of these courses teach you skills that you can use on land as well as in water.

There are many different names for this course depending on the agency that is giving it—sometimes it is called Rescue Diver Upgrade, sometimes Stress Upgrade. You might learn some up-to-date emergency techniques or have fun at the beach while role-playing to save "victims," but the best part is that the knowledge and experience you gain may someday save someone's life. Such knowledge might include basic first aid or even CPR using an automatic external defibrillator (AED). But your gift to someone else in the future doesn't necessarily have to include CPR or using an AED. Panic is one of the first things you learn to deal with in a rescue course. You'll learn how to inflate a panicked diver's buoyancy compensator for him in a way that prevents him from endangering you too, by either moving around behind him or by approaching him from underwater.

Your below-the-surface training will include how to help another diver stop, think and then problem solve. Practice scenarios will teach you how to assist other divers on the surface as well as different methods of towing another person back to shore. You'll learn how to address emergency situations such as preparing a search and rescue party, soliciting the aid of others and becoming familiar with the type of questions medical providers will want answers to in an emergency situation. This may also be the first time you have hands-on experience with oxygen bottles, continuous flow masks or setting up an oxygen delivery system and depending on the type of course offered, you may become CPR- and/or AED-certified. This type of aid can be vital to someone in need to avoid a tragic outcome.

I don't know how many people I've been able to help out over the years due to my own training, but I know I haven't helped as many as some of my rescue-certified students have. It's always good to hear how a former student helped a tired swimmer who was stuck on some rocks to get back to shore, calmed distressed divers so they could help themselves, gave someone in need a little oxygen or called for medical help and helped the responders save time by gathering critical information in advance.

I think a rescue course just makes you more aware of those around you and in turn makes you the kind of diver that everyone would like to have around. I know I'm not the only one who feels this way because some dive clubs give discounts, membership credit or special recognition to members who have become rescue-, stress-, or emergency-qualified divers. However, the best benefit by far has to be the feeling you get when you are able to help a fellow human when they really need help the most.

To find out more about this and other dive upgrade programs, visit your local dive shop or contact a dive instructor today. You never know when someone on the beach or walking down the street will thank you for not putting off this course one more day.

Dive Buddy Savvy

A while ago I went on a weekend retreat sponsored by a dive club, and just before we headed down to the water decked out in our gear, I was asked to buddy up with a woman member. I was new to the club and didn't know anyone so I didn't mind who I was teamed up with. I just wanted to get underwater and take pictures. I asked the woman the usual questions about how much diving she had done lately, and she gave me a vague answer then said she used to dive all the time. We were standing in our gear ready to go, so I didn't pursue the subject. This was my first mistake. I also assumed that everyone in the club was experienced and comfortable with diving. This assumption proved to be my second mistake.

As we put our masks and fins on in the water, I noticed she seemed a little slow putting hers on, but after we did a gear check on the surface, the two of us descended underwater. It didn't take long to see that she was totally uncomfortable with the entire situation.

She was slow to reply to my "Are you okay?" signal and she moved her body very slowly with her eyes wide open staring at everything. She finally signaled that she was okay, but the fear on her face told me otherwise. I turned off my camera and swam up next to her, but when I pointed towards shore, she didn't want to go in that direction, so we spent some time diving around an adjacent rock formation. While she looked at the local inhabitants, I kept one eye on her pressure gauge and my other eye on her.

Her eyes eventually reduced to a more normal size and she started taking deeper and slower breaths. I noticed that she wasn't going through her air supply as quickly as before, and she even appeared to be having a good time looking at all the tiny creatures. Then by mutual consent we descended to a depth of 20 feet and I checked her air pressure again. We spotted an octopus hiding within a crevice. . . well, to be exact, we saw one of its arms slither back into the dark recess. . . and I checked her air supply again and found she had already gone through half her tank. I motioned for us to return to shore and she acknowledged my request with an affirmative nod. We took our time making our way back to shore, and she left the water after thanking me for being her buddy and apologizing for not giving me a chance to take pictures. I told her I had a good time, but I really felt like I had just been put through a very precarious and unanticipated potential dive-buddy-rescue scenario.

After she went to the women's showers, one of the other club members came up and thanked me for diving with her. He said she had spent some time in a decompression chamber a year earlier and this was the first time she had got up enough nerve to go back into the water. They hadn't been sure if she would ever go back in again. I felt like the village idiot when I heard this. When you get hooked up with another diver, you don't think about worst-case scenarios. You can anticipate being partnered up with someone a little rusty, but not with someone prepared to bolt for the surface at the first sign of distress.

When you dive with a variety of people on a regular basis I've found that you can't afford to bypass the little details. You might want to think about what you want to do on the dive and hope your assigned buddy won't slow you down, make you move too fast or alter your plans in any way. However, when it comes right down to it, if you are diving with a buddy, your responsibility for her overall safety and welfare supersedes all the personal goals, desires and plans you had in mind.

In the end, I find the best part about every dive is the conversation you and your buddy have about your just-completed underwater experience. These conversations start the very minute you break the surface after the dive and continue whenever you remember good times.

Solo Diving

My father was a solo diver back in the late fifties when all you had to do was borrow or buy some used scuba gear and you were good to go. This was in the days of the J-valve tank. When the air pressure in the tank got low and the air became harder to breathe, you knew it was time to pull on the metal rod that connected to the tank valve, and if the valve hadn't already become accidentally engaged, you had another 300 to 500 psi of air left in your tank to make it back to the surface. This was before air gauges, quick release harnesses, buoyancy compensators (BCs) and other dive-gear innovations had come along to make scuba diving a considerably safer sport.

One of the first things to make diving safer was making it mandatory for all divers to show evidence that they had been properly trained before they could get their air tanks refilled. Rather than submit to a certification program, divers like my father, who had already been diving for some time, quit diving for the next 30 years, but the improved level of training as well as the safety performance of equipment did begin to make

The giant stride is quick to master and a favorite method for divers to abandon a perfectly good boat.

it a safer sport. Training agencies promoting the buddy system also helped to make it safer and reduced the number of dive-related fatalities. Some destinations such as Edmonds Underwater Park instituted a potential $1,500 fine for diving without a buddy, and the safety record at the park increased after this was introduced.

One thing that hasn't changed over the years is the debate over solo versus buddy diving. Even back in the early days, if you were talked into going on a dive you weren't comfortable with or a dive you wouldn't even dream of attempting on your own, you might have been lulled or pushed into thinking that it was safe to dive if done with a buddy or in the company of others. This is one of the issues that still lingers over the world of sport diving: no matter how perfect all the gear and technical innovations are, only you know if you are ready for the next dive. Technical divers go even further and state that if at any time and for any reason a diver wants to end a dive, that dive is ended with no questions asked.

As a technical diver I plan every dive as a solo dive. Although I prefer to dive with others and I enjoy their company, if my buddies alter the planned depth or dive time, I may not be able to remain with them. Each tech diver has to follow a strict set of dive tables and can ascend only at appropriate rates for pre-calculated sets of timed intervals. Ascending too late, diving too deep or shortening the decompression stops is not an option. Once the dive has begun and my buddy chooses to change her dive plan, I could find myself decompressing at the end of the dive as a solo diver.

Tech divers prepare for such solo diving situations by using redundant dive gear. You'll see them wearing dual tanks on their backs with two independent first and second stage regulators, stage bottles with independent regulator systems, backup reels, lift bags, dual bladder buoyancy compensators and maybe even a spare mask tucked away in a pocket. Recreational divers, on the other hand, depend on backup gear attached to a buddy.

Some may argue that diving with a buddy is safer than diving solo, but I think that it depends on your particular buddy. One who stays close by and has the same level of training or diving skills as you do may prove to be an asset if assistance is required, whether it is for sharing air, retrieving a lost weight belt or just catching crabs. If buddies routinely signal to each other how much air is in their tanks and they both remain alert, they'll both avoid any unexpected diving situations or aquatic inconveniences.

An unfocussed buddy, on the other hand, could be a liability. What do you do if your buddy shoots down beneath the waves like a rocket? Do you go after him? And if you do, down to what maximum depth do you search? What if your buddy power-kicks his way into a thick forest of kelp? Do you follow this irresponsible diver who may be putting your life at risk too, without a single thought? And what if you and your buddy plan a dive, but your buddy decides for some reason not to dive the plan? He has just effectively made you a solo recreational diver. I've had it happen to me a couple of times. One of the last times it happened, I looked around for a minute before I surfaced then called out to the boat crew. They just said, "Oh, that's just Frank (name changed)! He does that all the time. Don't worry about him. He'll show up."

I've had some very interesting dive buddies over the past 28 years and I'd like to dive with most of them again, but a few have been prime examples of when and under what circumstances solo diving may be safer than buddy diving. If you have the right equipment, the right training and 100 previous dives logged, solo diving may be right for you too. And just as enriched air (Nitrox) was shunned in the early days by the large recreational training agencies that later came around to embrace it and teach courses using increased levels of oxygen in air mixtures, solo diving will lose its negative stigma. Then through specialty education, such as the SDI solo diver course, it will be embraced with understanding, respectability and unbiased acceptance.

On a lighter note, I've lived less than 20 minutes from popular dive sites for over half my life, my tanks are always filled (since I'm a dive instructor) and I could dive every day of the week, but I don't. If I have a mission such as retrieving car keys, trying out a new piece of dive equipment or taking photos for a magazine, then I don't mind wearing my tech dive gear and going solo. But in my mind I don't consider these types of activities diving; I consider them work. Diving is an experience to be shared with others. Seeing a giant octopus with a buddy is not only fun, but it creates shared memories that you can talk about for the rest of your lives. For some, being a certified solo diver may suit them well, but for others, joining a club or tagging along with other divers is the only way to enjoy the overall scuba experience. Perhaps that's why I'm sitting here writing this instead of heading down to the beach solo like my dad.

P.A.N.I.C.

Depending on what accredited dive instruction course you attended, you most likely became familiar with a few tried and true acronyms. Now here's one more to add to your list with the sole purpose of helping you avoid what the upper case letters spell out.

P is for Prepared.

Diving is all about being prepared. On every dive it's critical to do a buddy check and make sure you have the right gear for the right dive. Does your buddy have an alternate air source? How and where is it clipped on? Do each of you know where to place your hands and arms while assisting in an out-of-air situation and have you practised the current donor and receiver techniques? Do you know how to release your buddy's weight belt? If your buddy is wearing a drysuit, do you know how and where to disconnect the air intake valve and is the zipper really closed all the way? Just a slight leak in a drysuit can make an unprepared diver suddenly bolt for the surface, and an open zipper can make a diver panic on the surface, forget to inflate his BC or even release his weight belt.

To a seasoned diver a sudden sharp surge of chilled water in a drysuit is an inconvenience that can't be ignored, but there is no reason to panic. You may even realize what is happening and unwisely want to dive a little longer, even with that flooded drysuit, before returning to shore or the boat. However, you can't avoid the increasingly chilled feeling as the heat from your body is conducted to the cold water, and you have no logical option other than to get out of the water before the first signs of hypothermia set in.

Pressing the valves and putting a little air into the drysuit is a good way to buddy-check and confirm that drysuit valves are connected and working properly. The same goes for your BC. Prior to entering the water is the best time to check everything before you really need things to perform properly at a later critical juncture.

A is for Aware.

First, knowing where your buddy is at all times is critical since he is essentially carrying your backup air supply (and possibly the keys to the car), but more importantly he is your second pair of eyes and ears. Second, being aware of the surrounding environment is just as important as knowing where your buddy is located. You can spend the entire dive avoiding discarded fishing line and watching for signs of changes in the current and the movements of stinging jellies, but if you let your guard down too soon, you may still get knocked over by a rogue wave as you step out of the water.

N is for Neutral Buoyancy.

If you are under-weighted and you are wearing aluminum tanks, you might find yourself floating as your air supply nears depletion (500 psi) at the end of the dive. This could frustrate your attempts to remain submerged to perform a decompression stop. On the other hand, a diver weighted too much could shoot downward like an anchor, giving him little time to clear his ears or sinuses. Weighted correctly, a diver can descend like a slowly falling leaf, giving him plenty of time to equalize and set up a camera system as well as keep an eye on a buddy and the surrounding environment. This technique also allows him to come to a stop easily or just hover above the substrate, thus avoiding unwanted abrasions, cuts and environmental faux pas.

I is for Instruments.

Checking your instrument gauges before the dive is always a good idea. If your depth gauges, air pressure gauges and bottom timers are battery-operated, you don't want to dive to 110 feet only to find yourself looking at blank screens and realizing you need new batteries. Never letting the air pressure in your tank drop below 500 psi gives you a good window of safety and reduces the margin of error. If your pressure gauge reads 3,000 psi on the surface but only 50 psi after you descend to 20 feet, chances are your tank isn't turned on all the way—or more likely it is barely cracked open. If you are ascending at the end of your dive and only have 50 psi left in your tank, you haven't been monitoring your air consumption or repeatedly verifying air pressure readouts with your buddy. Perhaps you have just started to hyperventilate, or your pressure gauge could be off by as much as 200 or 300 psi, or your tank could be leaking. No matter the reason, you need to get to your buddy to share air immediately. If I'm with a buddy who doesn't like to check his remaining air pressure on a regular basis, I'll usually unobtrusively check it for him and then pick a new buddy for my next dive. There's no need to worry about an out-of-air situation when routine monitoring can help avoid that situation entirely.

C is for Control.

You may not have complete control over the environment, but you can have control over your own actions within it. I once witnessed a diver with another group who had run out of air when he was down at 100 feet. He shared air with a member of our group and after we surfaced he told us that he thought his computer automatically allowed an extra 300 psi of air when the instrument read 0 psi. Why anyone would go so deep without extra air for a safety stop was another separate issue, but this guy's ill-conceived logic made him a panic case waiting for a place to happen.

If you plan your dive and dive your plan, you'll have great control over each dive and the possibility of panic situations will greatly be reduced or minimized to almost non-existence. Altering the depth descended or time spent at depth by just a few increments can alter your entire dive profile, your overall perceived amount of control, possibly add a mandatory safety stop and reduce your margin of extra air.

Dive manuals always say that to avoid panic you must stop and think before committing to an action, but if you adhere to the acronym PANIC, you can avoid what it stands for.

Northwest Diving is Cold

Whales and seals have blubber to thermally insulate them from the outside environment, but my excess fat tends to concentrate around my waist, which doesn't necessarily keep my chest area insulated when I plunge into the water. In Hawaii and the Caribbean I'll cheat and wear a 3-mm neoprene body suit when I go diving. Not only does this type of wetsuit keep the jellies from ever touching my skin, but it also keeps me warm enough for a few dives or a couple of hours, whichever comes first.

In colder or deeper water divers gravitate towards 7-mm suits, which will probably keep them warm for the first dive, but might be pushing it to wear it for any extended period of time or return to the water for a second dive. Besides, 7-mm suits are thick and stiff and you feel like Gumby trying to flex your legs and arms. This fact could explain why I find so much dive gear lying on the beach. If a wetsuit diver drops a light in the sand, he may just leave it there because it just takes too much effort to bend over in thick, inflexible material to pick up an object. Besides, after a long dive all wetsuit divers want to do is hurry back to their cars and get warmed up.

Below is a list of tips I gathered from other divers or learned the hard way. You may not need any of them to make it through a single cold-water dive, but adding extra warmth even on one dive can make a world of difference towards extending your dive time, remaining comfortable and building your overall level of enjoyment.

- Drink plenty of warm, non-caffeinated liquids prior to and between dives. A thermos of hot cocoa or herbal tea should do the trick.
- Carry a five-gallon insulated container of hot water to be applied liberally on exposed or cold body parts after or between dives. This feels especially good when poured on wet hair and hands, and down the front and back of your wetsuit.
- After any dive take off your wet hood and gloves and dry off quickly. Try to avoid strong winds too. You probably remember from your open-water course that water conducts heat away from the body 25 times faster than air. Getting dry can play a crucial role in your level of comfort, especially if you are intending to make a second aquatic excursion.
- Get plenty of sleep the night before the big dive. Lack of sleep or being jet-lagged can contribute tremendously towards a feeling of coldness and the onslaught of some of the first symptoms of hypothermia—shivers and goose bumps.
- Never give in to the primordial urge to relieve yourself in your wetsuit. The abrupt, warm, tingling sensation widens

blood vessels and capillaries and allows vast amounts of body heat to be suddenly released into the surrounding cold water. The net resulting heat exchange is negative . . . not to mention the long-term social effect and the increasing level of outright displays of avoidance behavior by fellow divers.

- Hot soup and hand warmers can go a long way towards keeping you warm. Hand warmers can be electrically or chemically activated. Hot soup can be pre-made and carried in an insulated container, or it can be cooked right on the beach over a gas camp stove inside a wind resistant three-sided tent and served in a fine china bowl. Of course, thick wetsuits are great if you only dive a few times a year, but hey, we are talking about the Northwest where diving is spectacular year-round. A little snow on the ground during the winter months shouldn't deter you from viewing purple cabezon eggs in 100-foot visibility. And when you're wearing a drysuit, you can be warm and toasty from the moment you suit up until the moment you unzip. In fact, you can actually find yourself sweating in a drysuit if you dress too warmly.

When people first come into a dive store, they tend to gravitate toward the wetsuits. I don't blame them. Wetsuits are less expensive, but in some cases a low-end model drysuit can be purchased for just a few hundred dollars more. While some new divers purchase wetsuits and dive for less than a year before drifting away from the sport except while on vacation in tropical waters, new divers who purchase drysuits tend to dive often and end up lifelong divers. They also join dive clubs, travel all over the Northwest, meet other committed divers and make lifetime friends.

Some dive shops train their new open-water students in drysuits. If you can find one of these facilities nearby, I highly recommend going this route. If you are initially trained in a drysuit, by the time you are certified you will be proficient as a drysuit diver and ready to purchase one as well. And if you've been out of the water for a while, this option also makes a great refresher course.

If you're already a certified diver, try to find a shop that rents drysuits. The only catch will be that they won't rent you one unless

Sea lions charge outrageous fees to work as divemasters and usually prefer to just hang around buoys.

you have proof that you already know how to use it; it's a well-founded liability issue. However, they may offer drysuit training for a reasonable fee depending on instructor availability. The final method of making the move into a drysuit is just to take the plunge and purchase a new drysuit along with pool time and/or open-water instruction.

Drysuit divers have it easy keeping warm. All they have to do to increase the heat is to add extra layers of clothes, polyester long johns or state-of-the-art non-cotton apparel. I've been known to head to the water straight from the airport wearing business attire and don my drysuit. The only thing I take off is my tie and black shoes. Provided that I zip up correctly, I can be guaranteed almost 100 percent warmth and dryness and totally disregard local weather conditions.

When you decide to advance to drysuit status, don't forget to upgrade to dry gloves too. This way the only part of your body ever to get exposed to water will be your face and the hair under your hood. However, there are dry hoods on the market now if you really want to make sure that only your cheeks and lips get wet during a dive, and wearing a full face mask will even keep your lips dry.

Use argon gas instead of air inside your drysuit. Argon is touted to keep you 10 percent warmer than air insulation. I put argon gas inside my drysuit every chance I get, even if it means coming up to a fellow diver and asking for a hit right into my drysuit intake valve. Not only does this dense gas keep you warmer but also it depresses undesirable urinary urges.

If all else fails or you have plenty of extra money to figuratively burn, then invest in an electrical heating pad system that fits right inside your drysuit.

Gaining weight can add insulation and therefore warmth, but I prefer other more conventional options. If you don't feel appreciably warmer after following any or all of the above tips, then perhaps you are one of the few true blue-blooded tropical divers. There's nothing wrong with being an all-inclusive warm-water diver, but you will miss out on a chance to dive with harbor seals, giant octopuses, wolf-eels, thousands of rockfish and swimming scallops and miss the chance to come face to face with a rainbow trout or have a close encounter with a playful juvenile gray whale. I don't guarantee that you'll see any or all of these miraculous sea creatures as you glide through cold waters, but I do know that you will stay warmer if you follow even some of the aforementioned tips, and that in itself should make your next underwater adventure more fun and memorable.

Ice Diving:
The Ultimate Cold-water Rush

I'm not going to sugar-coat it and say that ice diving is for everyone, but if you are always looking for a new dive experience or point of view while thriving on a planet composed mostly of water, then ice diving might be an adventure worth exploring. And if you've ever watched a *National Geographic* special on life under the polar ice, you will know how spectacular the ice world is. This is a sport where the planning can involve hours, but the actual dive may only last 20 minutes. So why go? Well, apart from the knowledge gained by the experience, you'll encounter fish and see aquatic terrains that are typically obscured by plankton during warmer seasons. You'll discover search and recovery methods that can be used any time of year, and most importantly you'll learn what it's like to dive with a limited overhead environment of solid ice.

Of course, to take advantage of the ice environment you should be comfortable with night diving, deep diving and underwater navigation, and you should have a minimum of 9 to 20 logged dives (depending on your instructional agency). You will also need to take a course that will prepare you for the equipment and communications to be used as well as the safety procedures.

Here in the Northwest it's surprisingly hard to find active ice dive locations. Bud Gray from Bubbles Below dive shop in Woodinville had a few instructors who previously took groups to Alaska to do the course, but the ice isn't as thick there as it used to be, so those locations have been abandoned. Several years ago when I was a scoutmaster, my troop and I came across an opening made by ice divers on Fish Lake close to the Cove Resort boat launch near Wenatchee, but I was recently told that that site hasn't been used for a few years. And six or seven years ago James Mankin of the Scuba Center in Spokane took a group of six divers to Davis Lake, 45 minutes north of the dive shop. James said the water felt like 24°F. They had 40 feet of visibility under the 10 to 14 inches of ice, but the fish were down deep, hiding and hibernating. The divers also found crayfish (crawdads) in a dormant state.

Earl Norton, an instructor out of Eugene Skin Divers dive shop, recently started taking groups of divers up to Diamond Lake, an hour away from Roseburg, Oregon. The first year he went with two other divers, the second year he had six divers interested. The ice was 12 inches thick with four or five inches of snow on top of it. The water was a balmy 34°F. Earl says the site is close enough for a day trip but you can spend the night in accommodation in Roseburg. With the extra snowfall as a top layer, he reports that it is dark underneath the ice, and you have to use lights to see anything at all. Apparently all the divers involved enjoyed the experience and plan to return. I think this could become an annual event.

Ice diving sounds easy when you're told that all you have to do is cut a hole in the ice and dive in, but in reality some groups spend an entire day just cutting out the necessary large, triangular hole. First, you need to find ice greater than eight inches thick. Then you have to don crampons or spikes on your dive boots and sprinkle sand on the ice to get traction and wear a rope and harness over your dive suit in case you fall in while using a chainsaw to cut through the ice. Earl explains that they use Saffola oil to lubricate the chain and not harm the environment. They also shovel off the snow that is on top of the ice in a 100-foot wagon wheel spoke grid around the entrance hole so that the lighter areas of the grid lines will help divers find their way back to the center opening. Just preparing the entry site can be hard work, and everyone has to keep warm without perspiring during this phase.

The dive equipment must consist of environmentally sealed regulators (regs), independent first-stage air sources and harness. There is always the chance of one reg freezing up at the surface or at depth as greater flow demands affect their performance too. With air consumption the divers typically follow the rule of thirds with one-third of their air always left in reserve. For hands-on training, divers use ropes attached to each other to lead the way underwater, and a surface tender communicates with them via rope tension and pulls. It's also a good idea to have two divers on the surface all suited up and ready to go as backup safety persons.

Your instructor will explain why dive times are adjusted by 10 feet or more on nitrogen charts when diving at altitude and how air consumption is also affected by metabolic rate in cold environments. You will also need to know the signs and symptoms of hypothermia and what to do about it. I have by no means listed every requirement for a safe ice dive, but my intent here is to let you know that it is only after the serious business of selecting the dive site and planning the dive that an ice diver in training can safely experience a world covered by ice that is seldom seen or visited by others.

Weight Placement

Some divers think of weight placement as a theory that needs to be constantly tested and altered according to the local diving conditions and the type of equipment they are using. Others feel that it is more like a theology, and it's going to take a leap of faith before they try a different weight system or placement. Having used nothing but lead weight belts for the first 15 years of my dive career, I will admit that I was slow to convert. But now that I've seen the light, my waist and back are not as sore and my margin of safety has arguably increased.

Weights are needed to offset the lift generated by the volume of water displaced by your body. If you don't wear enough weight, you'll float like a duck. If you wear too much, you'll sink like a rock or waste tons of air trying to inflate your buoyancy compensator device (BC) just to float, let alone maintain a level of control while moving up and down the water column. To see if I'm weighted properly, whenever I change my dive gear setup, I like to dive down at least six feet with only a reserve amount of 500 pounds of air in my tank and test how little weight it really takes to keep me from lifting off the substrate.

The other important factor in the buoyancy equation is weight placement. Not only should the placement make the weights comfortable to wear but in most cases it should also allow you to come to rest horizontally in the water column as you glide, kick or remain stationary while taking underwater photos. Moving through the water at a slight angle to the horizontal causes laminar flow resistance and forces you to work harder to maintain a specific depth. If your head and torso are tilted slightly downward, you will constantly swim slightly downward. If your legs and fins are tilted slightly lower than the horizon, then you are in effect constantly swimming upward as well as kicking up an excessive amount of sand and silt with every fin kick.

Lead weight belts have been used in one fashion or another for many hundreds of years, so it's no surprise that some divers will only wear what is tried and true (as well as what costs the least) no matter how uncomfortable. Soft-sided weight belts such as the SeaSoft brand did much to change the image of the uncomfortable weight belt, but the biggest change of all came with the advent of the weight-integrated BC. Now you could put all your lead weights right into the special BC pockets set up to rapidly release their contents if required. On some models of integrated BCs the pockets even allow you to adjust the placement of the weight to help make you float horizontally underwater. With these introductions the diver no longer needs a weight belt; the only weights he might need—apart from that in his weight-integrated BC—are ankle weights. But there has been a big change here too.

Ankle weights are to diving what training wheels are to bicycling, so it was dive instructors like myself who wanted to get students comfortable with their new drysuits as quickly as possible who helped make ankle weights popular. They get students into the water quickly, keep them from frequently turning upside down and reduce the number of times new divers with too much air in their drysuits float feet first toward the surface. As they get more dives under their belts, they find it easier to get the excess air out of their drysuits, and they also find it easier to roll out of those awkward upside-down positions. However, it's not uncommon to see divers with more than 100 dives under their belts still wearing ankle weights, oblivious to the fact that their feet tend to sink lower than the rest of their bodies when they try to remain motionless underwater. They just never got around to taking off their training wheels (ankle weights) and have no idea that they don't really need them anymore. They are just stuck in a bad habit. And I have to admit I was one of these divers too, until I took a tech diving class and they made me give up my ankle weights. It was almost as traumatic as giving up a favorite childhood blanket. Of course, there

Dive classes are a great place to meet other divers.

are some situations where ankle weights are still appropriate. If you have valves on the ankles of your drysuit that let out air whenever your legs rise above your body, you need ankle weights. If your fins are positively buoyant, you might need ankle weights. And if you feel naked without them, this might be still another (although questionable) reason to keep using ankle weights.

It's interesting to note that during the late 1990s some dive schools required their students to learn how to dive using a weight belt, even if they had purchased weight-integrated BCs and never planned to use a weight belt after completion of their diver certification course. And it really did look as if cold-water divers who carried upwards of 40 pounds of weight in their BC's pockets would never use a dive belt again. Warm-water divers who carried as little as 12 pounds of lead could go either with an integrated BC or carry a light weight belt if that's what the local tropical dive shop kept in stock.

However, the next wave of change saw the placement of weights in separate locations. Divers began to wear 20- to 25-pound weight belts plus another 16 to 21 or more pounds of weight in the pockets of their integrated BCs. This system makes the tank and integrated BC lighter and therefore easier to lift and put on. The separation of weights also keeps the catastrophic failure of a weight belt system down to a minimum; if the 20-pound weight belt slips off accidentally, the diver won't shoot to the surface as fast and as out of control as he would if he were wearing only a 40-pound belt. Another reason for separating weight involves higher levels of training. As recreational divers train to become tech divers, they can standardize their gear configuration by adjusting where they place their weights. Let's say that as a tech diver you have two 100-cubic-foot steel tanks with a 15-pound lead weight bar that fits snugly between your dual tank system. You also wear a 25-pound weight belt. For a recreational diver, you use this same 25-pound weight belt and add 16 pounds of weight to your integrated BC pockets. Now you have one weight belt that can be used for every dive while the rest of the necessary weight is already set up for whichever type of dive adventure you want to go on next.

Lately the move is once again away from weight belts to new products such as the DUI weight and trim system. It looks a lot like a weight belt, but the attached shoulder straps take the weight off the hips and keep it from ever slipping down the sides of the body. The two pockets each hold up to 20 pounds of lead, which can be released independently to control the rate of an emergency ascent.

> **For more information about weight placement systems:**
> www.dui-online.com
> www.customdivetech.com

Custom Dive Tech has made the next logical step by stitching 12 pounds of soft lead weight into the back of a trim vest that has two side waist pockets that can each carry up to 15 pounds of weight. For emergency purposes these side weight pockets may be independently released. This method seems closer to the weight separation method employed by tech divers, and it uses part of the weight as a comfortable back cushion while taking some of it off the lower back. It's the best weight system I've seen to date. Layering gear just like layering outdoor clothing lessens the weight and stress and ensures that even infrequent divers have a good experience gearing up.

Keeping 45lbs of weight off your ankles is a good thing. DUI WEIGHT AND TRIM SYSTEM, DIVING UNLIMITED, INC.

Although I've mentioned several weight systems and placements, the final decision on your own weight placement is up to you. Unless you ask someone else to check your weight placement and how level you are when suspended motionless underwater, you may feel you are level and horizontal, but you'll never know for sure. A buddy may be the last person to ever give you any constructive advice because she might not want to offend you or be too busy catching crabs. However, dive instructors would be good candidates to ask because their overriding goal is to make you a better diver. If by adjusting and moving a few lead weights from here to there or removing ankle weights you can gain the ability to remain horizontally motionless underwater, your air intake will reduce so that a tank of air will last longer, less silt will be kicked up by your fins and your ability to relax and enjoy your next dive will only increase.

A Passion for Compasses

Just as you wouldn't dream of getting into a car without first knowing where you are going, a good diver always checks and sets her compass before diving into the water. It is like looking at the map before heading down the road. How can anyone drive or dive a plan without first knowing where they are going and how to get there?

On a night dive it's easy to remember to set your compass and write down the readings. It's during the day when the sun is out and you can see the shoreline or look up and see the outline of the boat that it's easy to forget to use your compass. You need to remind yourself that during summer it's not uncommon to find yourself swimming through a plankton bloom where visibility can drop to just past the tip of your nose. Other times you may descend on a clear day, but by the time you ascend, fog has rolled in and the nearby shoreline or the familiar boat outline is nowhere to be seen. A compass also comes in handy when you find the perfect wreck, reef or hunting area. If you make a note of the site by using your compass, you'll be able to relocate it quickly and easily any time you desire.

If you've only used a compass a few times in the past or if you misplaced your compass somewhere along with your Ouija board, tarot cards and sundial, then it might be time for a refresher course. Most advanced courses include at least one navigation dive that goes a little past the basics. A navigation specialty course will cover the basics, but you'll also learn how to dive square and triangular patterns as well as search and recovery grid patterns such as the expanding square and continuous U. Using the U pattern has saved me hundreds in lost camera lenses, masks, flashlights and other assorted dive gear.

Another benefit of using your compass on every dive is that not only will you know where you are at all times, but you will also be much more in tune with how the currents are affecting your overall underwater position, much like having a built-in GPS locater. You'll soon be unconsciously correcting for cross currents as you navigate and making course corrections as you make your way towards your intended destination. Referring to a compass throughout the dive ensures that if your navigation is affected by magnetic anomalies such as metal and iron wrecks or buried treasure, you won't be caught off guard. Last but not least, a diver who routinely checks his compass throughout the dive is also the type of diver who is more likely to check his depth and air pressure gauges on a more frequent basis too.

Good habits like wearing and frequently checking a dive compass mean being prepared for almost any event; there's nothing worse than dealing with a situation when you don't even know where you are. (Perhaps that's why so many people who wake up in a strange bed in a dark hotel room feel panic-stricken until they are able to locate a light switch.) And while anyone can get turned around underwater while viewing the scenery, knowing which direction is shore or where to find the boat can be self-empowering and make you a more secure and confident diver. It's also nice to know that your good habits may just make you a desirable, if not high-in-demand, dive buddy.

Dive Flags

Do you know your local dive flag rules and regulations? If not, you could end up paying a small fine or, in some Washington State counties, even wind up with a misdemeanor charge. This will lead to a mandatory court date, possible jail time and/or a hefty fine. The word "misdemeanor" means "lesser crime," the kind of crime associated with sentences of less than a year in prison or perhaps no jail time at all unless you have more than one misdemeanor charge on your record. Now I'm not an attorney, but this seems to put scuba diving without a flag right up there with prostitution and petty theft. As ridiculous (or serious) as that sounds, an officer of the law who witnesses your failure to use a dive flag may not be able to let you off with just a warning, especially if you are endangering yourself or others. Keep in mind too that any time you dive near fishermen, fishing lines or boaters in general, if those affected are not happy with your scuba manners or questionable dive behavior, they can complain to the police. So it is just safer and better in the long run to have a dive flag visible. It is also good to remember that ignorance of the rules is no excuse in the eyes of the law and more importantly, ignorance has no place in a safe dive plan.

There are two kinds of dive flags. The white diagonal line across the red background on the diver's flag—acquired from an old navy flag that signaled "danger"—denotes the location and, depending on state and county rules, may also denote that divers are directly below or within a 25-, 50- or 100-foot radius. The blue and white "alpha" flag is a United States federal requirement for boats working with divers and signals that the boat has limited mobility due to divers in the water. It doesn't point out where the divers are located, just that the boat is tending to divers.

Commercial boat operators know about the alpha flag and most likely the dive flag too, but the local boater who got his craft for nothing down and $99 per month may not have a clue about either of them. In Washington State a boater education course and the associated boater's card, which both mention dive flags, are not required of all state boaters until January 1, 2016, and until then, depending on your age, boating is a right, not a privilege like driving. Therefore, if your craft floats and you can get it to travel somewhere at less than the speed of sound, you can still be a recreational sailor. In British Columbia's waters, divers must use the alpha flag when diving from a boat, but use of the red and white dive flag is encouraged but not legally required. However, Canada is seven years ahead of Washington State with its boater card program; as of September 15, 2009, all boat operators there will have completed the Pleasure Craft Operators Certification program and will have gained some knowledge of divers and dive flags. Currently, Canada allows non-resident boaters to visit the country for less than 45 consecutive days provided that they have proof of boater competency from another country or state. Once boat operators on both sides of the international border are educated and carrying certification cards, boat accidents and incidents involving divers should decrease.

But going back to the diver's side of responsibility, let's say you are diving near Octopus Hole on the Hood Canal in Mason County, Washington, without a dive flag. Chances are an officer of the law might be magnanimous and just give you a warning for not using a dive flag. But what if, while you are diving, a boat comes along and parks right above your dive location? The level of possible personal injury has just gone way up. Now an officer might be inclined to give you an autograph that includes consequences.

In the past two years I know of only two occasions on which a ticket was issued. The first involved a pair of divers with no dive plan who got separated underwater. One of them made his way back to shore and called 911. However, after the local search and rescue team and another 75 people who serve in different rescue capacities had been alerted and the rescuers had raced at 80-plus mph down narrow, twisty roads, the diver wasn't even sure where his buddy might be. A dive flag could have been a big help in locating him. Fortunately, the lost diver came walking out of the water on his own. He apparently didn't need rescuing—or, for that matter, a buddy. Because of all the work involved and the potential for needless injuries to the rescuers who were trying to respond to this emergency situation, these divers were ticketed.

During the second incident two divers swam out in shallow waters under boats that were jockeying for position while trying to fish for salmon. The divers ascended after running low on air and had to surface-swim between the boats in order to return to their entry point. In this case, a picture was worth a thousand words. The potential for injury was enormous and tickets were issued.

These incidents underline a couple of safety points. Dive flags let others know where we are and therefore give a point of reference in case of emergencies. They also signal to boat operators to be cautious and considerate, but in return, divers should be considerate of boats and fishermen.

I have to plead guilty to not always using a dive flag. On Oahu 25 years ago my brother and I were diving for lobsters when a sailboat stopped directly above us and the operator threw his metal anchor over the side of the boat. With the entire ocean to choose a location, the anchor landed two feet from where I was busy peering inside a crevice. My brother tapped me on the shoulder and pointed to the crude metal object resting next to me. My first reaction was disbelief; my second was "we need a dive flag."

In the past I always used a float and flag when teaching dive classes, but not so often during my own recreational dives. Now I take my dive flag wherever I go, not just for safety but to set an example and to keep the cost of diving down to the price of an air fill by not collecting expensive autographs. I also learned from my experience in Hawaii that the bigger the dive float and dive flag the better—although I've had motorboats driven by guys drinking beer or inhaling questionable substances run right over my dive float and flag! Covered inner tubes with zip-shut tops and side handhold rings make great floating bases for large dive flags. I have also used my dive flag floats to hold extra gear and help rescue divers in distress. A stainless steel stake tied to the end of the rope and augured into a sandy bottom keeps the flag and float firmly in place over a fixed dive site.

I have empathy for divers who have to learn the hard way, but hopefully in the near future we can come up with some state park rules, regulations and information about dive flags for all safety-conscious boaters and divers.

Logbooks

The other day I was moving some cardboard boxes in the garage and I came across a collection of my old dive logbooks. The first entries dated back to 1980 when I was living in Hawaii. My brother had talked me into taking a Professional Association of Diving Instructors (PADI) class that was offered by a local dive shop, and the details of the dives we did after our graduation are permanently stored in the pages of my logbooks.

Our first dive after our open-water class was at Poipu Beach on the south end of the island of Kauai. This was 12 years before Hurricane Iniki swept over Kauai and its 140-plus-knot winds damaged or destroyed some 14,000 homes. The heavy wave action alone wiped out the Poipu Beach Hotel along with 63 beachfront homes. Needless to say, this wave action altered the adjacent shoreline and left pieces of debris and PVC piping strewn about the reef. Fortunately, the nearby Sheraton Hotel and its section of the shoreline survived the assault.

I was only 23 at the time of that first log entry. I dived with a used Dacor 200 regulator and old jet fins. Later I upgraded to a Pacer XL regulator and high-tech, resin Power Plana fins, and my brother and I were two of the first on Oahu to own the latest and greatest Stab jacket-style buoyancy compensators. I know all this because I listed my gear inside my logbook. I even wrote down the model and size numbers as I upgraded my gear in case I needed rental information when I was traveling.

The pages of my logbooks became wet while I was living in the islands, and over time some of the ink smeared so it's hard to read certain words, but that doesn't matter. Looking at maps I drew on the pages, I had a chance to relive some of my earlier dive exploits. I had almost forgotten that my brother and I were crazy about slipper lobsters in those days, and we mapped the cave entrances to all our most popular lobster spots. One of them was right off the park next to the Ala Moana shopping center, but unless you knew where the caves were, you could dive all week out there without ever seeing a single lobster.

In those days boat captains never checked your logbooks to see how many dives you had done or where you had been. Experience wasn't an issue in the remote corners of the world. There seemed to be just one simple rule: if you had cash in deep pockets, you could dive deep. Now in more responsible days, a boat operator may actually look at your dive logbook and pair you up with a dive buddy of equal qualifications and experience. And without the logbook as proof of your qualifications, you might even find that they won't let you dive a specific site. I guess this saves divemasters headaches in the long run, but the overall experience can be disappointing for a relatively new diver traveling without a logbook or proof of experience.

After several hundred dives I found myself with a good-sized collection of little logbooks, although I only carried the most recent edition with me. I put as much detail in as I could about visibility, water temperatures, depth profiles and dive time, but after a few years I quit counting up the total accumulated dive time. Now I use the records in my most recent logbooks to remind me where the harbor seals hang out, when and where the Dungeness crabs congregate for mating and other bits of information

A few notes jotted down in an inexpensive logbook can turn into a treasure of memories and great dive site references.

on marine life that I have just acquired through long-term casual observations.

It's a good thing to keep a record of types of dive gear and sizes. It might also be nice to draw maps of dive sites, have a record of your experience level and past air performance. I think that keeping notes on when and where you saw your favorite wolf-eel and what it liked to eat may be interesting to remember too. But in my opinion the best reason for keeping a logbook is to look back at the dives you did with your brother or friends 20-some years ago, relive the details and enjoy the memories of times you might otherwise push to the back of your mind for good.

Nitrogen Narcosis

You might recall the passage in your first dive course book that explained nitrogen narcosis. It probably called it the rapture of the deep or pointed out that each 33 feet (1atm) you descend is equivalent to drinking one martini and that a diver at 100 feet has the cognitive reasoning of a person who has consumed three martinis. You might also have seen a shirt at the dive shop that read something like, "If strange fish suddenly offer you candy, you might be suffering from nitrogen narcosis." All these statements are true, but none of them really prepares you for exploring locations deeper than, say, 60 feet.

Over the years I've trained adults who don't even drink beer and 14-year-old Boy Scouts. Telling them that, like alcohol, nitrogen under pressure affects everyone differently and that diving deeper than 80 feet may impair complex reasoning by 33 percent or the equivalent of drinking three martinis doesn't prepare them for their next deep dive. However, listing the effects of nitrogen narcosis and teaching them what signs and symptoms to watch for and how to deal with them does give them information they can readily use and keep in the back of their minds on every dive. So let's start with some basics of nitrogen narcosis and gradually move to the topic of maintaining control under pressure.

Nitrogen narcosis is the effect that nitrogen gas has on a body under pressure. Nitrous oxide or laughing gas is a compound made from nitrogen. The gas has a narcotic effect at sea level and is used to relax patients in the dentist's chair while he drills, jack hammers and otherwise gently works on their teeth. For the majority of divers nitrogen gas at 100 feet has a similar affect, but for a few divers nitrogen at this degree of partial pressure may cause hallucinations or paranoia.

Nitrogen comprises 79 percent of the gas in the air we inhale. Oxygen makes up most of the other 21 percent and the rest is trace amounts of other gasses in proportions too minimal for our current consideration. You might think that if we reduced the amount of nitrogen or increased the amount of oxygen that we put in scuba tanks, we could reduce the effects of narcosis at depth. The idea sounds reasonable—divers up the oxygen percentages in the Nitrox or enriched air that they use in their scuba tanks to increase their bottom times and avoid decompression sickness caused by the body's retention of nitrogen. However, it turns out that oxygen has similar narcotic effects to nitrogen, so using different blended mixtures of just nitrogen and oxygen does not reduce or alter our susceptibility to narcosis at depth.

Some people genuinely like being "narced" and feel giddy and euphoric with the effect of nitrogen at depth. Others, however, feel panicked or paranoid and the experience is unpleasant. No matter what symptoms you experience, the reduction in reasoning abilities, the sudden false sense of well-being, loss of judgment, reduction in dexterity, lack of concern and idea fixation may lead to an overall decrease in control over a deep diving environment. To put it simply, a diver down at 100-plus feet may not be mentally sharper than Big Bird on *Sesame Street*.

Here is one perfect example: off the coast of Maui the submarine USS *Blue Gill* rested sitting up in the sand at a depth of 145 feet with its radio tower rising some 60 feet above the sea floor. Iron bars had been welded over the sub's entry points. Dive boats would take groups out to the site and stress the dangers of entering the sub on a limited air supply. On board the boat this information was well received as good advice by all the divers, but once underwater and down at 130-plus feet, the occasional diver would abruptly decide that entering the sub with little regard for her own safety was actually a really good idea. Suddenly something that had seemed too dangerous to contemplate doing while she was on the surface prompted little concern at four atmospheres underwater. In 1983 the Navy moved the sub out to deeper water.

Besides experiencing faulty reasoning, narced divers lose track of time and may not pay attention to such routine tasks as monitoring air supplies. Studies have also shown that narced divers become chilled faster but fail to recognize this change in their thermal condition, which includes increased heart and respiration rates while on the road to hypothermia. Put these factors together and you've got a diver consuming tank air at an unanticipated and undetected fast and furious rate. This is just one more reason why deep divers use the rule of thirds when it comes to their air supply: one third of their air for the dive, one third to return to the surface and one third in reserve.

The biggest factor inducing or enhancing the effects of nitrogen narcosis is alcohol consumed within 24 hours before a dive. Alcohol works similarly to nitrogen under pressure on the cells of the brain, affecting transmission from one nerve cell to another by altering the permeability of the cells' lipid outer layers. This might explain how some narced divers become so fixated on a single task, just like the Cookie Monster's fixation on cookies. Other factors that affect nitrogen narcosis include rate of descent and CO_2 buildup in the body, as well as physical conditions such as body size, fat content, mood, tiredness and stress.

How do divers in good health, let alone fat divers who are in bad Oscar-like moods such as myself, deal with nitrogen narcosis? If you feel behavioral changes, paranoia or euphoria while slowly descending, the sensations will vanish by ascending again, sometimes by even as little as a few feet. In case you may not be aware that you are suffering the effects of nitrogen narcosis, it's always a good practice to test yourself; while descending, have your buddy ask you how many fingers he is holding up on one hand. You reply by holding up the same number of fingers. (A variation on this test is to add one digit to the answer. That is, if he holds up two fingers, you reply with three fingers.) If you reply quickly, chances are you're fine. If you are slow to reply or forget to reply, chances are your cognitive abilities have diminished with depth and you need to ascend. Another method of testing involves doing math calculations on a slate. If your buddy writes down "125 x 125 =?" and you are slow or can't figure out the answer or respond with "Have you seen my mask?" it's time to ascend.

When your dive buddy attempts to hold hands with a glove sponge it may be an indication that he is suffering from the effects of nitrogen narcosis.
BERNARD P. HANBY

Currently, recreational divers are encouraged to dive above 100 feet and only down to the maximum of 130 feet if they have had deep diver training. Deep diving courses under the direct supervision of an instructor give the diver the opportunity to see how well he tolerates nitrogen narcosis. Many divers can learn to tolerate certain levels of it and perform simple tasks at depth, especially if they have done them repeatedly over the course of many similar dives—provided that unexpected events don't intervene and make things too difficult to deal with mentally.

Many tech divers prefer to add gasses such as helium to their nitrogen and oxygen mixture for any dive below 100 feet. These well-trained divers would rather have high voices and calculate dive plans that rule out such things as high-pressure nervous syndrome than be caught at depth with air in their tanks and the combined mental faculties of Bert, Ernie and Rubber Ducky.

The bottom line is that if you respect the effects of nitrogen narcosis, are well trained to your current maximum depth rating, plan your dive and dive your plan, test your buddy as he tests you during slow, deep descents, and most importantly, allow any diver to end any dive at any time with no explanation, then even with a slight case of reduced mental capacity or nitrogen narcosis, you'll be able to maintain good control under pressure. And always beware of red fuzzy fish that look like Elmo.

Dehydration: A Worst Thirst Scenario

I once read in a tech diving book that dehydration may very well be the most significant predisposing physiological factor in decompression sickness or DCS. Treatment for DCS is also less effective if dehydration is not corrected. In dive lingo this means that the more dehydrated you are, the more likely you are to get the bends under certain conditions, and it's going to be harder to treat you until you are less dehydrated.

While temperature and pressure can influence body fluid volumes, diuretics such as alcohol, coffee and caffeine-laden teas and soft drinks are the main contributors to dehydration. Traveling great distances in moisture-robbing airplanes can also lead to dehydration if you don't drink enough water during the flight.

Dehydration reduces the body's ability to flush out the nitrogen that is absorbed during a dive. Think of your body's fluid as a road full of cargo trucks carrying assorted molecules such as oxygen and nitrogen to different destinations. Being dehydrated is like creating a large roadside distraction with drivers slowing down to rubberneck, forcing the delivery trucks to be delayed or rerouted. Add changes in fluid volume and fluctuations in gas dispersal abilities due to temperature and pressure changes, and you've got gridlock traffic or, in diver terms, a backlog of nitrogen that may require an extra 10 to 20 minutes to flush out of your body. If you have excess fat, then you can add on even more time for off-gassing due to the fact that fat absorbs nitrogen five times faster than other tissues. Fat will consequently need additional time to flush out all that extra nitrogen so quickly accumulated. And don't forget about how breathing dry tank air also takes moisture away from your body.

Dive tables have been redefined over the last 20 years to consider a wide variety of physiological factors and project conservative decompression times and limits. These tables do a lot to reduce the possibility of DCS, but they may not work for every scenario. Consider the obese diver who flies in the night before the dive, has a hangover from the arrival party and feels tired and dehydrated, and the two large cups of coffee he drank minutes ago just don't seem to be helping him wake up. Would you want this person as your dive buddy? I've seen this scenario many a time in the tropics. Mandatory deco safety stops, conservative dive tables, diving with Nitrox (enriched air) and keeping physical exertion to a minimum prior to or after a dive usually helps this type of person avoid DCS, but why take the risk?

The best way you can prevent DCS is to stay well hydrated. Drink non-caffeine fluids hours before a dive and again 15 to 20 minutes before and after dives. Water and Gatorade are good choices, but now divers can also choose liquids such as Scuba Fuel or Diversitea, two products specifically made for divers. Scuba Fuel has a lemon-lime flavor and contains antioxidant vitamins, electrolytes, ginseng to increase oxygen utilization, ginkgo biloba to improve mental alertness and ginger to settle the stomach and reduce nausea. Diversitea, hot or cold, tastes like mild tea and is made out of red clover, which contains molybdenum, a trace mineral that plays a role in discharging nitrogen from the human body. Galangal to prevent seasickness, hibiscus, rose hips, orange peel, Cran-Max and stevia all add to the special properties of this diver-specific formulated tea. And there's nothing like a thermos full of hot beverage served between cold-water dives.

The best way to check your hydration level is to see if your urine is clear and copious. If your urine is in short supply and yellow, you're a risky fellow. If you are feeling a little fatigued, chances

For more information on decompression sickness:
www.diversitea.com

are you are a little dehydrated. Don't refrain from drinking because you don't want to risk a certain urge while diving. A urine-related dive accident is better than a dehydration-related accident any day of the week. Also keep in mind that there are two types of divers—those who admit to having accidentally warmed up a wetsuit and those who tell lies. Staying hydrated actually has many benefits, but if it takes a DCS warning to make you stop, think and drink, then cheers to you.

Seasickness Made Easy

It's actually harder to become seasick than you think. You need the right weather conditions, the right location, appropriate attire and most of all you need the right mental and physical conditioning. So if you want to get seasick, just follow the advice of my scientific colleagues as detailed below. If for some inexplicable reason you don't want to get seasick, just do the opposite.

Weather is the number one factor in achieving your objective. A hot, dry, humid day is all that you really need. Sure, you can get sick during a windstorm, but a soft, warm breeze blowing after you've geared up too soon in a 7-mm neoprene wetsuit works even better. Zipping up a drysuit too soon can also generate excess heat even on a moderately warm day and make you sweat and feel queasy. Add rolling waves to this scenario and you are three-quarters of the way to aborting a dive. The point here is that whether on a boat or on shore, you will need to become unobtrusively and incrementally overheated.

Odors are another important factor. Whether you sit at the back of the boat or on the bumper of an old truck, those exhaust emissions work better than a pack of second-hand smoke.

Don't forget food. A big, greasy meal is a sure-fire method of becoming queasy. On a boat just looking at certain food groups can do the trick, so stay in the galley area as much as possible.

I didn't forget about boat motion. The rule of thumb here is that the more the boat tosses around, the more likely you'll toss up, but that's something you really can't control once you are out at sea. However, you can make it worse by looking for small rooms to hide in so you won't have to look at land formations or the horizon, and the stern of the boat will usually give the best wild ride for the money.

With shore diving it's all about how long you spend swimming on the surface in the surf. Even by swimming a foot below the waves, you could clear up any signs of nausea. So planning long surface-swims might just be a swell way to separate the men from their meals.

The mental and physical aspects work hand in hand. If you already feel bad, then going in the water will only make you feel worse, and there's nothing like a good hangover to promote such a situation. Even something as innocuous as drinking too many caffeine-laden sodas can help get you dehydrated and give you a sort of sick advantage.

Now if you have been following my advice to this point, you may want to plant your face in the water. There's no cleanup crew on aisle five on most boat operations, so do your fellow passengers a favor and let the seas sweep everything away. It's true that you can get sick in your regulator while underwater and still breathe fine, but I prefer a simple face-in-the-water technique any day of the week.

On the other hand, if you stay cool, get plenty of rest, eat right, keep your eyes on the horizon, avoid noxious smells and stay hydrated, you can be a big help to those who unwittingly follow the guidelines in this section.

How To Go Overboard

If you like extra personal space and if making friends with fellow boat divers isn't your cup of chowder, here are seven steps that are guaranteed to assure swift success:

1. Bring the largest plastic storage bin you can find onto the boat—ones with eight-inch rubber wheels and two-foot-long steel handles will work best. Those net bags are just too small for all the gear you'll never use, and they can get misplaced under seats and other out-of-the-way places. With a

large plastic two-piece container you'll know where all your scuba gear is all the time—and so will everyone else on the boat as they try to move around your container.

2. Set your tank up before everyone else then stand in everyone else's way while they set up. Of course, you can't be sure the other divers will set their gear up correctly unless your backside is right against their front side. This maneuver also keeps other divers from brushing up against the gear that you so meticulously cleaned, shined and set up in the first place.

3. Before you put on your mask, spit into it and then rinse it thoroughly in water marked "Camera gear only." The water should remove most stubborn stains and bits of crud from your mask, and the residue left in the water will give camera lenses a variety of unanticipated optical enhancements. It's like you're helping photographers to discover new artistic mediums.

4. The farther you are sitting from the entrance to the water, the more important it is to be the first diver off the boat. Putting your fins on first always helps in this tricky but classic maneuver. With your feet spread apart, push by the other divers who are gearing up and head straight for the dive platform. This helps them to develop proper balance techniques while donning dive gear.

5. Practise your buddy skills as soon as you have a free moment. You'll probably see your buddy before the end of the dive anyway, but why wait until then? Stay close to him as you descend through the water column; this could come in handy in case you forgot to turn on your air or put the regulator in your mouth. And hey, your buddy could hold some of your dive gear for you so you don't get task-overloaded during the dive. Who said a buddy has to be just an extra source of air?

6. Try to be the last diver back on the boat. Go shallow for the last part of your dive and switch to your snorkel if your tank goes low on air. While everyone else is busy writing in their logbooks, snacking, shivering and twiddling their thumbs, you'll have the entire back of the boat all to yourself, giving

you more room to disassemble your equipment. Remember that dive boats are like airplanes: the more time you spend on them and the more time you keep them out at sea, the more you are getting your money's worth. We all know that there are 24 hours in a day, so when they advertise a half-day dive excursion, you should be entitled to a full 12 hours on the boat. Technically you could get in at least eight dives during this time if it wasn't for those dive tables and nitrogen bubbles that everyone talks about. But some dive boat captain probably invented them to cut short our dive time.

7. As they disembark the boat, most people leave a five-dollar tip for the crew if the diving experience was good. But you don't. You want to stand out. You want to be different. And the crew definitely will remember you, so next time you'll get even greater one-on-one service as they try their best to keep you separated from those other poor unfortunate divers who lack your level of gifted and benevolent dive skills.

There are many other ways to get the recognition you deserve—such as leaving the restroom facilities wet and out of order, getting sick on the boat or (my personal favorite) faking a heart attack and using up the boat's emergency oxygen supply.

Good luck and may you get everything that's coming to you on your next dive.

Tech Diving from a Zodiac

I thought I'd tried everything until my friend Mike Salvador, who is also a fellow PADI instructor (Professional Association of Diving Instructors), and I tried a tech dive from a 14-foot Zodiac. What I learned was that diving from a Zodiac needs real team effort. We both had dual tanks, stage bottles, bags filled with dive gear, extra water, sandwiches and camera equipment tucked into every inch of free space within the rubberized craft. Despite all this equipment, our weights and our own gravitational forces, the craft sliced through the water at a very fast pace and proved to be a very stable platform when we arrived at our destination.

We had planned our dive before we ever left shore. Mike had added extra brass clips onto the rope that ringed the Zodiac, and at the dive site we used them to hang our stage bottles and camera in the water before we went over the sides. Preparing to get into the water is definitely a two-person operation on a small craft. Mike had a conventional cave diver harness with no boots on the bottom of his tanks, so the rounded bottoms of the tanks slid easily down the rounded side walls of the Zodiac, making it difficult for him to place the tank back plate and shoulder straps in the proper position before snapping the buckles and cinching down his straps. We figured that a small board or platform could help overcome this obstacle on future dives, but for this dive I gladly assisted him. The boots on my own tanks made mini-platforms on the rubber side of the Zodiac and made it easy for me to put on my own BC and dual tank system, although Mike did swim around the boat once he was in the water and helped me put my arm through one of my shoulder straps. I would have thanked him for this help any day because trying to put dry glove rings through unwilling shoulder straps can lead to drysuit seal leaks and tears. Once I had all my buckles and straps in place, I put on my fins and mask, put some air into my BC and rolled over the side backwards into the water. It felt good to get wet.

Mike and I each unhooked our stage bottles from the side of the Zodiac and hooked them onto our D-rings. Next I attached my camera. We then started our five points descent next to the anchor line. We passed a sunken barge at 110 feet and saw a few bright red nudibranchs in the nearby sand. At 140 feet we entered a mud flat area. We shortened our time at depth and came back up to the barge. On the way up we found a kid's tennis shoe and a few worn-out metal objects. Back at the barge we saw several schools of perch and some large iridescent rockfish. We stopped at 80 feet for two minutes to decompress then slowly worked our way back up to 40 feet where we encountered a mass of white lingcod eggs, but we couldn't find their male guardian. At 30 feet we switched to 50 percent oxygen in our stage bottles and swam slowly over to a smaller barge about 20 feet away where some Dungeness crabs were wandering back and forth across the barge's top planks. Schools of small fish swam above our heads as we worked our way up to shallower water. According to our own tables and our four computers, we had made a very conservative dive.

We surfaced and began reversing the process by hooking the camera and the stage bottles back to the clips on the side of the Zodiac. In addition, we got out of our BCs and tank harnesses, attached this equipment to the side of the Zodiac and then let everything float beside the craft. Getting into the Zodiac was easy. I just dipped down in the water, and as the buoyancy effect lifted me back up in the water column, I pulled myself over the side of the rubberized pontoon, 25-pound weight belt and all. Once we were both back on board, we lifted the gear aboard and stowed it in all the nooks and crannies. We then sat back, ate a sandwich, drank some water and watched in disbelief as the sun came out and shone down on us. It turned out to be a great dive and a great day. I'm ready to go back out on the Zodiac anytime.

Check Out Your Dive Gear

It's that time of year again, the time you set aside to inspect all your dive gear. You really don't want to be stuck with a rip, a bad o-ring or a dead dive light down at the beach. And remember that whether you dive once a year or two hundred times a year, salt and silt will get into you gear and ruin it—another good reason why you should thoroughly check out your gear at least once a year. You can make a list and check the items off as you examine them or start with the gear that goes on top, such as your mask and hood, and work your way down to your fins and booties, making sure that everything is really ready to go diving.

The best time to check out your gear is before the busy summer diving season begins. You don't want to wait until the night before the first big dive of the year to do this because there are bound to be problems that there won't be time to fix. Always plan for the worst-case scenario. If your scuba tank just needs a visual inspection, you may have to leave it at your local dive shop for the day or overnight depending on how busy they are. But what if your tank has rust in it or it's been five years since the last hydro inspection? Now you could be talking about up to three weeks before it makes it back from the testing, sanding or Nitrox cleaning facility.

If you dive a lot, you'll probably want to have your regulator serviced too. It's amazing how fast salt and silt can creep inside your system and make breathing more of a difficult chore than a passive event. Even if you dive only a few times a year, you still may want to follow the manufacturer's suggestion to service it annually, especially if you're not the type to rinse your regulator in warm water after every dive for at least 20 minutes and preferably for a few hours. The rinse process will help reduce salt corrosion, but silt will eventually work its way past the best and tightest o-rings and ultimately alter your regulator's level of performance. Keep in mind that it could take two weeks to get your newly tuned regulator back from the dive shop, especially if it was built before 1492 in a country east of Serbo Crustacea, because the special replacement parts may simply be impossible to find. Of course, if the dive shop can't locate the right parts, then you'll have a good excuse for upgrading to a new regulator.

Some shops do overnight regulator overhauls and other repair services, but this might cost you a rush fee, and you don't want to be lined up with all the other divers who waited until the last minute to check out their gear. So figure three weeks out for your regulator and tanks, two days to glue and dry any rips in your hood, booties or suit and a few more hours to go through your gear checking mask straps, latex rings, o-rings and other soft rubber parts for wear and tear. Mark those areas and fix them while the issue is fresh in your mind. Then make a list of all the replacement parts you'll need when you go to your local dive shop because—well, I don't know about you, but I can't remember a thing the minute I step inside a dive shop and see all those shining new products competing for my undivided attention.

Once you've visually checked out your gear, take all the loose items (minus your tank and regulator) and place them in a bin full of warm water and a product such as Sink the Stink. Masks can be cleaned with household dish soap to get off the oils that so frequently float on the ocean's surface. Use something like B.C. Life to clean out the inside of your buoyancy compensator (BC). Now is also a good time to inflate it in a tub of liquid and check for leaks. If a leak is coming from an o-ring it will be easy to fix, but if it is the result of a punctured bladder, you may have to replace the bladder and that could take time if the local dive shop doesn't have one in stock that fits your particular model. And that's especially likely if the model you're using was featured on the 1950s TV show *Sea Hunt*. If you have a BC-mounted regulator, be sure to have it overhauled too. Most manufacturers suggest servicing them every six months. If the deflation or inflation button sticks during normal operation, this is a good time to have this problem corrected as well.

On items such as flashlights and dive cameras check and clean o-rings and replace parts as necessary. Be sure to open flashlights and other battery-operated equipment facing away from you just in case there is residual gas buildup, and remember to clean off the metal springs that rest against the batteries. Corrosion can make you lose electrical contact and make any newly charged battery useless. Turn on lights and strobes and check the bulbs too.

This is also a good time to mark or re-mark your gear with your initials or Bar S brand. Use three initials if possible because, believe it or not, I've seen other people's tanks with my two initials on them. If you really want to make your gear stand out and easier for your buddy to find you underwater, place some reflective yellow bike tape on both sides of your fins and any other gear locations that you might find appropriate. The tape should hang on for a couple of years if applied dry to a clean surface.

Now that you've cleaned and dried all your gear, use a head-to-toe systematic approach and go through every piece of your dive gear again. Check the clasps, clips, seams and straps and wax the zippers—including the one on your drysuit. Tighten everything, because you don't ever want your dive buddy to be the one to tell you that you have a screw loose. And now that it's all clean, do you see any more holes, tears or material wear and tear? Being obsessive is a big plus when you are trying to keep your gear in tip-top shape.

Now lubricate any latex seals with an ultraviolet protection and rejuvenating liquid such as UV Tech, and lubricate other items according to manufacturer's specifications. Never use WD-40 except on dive knives and scissors that won't come into contact with rubber or other silicon-based parts. Wetsuits should be sprinkled liberally with a non-fragrant powder to allow easier suiting up. Fragrant brands of powder not only make one smell a little too fresh for a buddy to stand close to you, but the added chemicals may be harmful to the material in your suit. Most divers use the powder recommended by the local dive store, though I've seen divers douse their wetsuits with billiards (pool) chalk. However, substituting a powder such as pancake mix could cause your buddy to question your mental faculties and prompt him or her to leave the dive site before you ever get your gear assembled.

At this point in my check-up I like to see if my gear fits the way it did last year before that wonderful and inexpensive pizza place opened for business just down the street. (If you are married, please explain the next step in this process to your spouse before he/she reaches the wrong conclusion and dials 911.) Assemble everything (minus your fins and tank) and put it on as if you were going right out your front door and into the water. Be quick about this step so you don't overheat and pass out in front of the TV set. Put it all on and pull it off, turn it on, inflate it, deflate it, cinch it up, make it fit just right and re-familiarize yourself with how to hook up and operate all your equipment. Now ask yourself, is everything cinched up the way you like it? Are all your clips and buckles in place and not twisted? Does your wetsuit/drysuit still fit you comfortably? Is it time to get a StairMaster? (Oops, sorry! That's just my subconscious talking.)

Okay, so I had a little fun writing this section, but you should have a little fun while you check out your gear. Basically, if you intend to use it underwater, clean, lubricate and check it out on land first to make sure it's working as designed. I think airline pilots follow a similar plan of action before every take-off in one of those gravity-defying, winged aluminum tubes, and as any good pilot will tell you, a good pre-flight check is easier to complete than a bad post-flight check.

When you've completed your yearly mission, not only will you look shinier and brighter but you will also have your dive equipment operating skills up to peak performance level, ensuring swift reaction times and greater physical and mechanical dexterity. The next time you enter the water your comfort level will be near or at 100 percent and you will be significantly better prepared to undertake your next great dive adventure.

The Washington Scuba Alliance

For more than 15 years a group of energetic individuals has been working together on issues that affect the Washington State scuba community. You may not have ever heard of the Washington Scuba Alliance (WSA), but you may have walked down stairs they helped build, dived underwater parks they helped clean up or to some degree maintain, or you may have gained access to dive sites that WSA helped ensure would be open to all present as well as future scuba divers. The members do all this as dedicated volunteers and their various projects are financed by membership fees as well as public and private donors. They also work closely with government agencies such as the Department of Fish and Wildlife, Washington State Parks and the National Oceanic and Atmospheric Administration (NOAA).

The work is not always easy and sometimes they come away with more cuts and bruises from filling out government forms and fulfilling local, state and national regulations than they do from removing abandoned fishing line or working with cement products. Yet it's all worth the effort as the end results benefit not only scuba divers but entire local wildlife ecosystems and they boost the local human community's economy too.

A four-part mission motivates WSA members:

1. To be the voice of the dive community. WSA listens to the concerns of divers, dive shop operators and dive clubs and addresses their concerns to the governor, the legislature and regulatory agencies in Olympia. Note: if you see a televised news conference with Washington State Governor Chris Gregoire discussing the quality of local waters and standing right beside her are people wearing drysuits, chances are you're viewing members of WSA.

2. To focus on issues of access. This deals mainly with shore diving in places where progress, growth, cleaning up Puget Sound or transportation development—what Mike Racine,

WSA's current president, calls "incidental collateral damage"—has destroyed or impinged on access. For example, the building of a gravel facility could lead to the need for a new water access point for divers. The cleanup and removal of toxic creosote pilings in Puget Sound could also eliminate some dive sites without the help of state and local communities and projects being initiated by WSA. Or if the Department of Transportation expands, changes or moves a ferry terminal, there would be an immediate impact on local dive sites. Fortunately, the Washington State Parks Department is a great partner of the dive community in reaching the goal of this part of the mission.

3. To expand marine conservation. The WSA's intrinsic interest in the environment ensures present and future generations of divers access to dive sites rich with sea life. As divers, all of us are the eyes and ears of the media and government agencies. We can provide a first-hand account of the underwater environment, and our knowledge can be used to support or oppose legislation that would impact our waters.

4. To do volunteer diving. As WSA president Mike Racine put it, "We have a well-oiled practice of putting people in the water." In the past the WSA has been involved in community cleanups, the removal of invasive tunicates and tire reefs and reporting derelict fishing gear. NOAA, as part of Team Ocean, has recently certified six WSA members as volunteer "Citizen Scientist Divers," and their first mission was to complete a maritime heritage shipwreck survey of Neah Bay. There is a rigorous training process to obtain such a level of certification, but the rewards are measured by team achievements multiplied by individual self-fulfillment. WSA volunteering also includes the promotion of dive tourism in Washington State, as it has been shown time and again around the world that a well-developed dive destination is an economically sound goal for the entire community. The Bruce Higgins Underwater Trails in Edmonds is a prime example of how, between dives, thousands of divers bring hundreds of thousands of dollars annually to the local

community through hotel and motel stays, dining out, attendance at local events and the taxes on all of the above.

You may want to read about past WSA projects on-line, but one of the current projects is Saltwater State Park where the reef tires have been removed. Taking their place will be three long rows comprised of 20 to 30 individual rock piles with cement pillars strategically placed to provide a habitat for many species of fish and invertebrates. This dive site is also designated to become the next marine protected area.

Another important initiative, headed by WSA vice-president Jim Track, is the installation of buoys at 15 or more dive sites. His team, along with Swanson Brothers Concrete Company, Roberta's Custom Graphics, the Department of Ecology and others, just completed the stairs at Les Davis to make a safe and easy entrance to this popular dive site. Next they will direct the skills learned from this project toward the buoy project, which will ensure that in the future no anchors will be indiscriminately dropped at the more popular boat dive sites. Jim and his team will use a double buoy line attached to a helical anchor system that screws right into the substrate and only leaves a two-inch footprint instead of the large footprint left by cement blocks or anchors. At some dive sites where currents dictate the need, such as Possession Point in Island County or at Dalco Wall, a second buoy will be installed. Maury Island will also have two buoys and they have already been funded by donations from Olympic Sand and Gravel. Incidentally, each buoy will be labelled with the name of the granting organization.

The Titlow Artificial Reef project is another major WSA initiative that has been timed to coincide with the removal of the creosote pilings there. What board member and treasurer Karlista Rickerson and others would like to see is the removal of the current creature population from the toxic creosoted wood pilings and their transfer to replacement structures, such as cement reef balls, before the pilings are hauled out of the water. Otherwise there will be an immediate and devastating loss of all life on the pilings, however precariously attached.

Board member, dive instructor and marine educator Janna Nichols says that the best way to get ready for the next invasive species

WSA promotes diving by making sites like Les Davis accessible, safe and visually pleasing to divers and non-divers alike. JIM TRASK

cleanup or other volunteer-based activities is to join WSA and be ready. Sometimes there are lulls between activities just as there are lulls between invasive species outbreaks, but you can spend the downtime learning to become a NOAA citizen scientist.

For more information go on-line and check the WSA web site. You'll see that there are several different levels of membership and ways to donate. While on-line you can read more about board members, the Titlow Artificial Reef Project, visit 30 things you can do for the marine environment or become current with the Washington State dive flag rules. Also view the great slide show on the proposed Titlow Project produced by Bellarmine Preparatory School's marine chemistry program students.

You'll be impressed with what WSA members have accomplished over the past 15 years, making Washington State more accessible for those of us with flippers, masks and regulators while simultaneously increasing the number of safe havens for those with fins, frills and gills.

For more information about the WSA:

www.wascuba.org

The Northwest Dive and Travel Expo

In 2008 the Northwest Dive News Treasure Hunt, which has been an annual event since 2003, matured into an entire weekend of activities devoted to both current and future divers. This new annual event is called the Northwest Dive and Travel Expo and it is held in the Greater Tacoma Convention and Trade Center. It is the brainchild of Rick Stratton, publisher of *Northwest Dive News*, who also organizes the event. Rick and a host of volunteers spend thousands of hours planning for it and during the actual Dive Expo weekend 50 to 70 volunteers put in a few more hundred hours running the show.

At the first Expo in 2008 there were 140 booths in all; by January 2009 there were already 272 booths registered for the next one, representing gear, destination, resorts and charter providers as well as other dive-related businesses. Over 2,000 people attended the three-day event in 2008, and 4,000 to 5,000 are expected in 2009. These numbers compare very favorably with the approximately 11,000 who turn up each year for the 22-year-old Scuba Show in Long Beach, California, and the 15,000 who come to Beneath the Sea in Secaucus, New Jersey, a show that has been around for 33 years.

So what can you expect at the Northwest Dive and Travel Expo? The actual Treasure Hunt dive takes place on the Friday morning to make it easier for everyone to participate in all of the weekend's scheduled activities. The hunt takes place at Owens Beach and there's over a thousand dollars in prizes for the winners. Since the first Treasure Hunt in 2003 the event has been averaging between 125 and 250 divers, but one year there were 350 divers and that was just about all that the parking lot at Owens Beach could hold. In 2008 there was a respectable and comfortable turnout of 157 divers.

On the Friday there are also seminars for dive professionals similar to those held at the annual Dive Equipment and Marketing Association (DEMA) convention. Expo's seminars are specific to the dive industry but also include business seminars such as "Making the media work for you, instead of the other way around," or other vendor-specific hot topics. And on Friday night there is an informal social gathering for booth vendors and industry professionals.

Saturday is the day everything begins for the general public at the Greater Tacoma Convention and Trade Center. Events are geared to the interests of divers, inactive divers, warm-water-only divers and future divers. Exhibitors represent gear manufacturers, warm-water as well as cold-water dive resorts, travel destinations, charter operations, travel agencies and voluntary organizations. Expect to meet vendors from British Columbia, Washington, Oregon, Hawaii, Australia and even select Caribbean Island destinations. As Rick Stratton told me, "Anyone who wants to attract divers from the Northwest will be at this show."

Multiple seminars over the course of the day cover topics such as diving with sharks, diving the wrecks of British Columbia, how to take underwater images, from ships to reefs and the Washington Scuba Alliance (WSA), and there are even some on non-dive-related subjects such as the Puget Soundkeeper Alliance. You can expect to view slide shows, talk to experts and be able to get answers to most of your local and world dive-related questions. To reach out to children and future divers at the show, Deep Ambitions holds an Aquatic Career Fair, where hundreds of local school-aged kids can experience extracurricular marine-related activities and have a great time in the process. On Saturday evening the focus of activities shifts to the host hotel where you can see a film, view the

Owens Beach is busy with divers and dive families on the day of the annual Northwest Dive News Treasure Hunt.

results of the underwater video and photo contest and/or dance to live music until midnight. On Sunday the Expo hall is open again with additional seminars to enjoy besides all the vendor booths to visit. It's also a good time to ask all the questions you forgot to ask on Saturday.

The Pacific Northwest has the third largest diving community in the country behind Florida and California, but unlike those states, we have a vast dive empire separated by bridges, ferry crossings and national borders. Our Expo is a time, place and chance to bring together this expansive and diverse dive community and show off all the things that make this region such a great place to scuba dive. It is organized by local divers, dive club members, dive shop volunteers and others willing to lead or be a member of a committee. Their number one goal is to make the Expo a fun-filled and successful annual tradition. If you are a single diver, you may want to visit your local dive shop or club and ask if they are planning a car pool for the event. For dive instructors this is a great opportunity to mail out to former students and invite them to come.

The Northwest Dive and Travel Expo is definitely one event not to be missed by divers from British Columbia and all the way down the West Coast of the United States.

> **For more information:**
> www.nwdiveandtravelexpo.com

The DEMA Show and an Underwater Conference

The DEMA Show is the world's largest trade show for professionals in the diving industry. The acronym stands for the Dive Equipment and Marketing Association, although it began as the Dive Equipment and Manufacturers Association back in 1963, a full three years before Ralph Erickson and John Cronin got together to form the Professional Association of Dive Instructors (PADI). But it wasn't until 1977 that the first DEMA Show came into existence in a neutral territory called Miami. That was over 30 years ago and now each DEMA Show hosts over 1,500 booths, 2,200 registered buyers and 11,000 professional attendees. Since 2003 the show has been marketed very successfully by Adams Unlimited, a dynamic boutique marketing communications agency based in the media center of the world, New York City, and in recent years the four- to seven-day show has been alternating between Las Vegas and Orlando.

What surprises me most about this event is that so many dive shops do not insist that their instructors and divemasters attend. The shop owner sitting in his back room doing the bookwork may know all the intimate details about DEMA and dive gear and dive travel destinations, but he may have little time to pass this information on to his staff. And his staff, comprised of instructors and divemasters, may spend a tremendous amount of time with each individual student or dive shop customer, but may not even know what DEMA stands for. Why is this so critical? Because students ask dive shop staff where to go on their dive vacations. They ask them about equipment selection. They trust their advice on everything related to their present and future diving experience—in fact, with their very safety in the water. So a divemaster or shop employee who has attended DEMA is worth her weight in gold. This person will generally be more knowledgeable about dive gear in general and, after attending seminars and talking to representatives from worldwide travel destinations, she will be able to offer sound advice about travel destinations right around the planet. And the more the dive shop staff knows about the world of diving, the more overall credibility and loyalty that customers will give to that dive shop.

Dive professionals should expect the unexpected at DEMA shows. At the 2005 show I was one of 15 journalists who entered the pool at the Riviera Hotel and Casino in Las Vegas to set a world record. Al Hornsby, then president of DEMA, presided over the largest underwater conference ever attempted at that time. Underwater communication between the speaker and his audience of journalists was made possible by the participants' use of Ocean Technology System full-face masks complete with integrated microphones and listening headsets. These masks were surprisingly comfortable to wear and the quality of the voices was so clear that you would have thought we were all in a conference room. Speakers were set

With 1,500 booths to peruse and countless seminars to attend there is little time to think about lunch. Many thousands of us make DEMA an annual pilgrimage.

up topside around the pool so non-divers could hear the conference too. One video cameraman filmed the event while I swam around with my SeaLife DC500 digital camera and took pictures of the participants as well as represented *Northwest Dive News* for the event. Other journalists—including one from the UK's Deeperblue.net on-line magazine and one from *Octopus Magazine* (Russia's oldest and longest running dive magazine)—and international staff writers and freelancers also took part in this world record event. It seemed a little ironic, though, that out of all the world-class journalists, I was the only one present with an underwater camera. As soon as we surfaced at the end of the dive, we were met by a host of professional photographers: our underwater conference was not only a world-record event but part of the Riviera Hotel's 50th anniversary celebrations. We only held onto our world record for one year, though. In 2006 we were replaced by a European group that held up signs underwater in a lake.

While you may not come away from a DEMA conference with a world-class record, as a dive professional you have the opportunity to attend and have a great time at a world-class event. I know from having experienced the DEMA show myself that if I wasn't already a dive instructor, I'd get a job at a local dive store, become a dive-master, build a dive shop or design a new fin just so I could attend this incredible event.

For more information:
www.demashow.com
For images of the 2005 world record underwater conference:
www.deeperblue.net/printarticle.php/687/23
www.deeperblue.net/article.php/687/%200/1

A brand new Ocean Technology Systems full-face mask is on display at the Northwest Dive Expo, only mere inches away from my trembling fingers. What were they thinking?

DIVING GEAR

Odd Diver Out: Rebreathers

A while back I had the good fortune to go on a dive off West Vancouver, BC, with Ron Akeson from Adventures Down Under in Bellingham, Washington, along with two other experienced divers. All three of them were using rebreathers. I wore dual 100-cubic-foot tanks on my back and a 40-cubic-foot stage bottle filled with 50 percent oxygen under my left arm. Before I arrived at the dive site, I thought I had the latest and greatest in tech dive equipment, but one look at their rebreather systems and I felt like a sponge diver from the Middle Ages.

As previously planned, we unloaded our gear from the van at the head of a narrow dirt trail, hauled the gear down it and then down a set of wooden steps and over a few logs and stumps until we reached the gravel shoreline of a secluded beach. After putting my ego inside a small plastic film canister, I got my neolithic dive gear ready to go. As we worked at the water's edge, a small harbor seal popped its head out of the water to see if we knew what we were doing. Once we had checked and double-checked our gear, we swam out on the surface with the harbor seal in tow.

When we reached the outer edge of the small bay, we dropped

down to 100 feet, and there we let the current do most of the work as we drifted past rock formations and sloping outcrops. Anemones, tunicates and assorted small fish live down there and you could tell by their skittish nature that they didn't get a lot of weekend bubble-blowing visitors. I found it interesting yet eerie being the only diver blowing out bubbles on a regular basis. Between breaths, the surrounding area was quiet except for the sound of occasional waves splashing against the rocks somewhere up above.

A couple of years earlier I had dived with a rebreather at Captain Don's Habitat in Bonaire, and I had been able to get closer to the fish than on any of my previous 700-plus dives. I even had a four-foot-long barracuda as my unofficial escort on that dive. Although we train new divers never to hold their breath, when you're taking pictures and you want to get close to the fish, you exhale then hold your breath for what seems an eternity. Once you've taken the perfect picture, you get to breathe normally again, and the sound of the bubbles going out into that open system divers commonly refer to as "the ocean" frightens the fish, and suddenly the only thing left in the viewfinder is a drifting trail of fine particles and fish excrement. Not so with a rebreather. Your discarded breath goes through a closed or semi-closed system and the used air is cleaned and recycled. In a typical system carbon dioxide is scrubbed out and oxygen pumped in, turning used air into air good to breathe again. Because the used air is recycled, none or very few bubbles pass out into the ocean, and skittish fish are not scared away.

The other beauty of modern rebreathers is that they use computers and state of the art logarithms to monitor and adjust the gas mixture or percentage of oxygen to give you the best gas blend per minute per depth. If you've ever taken a Nitrox or enriched air diver course, you know how much you can extend your bottom time and reduce your decompression time with just a little oxygen added to your tank's air supply. But a rebreather diver can keep his nitrogen levels far below what we can do on a conventional dive, even if our tanks were filled with enriched air. Once we start a dive, our tanks can only follow one set of oxygen tables regardless of how fancy our dive computers are. Unlike a rebreather diver, we can't change or adjust the oxygen mixture in our tanks until we get back to the local dive shop.

After some 40 minutes of drifting at depth on our West Vancouver dive, our team started up the walls and began a series of decompression stops. The other three got a kick out of me at the deco stops, but it wasn't my diving technique that entertained them. It was the antics of the harbor seal that was chewing on my old, bright neon green fins. The other divers wore black ones. Apparently the combination of deco stops and green fins was too much for the young seal to resist. The more I tried to remain still, the more that seal had to gnaw on the tips of my fins. I just couldn't shoo him away. He didn't leave my fins alone until we reached 15 feet of depth and he found a big mussel to chew on instead.

Once we surfaced we swam around the corner and into Whyte Cove, the spot where most of the Vancouver, BC, dive shops train new divers because it's only 15 minutes from downtown Vancouver. A couple of classes were just getting geared up near the water's edge. A few dive flags were spread out in different parts of the bay, and two pilot whales were busy catching whatever was on today's lunch menu just outside the bay.

As Ron and the other two divers made their way out of the

Whyte Cove in West Vancouver's Whytecliff Park is very popular with pilot whales, seals, and saltwater divers.

74

water, all the people on shore stared, gawked and commented on their rebreathers. I was grateful that they let a noisy bubble-maker like me tag along on the dive. If you ever get an opportunity to dive with a rebreather, don't pass up the chance. I highly recommend the experience. Oh, and try not to wear green fins unless you get a kick out of attracting not-so-shy harbor seals with teething problems.

Tips for Selecting Your Next Regulator

It used to be easy to tell regulators (regs) apart. If there were visible holes in the first stage and you could peer inside, you knew at a glance that it was a piston regulator. If there were no visible holes, then most likely it was a diaphragm reg. Today, some piston regs are environmentally sealed with rubber collars covering the holes, so at first glance you may not be able to tell how it is internally configured. Piston regs usually have fewer parts, can deliver slightly more air at depth and are generally easier to service, but diaphragm regs do a better job of keeping out silt and sand. The latest buzzword in regs is "overbalanced," which has to do with increasing air flow to compensate for the increased density of air at depth so that each breath is easy no matter how deep you go. High-end regulators such as the Apeks XTX200 and Aqualung Legend LXACD Supreme incorporate this technology, and they breathe light years better than what we thought was top of the line a mere decade ago.

So how do you pick a regulator that's right for you? Let's talk about usage first. If you don't like to rinse your dive gear thoroughly after every dive (and you should rinse it), then you might consider acquiring a reg made out of titanium. It won't rust for centuries, but it will cost more. Atomic Aquatics T2X and Scubapro MK25T are good examples.

Most new regs come right out of the box ready to use for enriched air up to 40 percent oxygen. For Nitrox (enriched air) purposes from 40 percent to 100 percent oxygen, consider a manufacturer-specified reg that is constructed with green-colored parts, such as the Apeks XTX40/DS4 Nitrox or the Aqualung Oxygen Calypso O2. For Nitrox applications below 40 percent oxygen you don't necessarily need a color-coded reg. After all, you don't need a specially cleaned and serviced green drysuit valve or a Nitrox dedicated buoyancy compensator device (BC), yet both of these items may be inflated from oxygen-enriched air supplies.

If you plan on ice diving, get an environmentally sealed first stage with a heat exchanger on the second stage. The Mares Proton Ice or the Aqualung Glacia might work well for you. For your octopus or backup reg, consider an inexpensive low profile one, or you might prefer one built right into your BC inflation hose to be used as a spare air source. Keep in mind that the manufacturer may require a BC-integrated reg to be serviced every six months instead of once a year as is the case with most other reg configurations. The Apeks Egress and the Aqualung ABS are both low profile secondary regs.

With so many variations where do you begin? First, most new students want what their instructors, divemasters and fellow divers use. While all these divers may use different brands, their regs are being performance-tested on a frequent basis. Second, don't go cheap and shortchange your safety. Buy a good quality regulator from a licensed and reputable dive center near you, not from the internet. You can physically test it out right there at the shop, and it gives you a place to go if the regulator needs service, parts or both. It also gives you access to upgrades and information on recalls.

For tech diving I depend on a set of Apeks ATX100 regs. For recreational diving I prefer my Atomic T1 titanium reg. Not being environmentally sealed, the titanium one is good for about 120 dives a year before sand and silt creep in and its performance begins to diminish. However, some of the new titanium regs only need servicing every two years because of their enhanced, environmentally sealed construction. But titanium as well as aluminum regs share one drawback—they shouldn't be used around oxygen above 40 percent. This is really a concern for technical divers trained to work with higher levels of oxygen, so for my own oxygen and argon tanks I've cleaned and serviced some all-purpose inexpensive brands of regs.

Price doesn't have to be your main concern. Nowadays, several inexpensive brands can give the high-end brands a close run for their money. After all, can you really tell the difference in work effort between .63 joules/liter and .79 joules/liter while breathing at 165 feet of depth? I can't. At that depth I'm too busy watching strange fish dance naked around my air bubbles. For my purposes, I'm more concerned with how a reg performs at 130 feet or less.

The bottom line is that if you can afford the reg with hand-carved figures on the first stage, gold or titanium on the second stage and an awesome reg name etched by laser beams, by all means buy it. I have my eye on the Apeks XTX200 and the Aqualung Legend LXACD Supreme. Keep in mind, though, that other regs at the dive shop may in some cases perform just as well for your needs; these include the Dive Rite RG3000, the Apeks XTX50 and the Aqualung Titan or Abyss.

If you're like me, over time you'll collect several brands and models of regs and use each of them for a specific dedicated task. When it comes to modern regulators, the choices, value and performance have never been better, which in turn will make every breath a little easier on your next great dive.

Regulator Technicians: Your Air Is in Their Care

If you've been diving for a year or two and own your own regulator, then depending on the make and model, it's time to get it serviced. Some divers refer to this as getting it "tuned up" or "overhauled," but I think the word "serviced" encompasses a more widely accepted idea of what you want done to your non-peak-performing air delivery system. "Tuned up" suggests your reg might be made to operate better at greater depths and possibly under-perform at lesser depths. It also sounds like the screws are to be rotated but the o-rings will remain the same. "Overhauled" sounds like the dive shop will take your reg to an automotive shop where it will be hoisted up on a giant hook and chain system and half the parts randomly discarded across a cement floor. Then it will be repacked with chrome parts shipped in a month later from a country that doesn't mark its boxes with anything intelligible to a native speaker of English. I guess that's why asking a dive shop employee to have your reg "serviced" seems so simple and straightforward.

You may have wondered how they service a reg, and you might even have looked at diagrams of their internal parts, but have you ever wondered what sort of training it takes to repair and service regs? Even 25 years ago you had to be certified to work on the major brands of regulators. Courses are set up by each name-brand reg manufacturer that sells to dive shops. I point this out because some internet brands of regs may be made up of collections of parts or leftovers and may not be found in local markets, and neither service parts nor certified technician courses may exist for these collective products.

Most reg manufactures host repair training seminars at the Dive Equipment and Manufacturer Association (DEMA) convention usually held annually in a location such as Las Vegas, Orlando, Miami or Houston. Individual reg manufacturers may also host training sessions in local towns or they may train local dive shop personnel right on the shop premises. These one-on-one update and instruction sessions are the most costly way to train, but they build strong ties and bonds between manufacturers and dive shops.

The training sessions at the DEMA show may be open to anyone in the dive industry although subject to advanced enrollment months before the show. The manufacturer may require a store to have a prior identification code for that brand of reg, or the training sessions may be held by invitation only and be open to vendors who sell exclusively or above a certain quota for that particular manufacturer. I should mention that while some of these training sessions are free, some manufacturers charge a set fee to offset instructional costs. (It seems that just like foreign countries, reg manufacturers have their own concept of how the world works best.) Some offer training to anyone in the belief that the more people who know their product intimately and how easy it is to repair and how reliable it is in the field, the more word-of-mouth testimonials their regs will receive. A small minority of manufacturers feel that only stores that stock and sell their regs should have access to their repair information; all others need not apply and that includes independent freelance reg technicians no matter how good or experienced they seem to be. It may sound crazy, but then again what good is a trained technician who doesn't have access to their particular parts?

During the actual course, the repair candidates are assigned a set of tools (special proprietary tools may be required) to use while they take apart and reassemble regulator first and second stage kits. The instructors may use computer-generated slide shows as well as hands-on demonstrations to explain the particulars of their regs, what makes them unique and the special tricks of the trade for use when repairing specific models. The instruction may last a few hours or encompass a series of days, depending on complexity and number of models to review. The instructor examines the work in progress to make sure the candidates understand the reg completely, including every stage of replacing o-rings, chrome and plastic parts. It's in the manufacturer's own best interests to leave everyone knowledgeable and technically enlightened. Once the candidates have completed the assigned tasks, they are either given certificates right on the spot or have them mailed to their homes or dive shops.

Now that you know how regulator technicians are trained, you should feel a little more reassured when it comes to who's working on your lifeline equipment. Keep in mind, though, that even a highly experienced technician can't take an old reg and make it perform like the modern models, just as the best car mechanic can't make an old Volkswagen bus run like a new Porsche.

If you want to know more about regs, my advice is to take a specialty course in equipment or, better yet, become a divemaster at your local dive shop. Not only does it give you a legitimate reason to hang out there and learn new things, but divemasters can go to the DEMA show where the bulk of the technical classes are held. The only downside to becoming a divemaster is never wanting to leave the dive shop unless specifically scheduled to go on a dive.

Tanks for the Memories

Back in the early eighties when I first started diving, everyone seemed to use 72-cubic-foot steel tanks, but aluminum 80-cubic-foot tanks had just come on the scene. Not only did these aluminum tanks look cool but with that extra 8 cubic feet of air, we could also stay down practically forever. At least that's what we thought at the time.

Lately there have been a lot of articles on scuba tanks in dive magazines and updated information in instruction books. They tell you everything about scuba tanks except one thing, and if you're like me, it's the one thing you really care most about—which scuba tank is right for me and my world of diving?

Today, a high-pressure, 3,500-psi, steel, 80-cubic-foot tank is probably one of the best overall choices for recreational diving. These tanks are smaller than their aluminum 80-cubic-foot cousins so they are not as likely to hit the back of your neck or dig into the back of your legs. In addition, they require 6 pounds less weight to keep you negatively buoyant when they are reduced to 500 psi of internal tank pressure. Six pounds may not seem like a lot of weight to someone diving in the tropics with a 12-pound weight belt, but to a Pacific Northwest diver wearing a 7-mm wetsuit and over 40 pounds of weight rubbing against his hips, 6 extra pounds of lead is an additional amount of liability to deal with. The majority of experienced divers know this and dive shop owners know it too. That's why so many dive shops on the West Coast now offer steel tanks in their rental departments. Aluminum 80s are best left for tropical dive resorts, divers who are trying to save a few dollars on the cost of a new tank or young bucks who have strong backs and don't mind the extra weight.

Most tech divers prefer a high-pressure (HP) 100-cubic-foot tank or greater because it will give them a great supply of air in a tank not much bigger than the average aluminum 80-cubic-foot tank. Besides being smaller and more streamlined than regular steel tanks, high-pressure tanks have DIN valves, which add a theoretical safety margin during tank usage. Standard yoke valve tanks are only filled up to 3,000 psi, but I've heard that in Europe some high-pressure tanks are rated up to 5,000 psi. In the US we can only fill that same style of tank up to 3,500 psi or so; I don't know if this is because we have more stringent safety standards, more lawyers or both. A regulator technician friend of mine in Miami did tell me once that HP tanks filled beyond their limits could cause permanent damage to the first stage of some very expensive regulators, not to mention burst disk problems and premature metal fatigue. But that's a topic for another story.

So do I only advocate HP tanks? Not necessarily. When we go diving in British Columbia, we always take low-pressure (LP) steel tanks with us because some of the best places to dive simply don't have the facilities to fill tanks past 3,000 psi. I prefer a low-pressure, 2,400-psi, 98-cubic-foot tank myself, since even the smaller portable air compressors can quickly and safely fill a 2,400-psi tank (plus 10 percent overfill if the tank is marked +). A 3,500-psi 100-cubic-foot tank filled to 3,000 psi contains about as much air as an aluminum 80. A friend of mine even goes one step further; he packs two LP 98-cubic-foot steel tanks with him when he goes diving in the South Pacific because in his book the aluminum 80 tanks that they rent or supply you with there just don't cut the

From left to right, we have the old "J" valve 72cuft tank, a steel short HP 80cuft tank, a tall HP 100cuft tank and a LP 100cuft tank.

mustard. When diving on World War II artifacts that extend well past the 130-foot recreational depth limits, my friend just likes the extra air as it provides a greater margin of safety. As an instructor, I too like to carry around more air than I really need.

So does that mean I'm completely against aluminum tanks? Not at all. I use them while on vacations in the Caribbean. My 40-cubic-foot stage bottle and pony bottles are aluminum, and I use a little 50-cubic-foot aluminum tank when teaching pool sessions. I just prefer not to use aluminum tanks anytime or anywhere I can get the lead out or travel with more air.

It's amazing the amount of diving we used to do with the old steel 72-cubic-foot tanks. But it's even more amazing the amount of diving you can do with the new steel HP100-cubic-foot and LP 98-cubic-foot tanks.

Are You Thinking about a Pony Bottle? You Should. It's a Gas.

There comes a time in your dive adventures when you just want a pony. You've seen divers carrying various sizes of pony bottles or tanks hooked onto back plates, attached to brackets on their main tanks or clipped to chest level D-rings. But which pony bottle and configuration is right for you? Or better yet, what can a pony bottle do for you? Let's take a look at a few examples.

A regulator attached to a pony bottle makes a good independent backup source of air. I've seen divers skip a recommended safety decompression stop just because they were low on air. Having an extra bottle can give you a big safety advantage. Even if you know you always have enough air for your mandatory safety stop, having a pony bottle filled with enriched air may be an even better solution for off-gassing.

If you're conservative with your breath consumption and return from dives early on a regular basis, you still might want to carry around a small pony bottle just in case your buddy or an unfamiliar or unannounced diver swims up to you and signals that he is low on air. You planned how much air you needed, but how can you plan for the unexpected? A little extra air might just calm down a fellow diver or turn out to be a lifesaver.

A first stage and low pressure gauge attached to a clearly marked pony bottle creates a good source of argon gas for filling drysuits, keeping you warmer and saving the main tank of air for breathing purposes. The most popular style for this use is an orange steel, 13-cubic-foot bottle with a big argon sticker on its side. The small steel tanks are less buoyant when empty than aluminum tanks, and with a steel pony bottle you might even be able to take a few pounds of lead off your weight system. You'll usually see this bottle attached to the back right side of a back plate or attached to the main tank by a lock and pin system held in place by stainless-steel tank bands. Pin-mounted bracket systems are favored by open-water divers who don't want gear jiggling back and forth or moving around in splash zones and in currents. Argon gas in your drysuit creates a better barrier than air does and reduces your heat loss to the point that you don't get that excruciatingly painful urge to turn your drysuit into a wetsuit. An argon pony bottle may also let you reduce the thickness of your drysuit undergarments so that in the summertime you don't overheat on your way down to the beach. An argon bottle could last you 8 to 20 dives before you need to refill it—it just depends on how deep you go and how much of your argon supply your buddies pump into their own drysuits once they realize the overall benefits.

Most recreational divers start off with a 13- to 19-cubic-foot aluminum pony bottle. A rule of thumb is that the deeper and longer you go the larger the pony bottle you'll need. Most technical divers prefer a 40-cubic-foot tank or larger. Deep tech and cave divers plan for and use tanks that are 80-cubic-foot or greater.

So you've picked out a nice little 19-cubic-foot aluminum pony bottle. You've attached a regulator to it along with one of those cute little pressure gauges no bigger than a dime-sized lug nut that screws right into the first stage assembly. This set-up will let you know that your tank is close to full, but a full-sized pressure gauge, which will be a bit too bulky for most rec divers, will give you an exact PSI reading without straining your eyes. Tech divers use surgical tubing, neoprene straps and other materials to hold the regulator hose and second stage close to their pony tank.

Now where do you hitch your pony? With a 13- to 19-cubic-foot bottle you have a couple of options. Placing it on your back right side and mounted to your main tank or back plate is one choice. Some divers like to turn the pony upside down so they can reach back with little effort to turn the bottle valve knob on, and this configuration works great provided it doesn't hang too low and bump against any substrate. If you set your pony upright, then you have to raise your arm and reach back to turn it on. This is easy in the tropics but not when in cold water while wearing a 7-mm-thick suit and feeling as nimble as Gumby. This maneuver is best done on shore.

A small air-filled aluminum 19cuft tank on left, a steel 13cuft argon-filled tank and a 50% oxygen-filled 40cuft aluminum tank on the right. KRISTINA HUGHES

Lately a lot of divers are attaching their ponies to their D-rings on the left front side. Not only does this placement make one look like a cool tech diver, but this placement makes the pony easy to get to, turn off and on, hand to people aboard a boat or just reposition. Larger pony bottles are usually clipped on this way and are referred to as stage bottles. Tech divers may have several of these bottles set up or staged at different points along their dive; they usually turn them on then off again before leaving shore just to pressurize the systems before they enter the water. No sense in letting water get a chance to seep between the tank and first stage when the system is not in use.

A strong, braided, rot-resistant rope is tied around the neck of the pony tank and allowed to extend two-thirds of the way down the length of the tank where it is tied off to a stainless steel band. A piece of soft plastic hose is placed over the rope so that it acts as a carrying handle. Clip-on devices are attached to the rope near the neck of the pony tank or stage bottle, and it is attached to a shoulder high D-ring, while a clip device near the lower end of the D-ring is attached to a waist high D-ring. The clips are tied onto the rope and never held in place by metal. This way you can cut them off if for some reason they won't unsnap from your D-rings.

Nowadays you can also purchase a very well-designed clip and handle system for your pony/stage bottle. These new kits, which meet the recommended specifications of most dive organizations, come with the parts already assembled. Keep in mind, however, that some dive organizations follow their own guidelines for types of material and clips, and some organizations promote only the gear they produce and sell. Also, what may work in cave diving might not be the best choice for environments that deal with fast currents, changing tides or non-ideal surface conditions. Your local dive shop can recommend for specific nearby dive sites. Another good way to learn more about pony tanks and stage bottles is to take a related specialty dive course or ask your local dive instructor.

Stainless steel bands and aluminum brackets with a quick release pin keeps tanks from jostling around during the dive.

I hope you have a gas on your next dive and enjoy the added security and/or warmth you can receive by owning your very own pony . . . bottles.

In Search Of the Perfect Buoyancy Compensator

Buoyancy compensators or BCs are to a diver what ski poles are to a skier—they are used to fine-tune your movements while descending through a defined medium. And just as ski poles also help to hold you up when you are stationary in the snow, a BC can hold you up at any level underwater as well as while resting on the surface. Normally I give my BCs a workout while practising rescue diving scenarios, but as a drysuit diver that's about the only time I use them underwater. Normally once I'm underwater, my BCs are restricted to use as attachment points for various objects because, in effect, my drysuit becomes one giant air bladder. As a wetsuit diver, during the course of a dive you will typically inflate and deflate your BC as buoyancy requirements dictate. I could never see diving without a BC, but I like to use different types of BCs for different types of diving.

As a cold-water diver, I tend to classify BCs into three main categories: tropical, cold-water and technical.

Tropical BCs should be low profile and may have less than 25 pounds of lift capacity in warm water. Chances are that while wearing even a 3-mm wetsuit you'll need less than 18 pounds of integrated or non-integrated weight to make you neutrally buoyant. Enlarged BCs with surplus lift capacity just mean more drag or water resistance while moving through the water. Pockets are great for storing C-cards, but otherwise you could do without them. One or two D-rings for clipping on a camera or a small flashlight when it's not in use pointing out spiny lobsters may come in handy, but that's about all you need. The whole system should be sleek and unencumbered by hanging objects that might snag or scrape against pristine coral reefs. Smaller, close-fitting BCs are easier to pack in roller bags to take on trips. Several companies make excellent models such as the Seaquest Passport, Oceanic Excursion, Aeris Reef Raider or the Sherwood Tortuga. Tropical BCs seem to come in unlimited colors, styles and price ranges, but be cautioned: I've seen some BCs that were ordered on-line and the problems divers had with them. The best way to see which one fits your tropical needs is to visit your local dive shop. This way, your BC will be guaranteed, you can get immediate answers to your questions and you can save yourself the hassle of unanswered emails and unexpected postal charges.

Cold-water BCs come with integrated weight compartments or non-integrated weight systems. If you don't dive often, I recommend getting a weight-integrated BC. A few days of horizontal diving with a 25- to 45-pound weight belt around your waist when you're not used to it can really pull on your lower back muscles. Integrated weight BCs or additional weight harnesses help take the pressure off your lower back. On cold-water BCs I want to have four to eight D-rings and two or more zipper pockets in addition to any weight release pockets. I want to carry backup flashlights, camera equipment, crab gear (including a net bag and crab measuring gauge), pony bottle, argon bottle, notepad, lift bag, reel, signal beacon and any other home or yard appliances that I might be able to use underwater. As a recreational diver, I want to look like a Christmas tree displaying every object sold at the local dive shop. The DUI Delta and the Ranger BC work well for this task. Once underwater there's too much to see, and as a former scoutmaster I want to be prepared. I may have planned the dive to take pictures, but who can resist bringing home some Dungeness crabs if the season is open?

I mention technical BCs because some cold-water BCs with 65 pounds of lift capacity, like my Tech Ranger BC, are used interchangeably with recreational set-ups as well as technical gear set-ups including dual-tank configurations, and these work well in the open ocean. Cave divers prefer BCs that consist of a back plate, one or two sets of winged bladders, few buckles and one continuous interwoven strap/belt system. This type of system is the mix-and-match dive piece approach that when put together firmly attaches to your back. Advanced training is required before using such a system, and the extra weight may be too much for the occasional diver. Halcyon, Dive Rite, Apeks WTX series and OMS all make great tech diver configurations.

The first time I took my Ranger BC with 18 pounds of integrated weight to the Cayman Islands, I had one full suitcase and its full weight almost broke the local divemaster's back. I didn't have the heart to tell him that it was 25 pounds lighter than what I dive with back in Seattle. On my next trip I took my Seaquest Spectrum II tropical/pool instruction BC to Mexico. I had to wear a 17-pound weight belt with it and by the end of the week my back was sore. When I returned to Seattle, I started wearing a 25-pound weight belt even while wearing my integrated BC. That way, come my next vacation, I was ready for any weight system. I also liked the fact that by separating the weights, I couldn't accidentally release them all at the same time. I could also ascend in stages at a speed over which I had more control.

There are lots of options with BCs, but the more lift you need the more likely you'll need two different BCs to meet all of your diving needs. In cold water you can never have enough extra lift capacity and in tropical waters you can never seem to reduce enough excess drag. A BC for each environment may be the best way to solve this dilemma. After all, who isn't in favor of collecting more dive gear?

Incidentally, Seasoft is now making BCs specifically in children's sizes, so divers will be able to start their gear collections at an even younger age. The new Aqua Lung Pearl is made for women and features a sports bra-style front and a scalloped hip region.

The Custom Dive Tech Vest

Recently I had the opportunity to try out a new dive product whose best feature is that you don't even know you're wearing it. I'm talking about a weight-integrated vest produced by Custom Dive Tech and invented by Allen Rolfness, a PADI divemaster and scuba diver since 1980. This rather streamlined vest is made out of ballistic cloth and incorporates 10 to 12 pounds of lead weight evenly distributed across the middle of your back. There are two side pockets that each hold up to 15 pounds of additional weight, and the contents of these side pockets can be immediately discarded in an emergency by pulling on their easily located quick-release handles.

For years tech divers have been putting additional weights between their tanks and knowing this, the manufacturers of buoyancy compensators have routinely installed soft cushion pads where your scuba tank rests against your back. Allen, with a background in sewing upholstery products, has combined these two features and designed a weight-integrated vest that not only takes the weight off your hips and therefore prevents your weight belt from falling off ever again, but he has also made one that feels so comfortable you'll forget that part of the weight is in the back lining.

At Octopus Hole on the Hood Canal in Washington State, Steve Drynan, Allen and myself all wore one of his weight-integrated vests under our integrated buoyancy compensators. I discovered that the vest can be easily adjusted for a wide variety of body types, so I tightened the waist belt buckle and cinched down the shoulder straps until it felt comfortable yet firmly in place. For recreational divers the division of weight placement is a welcome relief. Now anyone can help you pick up your tank and BC, move it around or help place it on your back without the burden of all that extra weight. I set my tank on the tailgate of my truck and Allen assisted me as I put on my BC—I think he used one finger to lift up my BC shoulder strap as I inserted my right arm. I cinched up my BC and

Fixed soft lead weight sewn in the back of this vest acts as a cushion against a tank and backpack.

was surprised to find that the vest barely increased my overall volume. Not only had my BC been easier to put on with minimal assistance, but the vest also felt as if it had always belonged there. I now had two extra weight pockets in my BC so I immediately put a flashlight in one of them. With my pockets zipped up and gear ready to go, I reached down and checked the placement and position of the quick-release handles just below my BC. The handles were easy to locate and the weight would be simple to release in case of an emergency. I liked the fact that even if I dumped both side pockets of weight, still having 12 pounds of lead spread across my back would help slow and control an emergency ascent. More instructors and dive agencies are coming to the conclusion that dropping portions of weight is better than having to drop all your weight and shooting up to the surface like an uncontrolled rocket.

We went out on the dive and the vest fit so well that I forgot it was even there. There was no weight belt to slip or roll, and I just swam smoothly and fluidly through the water column while my mind concentrated on finding a giant Pacific octopus to show Steve and Allen. Back on shore after the dive we talked about the vest and what we had seen on the dive while we let Washington's finest liquid sunshine sluice the salt water off our drysuits. It was at this point that I noticed another innovative feature of the vest. Below each of the side weight pockets were small attachment D-rings where you could clip on a pouch or additional pocket to carry a spare mask or reel.

Allen explained that the vest is evolving on a daily basis with new innovations such as quick-release shoulder clips and optional crotch strap. However, he already has a product fit to ship to tropical destinations where snorkelers and divers just want to be neutrally buoyant without a cumbersome weight belt. It's also a product that both cold-water tech and recreational divers will love because the weight is removed from the hips, and one that will give divers with integrated BCs more options and pockets than they ever could have imagined possible. It is sold at Salem Scuba and Travel, Inc. in Oregon, as well as on-line at www.customdivetech.com.

Masks: A View on What's New

When you signed up for your first scuba course, you probably purchased your first dive mask. The dive shop employee showed you how to get the right fit for your specific facial features, explained the benefits of low-volume, hypoallergenic silicon, high-impact polycarbonate frames and tempered glass. Of course, the low-volume feature didn't concern you until you jumped into the pool and the instructor made you flood and clear your mask 5,000 times. But now that you owned a mask, you probably thought you were set for life. Not so fast. Just like shoes, there's a mask for every occasion. You might want to purchase a mask because of the way it looks or because its color goes well with the rest of your gear, but while there are ultimately too many types of masks and related features to list here, if you need to justify your purchasing decisions, here are some reasons and overall benefits that might make you want to enhance your mask collection today.

First, let's talk about lenses. Masks with red-colored lenses let you see more color with depth. Remember how everything starts to look dull and gray the deeper you go? Filtered lenses put the red back into your eyes for a more enhanced colorful view of the underwater world.

Masks can come equipped with special optical lenses to overcome personal vision deficits. Lenses or entire masks can be ordered to correct for astigmatism or other prescription requirements. Check out on-line sites such as www.prescriptiondivemasks.com. Multiple lens masks may provide a good field of vision as well as give extra areas to insert or stick on small auxiliary reading magnification lenses, but this type of mask does increase overall mask volume. A new style of mask recently on the market comes fused with a gauge-reading lower lens section with a diopter reading of +1.75. This is a great tool for the life-experienced diver who tends to be "macro-alphabetically challenged."

I had the opportunity to try out some great innovative dive gear from IST, and my favorite piece of equipment has to be their Pro Ear mask. I had seen them around but never had the chance to try one out before. It is a must for any diver with ear or sinus problems because it is designed to keep the ears dry, which is a good thing if you readily suffer from swimmer's ear, and the tubes from the ear compartment to the main mask area make it easier to equalize the pressure in the ears upon ascent and descent. During pollen season I always have equalization problems, which as a dive instructor I just can't afford to waste time on. I don't recommend ever diving with blocked sinuses, but if you are the type that just takes a little longer than everyone else to get underwater, then by all means try this mask.

I'm told that because the Pro Ear mask keeps your ears dry, you can hear sound directions more easily too, but with my cold-water hood on and my poor hearing (according to my wife), I can't really validate this claim. But I'll test the mask again on my next tropical dive. Although they recommend wearing the Pro Ear mask on the outside of a hood, I found the best way to keep your ears dry was by actually wearing it under the hood. IST's two-layer drysuit hood makes this an

HydroOptix MEGA 4.5DD mask. © 2009 HYDROOPTIX LLC

easy process, but it means that you'll either have to dive without a clipped-on snorkel like a tech diver or have to rig a Velcro strap on your hood to clip a snorkel in place. However, it's a minor inconvenience when it means relief from equalization and other ear problems.

Full-face masks make it possible to communicate verbally underwater to fellow full-face dive buddies. A frameless mask may be a good choice for a backup or travel mask. Tech divers love the way these lightweight masks fold up and fit into small pockets. Clear silicon masks are great for photography and relieving claustrophobia, while black silicon or rubber masks keep unwanted light from reflecting back through the lenses.

One of the latest and greatest scientific breakthrough masks has to be the HydroOptix, which has a bubble lens similar to the fish bowl lenses you see on some dive camera housings. This fish-eye approach gives you better depth perception, less visual distortion and a better overall view of underwater vistas. In fact, wearing the HydroOptix mask is like viewing underwater on an 80-foot-wide Imax screen. It makes using a conventional mask feel like looking at a show on a 13-inch TV.

So why isn't everyone rushing out to get a HydroOptix mask? Well, for one thing it is double the price of the average mask. Of course, high definition TVs are 10 to 20 times the price of a flat screen TV, and people are going out in droves to purchase those items. But perhaps another turn-off is that if you have 20/20 vision, you will have to wear contacts to make you nearsighted in order to obtain the visual benefits of the HydroOptix. And if you already have to wear contacts, the system gets a little more complicated. While on the surface you may also need to use the special plastic eyewear that attach to the mask, but this is a small price to pay to put the power of physics on your side.

Fortunately I'm already slightly nearsighted, so just wearing the HydroOptix mask without contacts gave me a better view than a conventional mask. However, this technique is better left for younger eyes; because of my age, prolonged use of the mask without contacts could result in headaches.

The main reason this mask is so awesome and worth the fuss of wearing contacts is the incredible wide-screen view it gives. Not just more peripheral view but a closer, wide-screen view of everything in front of you. The overall effect is dramatic. The second reason is because you see everything the way a fish-eye camera lens sees things. You have less optical distortion and therefore you see close objects more clearly and distant objects stand out instead of blending in with the background. You'll see things your buddies who are wearing conventional masks just can't see: you'll see the faint outline of a wreck ahead while they see only a blurred gray landscape. The third thing I like about this mask is that it magnifies everything so that the little numbers on my gauges and computers are easier to read, and while doing a decompression stop, I can observe shrimp in more detail.

One of the downsides to this mask is that it requires more care to avoid scratching the plastic lens. Appearance-wise, it makes the diver look like a giant insect, and the contact aspect may be a bit too much for divers who have never worn contacts before. However, the

> **For more information about masks:**
> www.prescriptiondivemasks.com
> www.HydroOptix.com

company is coming out with a new model for divers who don't want to wear contacts. I tried on the prototype and it is flat in the front like a conventional mask, but I still got the great peripheral vision of the advanced mask.

Personally, just as I'll go to great lengths to see certain movies on Cinerama-sized screens, I'll wear or put on anything to enhance my underwater view, and I fell in love with this mask at first sight. For people who spend thousands of dollars to travel to particular dive sites for the views, the HydroOptix would be worth the extra cash. The bottom line is that there's nothing even close to the view you'll get using it.

Note: sometimes the only way to justify acquiring a cool new mask is by "accidentally" leaving your old, outdated and faded mask on a conveniently located picnic table.

Snorkels

Thousands of years ago, probably on a Saturday morning, someone got the bright idea of using a hollow reed to breathe through while moving underwater in order to sneak up on some unsuspecting ducks. The plan, the reed and that hunter's deed gave rise to the expression "just like sitting ducks." It didn't take long to find other applications for this novel aquatic invention, and soon everyone from prehistoric fish hunters to the first recorded salvage divers were getting low on reeds.

On the serious side, thousands of refinements have culminated with the state-of-the-art dive tool known generically as the snorkel. While there are many types currently on the market, to use the right snorkel with the right technical innovations, consider the following recommendations:

1. The mouthpiece should be soft and replaceable. A sudden sharp attack by teeth shouldn't make a snorkel obsolete.
2. Just below the mouthpiece there should be a large reservoir or drain chamber to keep water out of the direct airflow pathway. At the bottom of this reservoir should be a self-draining purge valve. Some models of snorkels may even have the purge valve tilted at an angle to move exhaled bubbles out and away from the face area. Without a reservoir chamber, annoying water droplets could work their way down past your throat, and no one likes a leaky pipe system.
3. Attached to the main tube just above the mouthpiece you need a flexible, corrugated joint, preferably made out of

silicone. This corrugated midsection allows the mouthpiece to automatically drop down and away from your mouth as you switch to breathe off your regulator. It not only frees up a hand that would have been needed to move the snorkel out of the way but also works as a swivel when you rotate the upper end of the snorkel tube to make it fit more ergonomically against the side of your head and create a better breathing angle when your face is planted just below the water's surface. This corrugated midsection and the snorkel tube itself should have a large bore diameter so that the active diver doesn't become breathless.

4. The top of the snorkel may come equipped with a splash-guard, protective baffles or some other system to reduce random wave and splash water intake. Such a system will keep a snorkel semi-dry on the surface. Dry snorkels include an additional patented valve system that will not only keep all the splash water out but also stop water from entering the top of the snorkel when the diver is on or below the surface. Most of these devices are water pressure sensitive and work best if cleaned with fresh water on a regular basis. IST has a dry snorkel that works so well that even when I tried to breathe forcefully through it underwater, the tube stayed dry—not that I recommend using a snorkel underwater. On the surface just a slight exhalation opens the valve and lets you inhale water-free. How easy is that?

5. Most snorkel keepers that come with new snorkels are quick release or "easy-off-easy-on" in operation. I always keep a backup snorkel keeper in my save-a-dive kit.

6. If you're a tech diver and can't use a snorkel due to gear restrictions, you might be interested in some of the new models on the market that roll up or periscope down and fit nicely into a spare pocket. They can quickly be attached to your mask for leisurely viewing of divers below and quickly stowed when it's time to get down to business.

7. There's also a new snorkel in town with a revolutionary design that pretty much puts it in a class of its own. In fact, you can't even compare the Kapitol Reef™ snorkel, introduced by Kadence Technology Inc. and designed by Mark

R. Johnson, MD, to a conventional snorkel because it has a dual tube system where the inhaled air flows in through an outer chamber and the exhaled air flows out through an inner chamber, giving you an increased oxygen and carbon dioxide exchange with less effort exerted. In fact, the gas exchange is so efficient that they recommend never hyper-ventilating while using the Kapitol Reef.

Swim tests have shown that the rate of respiration is reduced by 32 percent over a conventional single-tube snorkel design. I tried to do the swim test and count breaths between laps and do the math in my head, but the real difference didn't hit me until I was using it while resting on the surface between dives in Cabo San Lucas, Mexico. I had been using a rental regulator during the dives, and although it was a good one, it just required more effort to breathe

through than my titanium regulator back home, which as a regulator techni-cian I have finely tuned. So just like my rental regulator, a conventional snorkel still works, but it requires more energy and effort than the dual air exchange

Kapitol Reef's snorkel and exchange port.
KAPITOL REEF

design of the Kapitol Reef. However, you don't have to breathe deeper and with more effort using a conventional snorkel during a long surface swim just to realize the physical cost benefits of switching to a Kadence technology-designed snorkel. Just rest on the surface with this snorkel and notice the reduced amount of physical work required to breathe in and expand your lungs against the surrounding surface water pressure.

Now I have to admit that the first time I used the Kapitol Reef and heard a slight gurgling noise—which is common during usage—I tried to keep clearing it because a similar sound during use of a conventional snorkel means you're about to swallow water with the next inhalation, but the Kapitol Reef remains clear even with a little water in the reservoir chamber. Once you relax and remind yourself that the new design is working normally, you quickly get used to this new sound.

So, what's the only real downside to this snorkel? It takes a little more effort to clear it on the surface during initial use, but expelling air during your ascent to the surface takes less effort and is the recommended way to clear it. In this way, it is ready to go the minute your head pops above the waterline. And I should add that it also makes slightly more noise as it fills with water when not in use as you start your dive descent. So the downside is relatively minimal compared to the great benefits.

The bottom line: the Kapitol Reef is a great snorkel for divers who want to reduce their anxiety and apprehension about obtaining air while on the surface. It's even a better snorkel for divers who want to exert less energy while gaining greater oxygen exchange and airflow. For divers accustomed to years of conven-

For more information:
www.kapitolreef.com

tional single-tube snorkel use there is a short learning curve required before you recognize the overall benefits of this fantastic product. I recommend you see a design demonstration on-line, then take it on a couple of dives. As a dive instructor and snorkeling enthusiast, I believe that with the introduction of the Kapitol Reef, the world of diving and snorkeling has stepped up an evolutionary notch from the days of the single-tube snorkel as the only design choice.

Get a Kick Out of Fins

When the first jet fins came to our attention in Hawaii in the early 1970s, we thought there could never be more powerful fins, and we didn't care how much leg power it took to push them through the water because we could always stop and float while we massaged a leg cramp. Then in the early 1980s the semi-clear Power Plana fins came to the islands. They were made from a revolutionary thermoplastic rubber material called Tecralene and were supposedly 20 percent more powerful than the early jet fins. Better still, they reduced the number of leg cramps. About the same time a short split fin called the force fin also started to make its way up and down the West Coast, although I didn't really hear much about this one until 20 years later. In the 1990s we were introduced to Apollo Bio-fins. These full-length split fins were said to generate 30 percent more power than a conventional fin and leg cramps were almost a thing of the past. Nowadays every manufacturer seems to produce some derivation of the original split fin, yet old-style jet fins are still in vogue with cave divers where currents usually aren't an issue, and Plana fins are still a good medium-priced choice for people entering the sport.

So which pair of fins is right for you? There are many factors to consider. I prefer professional force fins, twin jet fins or split fins when recreational diving, but I would rather use regular old-school force fins, jet fins or conventional fins for technical diving. Too much force can silt up an underwater environment, and some brands of split fins turn from hard rubber into Jell-o when you kick fast or carry a heavy load. Navy SEAL teams discovered that while many modern split fins and other high output fins have a lot of initial power, during non-recreational activities they make the diver consume more oxygen per kick cycle. Fortunately, recreational divers need not be as concerned about air consumption during a dive as tech divers and inherently powerful load-bearing SEAL teams where a rate change in air consumption could be critical.

If all you are doing is a few dives a year, then a pair of conventional fins could last you a long time. In fact, I still occasionally use a pair of my conventional fins for tech diving (or when I want to attract harbor seals!). Rent them or try them out first if you can. However, if you can afford them or you dive more often, get yourself a pair of split fins, twin jet fins or the real original force fins. You'll get a lot more power and a lot fewer leg cramps for the extra money. These types of fins also allow you to move and rotate 360 degrees without much effort. IST's Talaria II fins are powerful split fins that have been curved so you don't have to keep your feet hyper-extended and angled back in order to position your fins level and straight in line with your body. This feature relieves a lot of muscle tension around the ankles yet still provides the power and agility you've come to expect from split fins.

Size is also an important criterion. Bigger fins not only require more leg muscle but they have a tendency to bump into things, which could be a negative issue in a silted overhead environment. And when traveling, you may find that your small fins will fit into a carry-on bag, but big fins may need to be checked in with cargo.

Now if you are one of those divers who likes to frog-kick underwater, then you might prefer conventional fins, real force fins or modern material versions of jet fins. Regular split fins propel a diver fast during slow to moderate scissor kicks, but some flexible varieties of split fins have a tendency to feel like mush when doing frog kicks.

The last few years have seen the greatest outpouring of styles, shapes and sizes in fins, but just when you think you've seen them all, someone comes along with a product that once you've tried it out, you know you have to have it. The Amphibian™ fin by Omega Aquatics is just such an I-gotta-have-it product. Yes, I know what you're thinking. What? Another pair of fins? But this fin flips up to rest vertically and gently against your shin while you walk on the heel/sole section of your foot as you would in a pair of flip flops or hardened sandals.

I took a pair of Amphibians to Miami Beach, Florida, to test them out, and I was surprised how many people stared at my bright yellow-and-black-bordered fins as I walked across the beach with them in the "flipped-up" mode. On a beach where clothing is optional I would have expected they had seen it all by now. The fins don't flip down and lock into swimming position until you give one or two strong kicks. Although the waves may pull the fins downwards as you walk through flowing water, without the strong kicks or bending your leg back then immediately straight forward or pressing down on the fins with your other foot or a helping hand, the fins will spring right back against your shins as the force of the flowing water diminishes.

At the end of the dive, to flip the fins back to the vertical position, all you have to do is run the heel of one foot over the latch on the top of the fin on the other foot. I practised the maneuver a few times, and before long I found that I could even float on the surface while I flipped the fins into the stowed position. With these scuba fins, you don't have to take them off before stepping aboard a boat. Just flip them up and climb up the ladder. You don't even need to take your fins off between dives either, just wear them around as if they're a pair of slightly oversized dive boots.

During my Miami saltwater test the fins worked as well if not better than most conventional fins. When I finished swimming around in the ocean, I kept them on as I waded through waist-deep waters. I quickly found that there was a slight water resistance pressing against the fins when I walked straight forward, but the

Bob Evens is the genius who invented the Force Fin. The design has been imitated thousands of times, but never equalled in power or performance. The Force Fin is a Navy SEAL staple.

Amphibian Flipfins, Omega Aquatics.
TY SAWYER

resistance diminished greatly when I turned and walked slightly at an angle, and I found that walking with the fins on in the flipped-up position in shallow waters was a breeze. From the beach I walked right over to the showers to rinse off, then I stepped over to the hotel pool and marched right in. You might say I got a kick out of double dipping, going from saltwater to chlorinated water without ever removing any of my dive gear.

Amphibian fins will change the way instructors teach diving too, as this fin can be slipped on at any stage of the gearing-up process. It no longer has to be the last thing you do before entering the water. Divemasters and instructors will also love the fact that they can have their own fins on and ready to go but still be able to enter and exit the water as many times as they need to without the additional effort of putting on and taking off their fins every time.

By placing my Amphibians in the half-flipped-up position, I was able to carry both of them inside my airline regulation-sized roller bag. Then I used the netted Omega Aquatics carry-bag that came with the fins to transport them down to the beach. It also has an outer pocket to insert a mask and snorkel so that the whole system travels well from plane to beach and back again.

The bottom line: while wearing Amphibian fins you may look a little like something out of a *Transformer* robot movie, but it doesn't take long to feel comfortable and accustomed to them, and with your hands freed-up while walking to and from the water's edge, you can more readily multi-task and carry extra dive gear. Getting off and on a dive boat need no longer be an orchestrated ordeal, and you can lounge about on the boat with your fins on, permitting you to be ready to lend assistance to fellow divers in or out of the water. The Amphibian may not be the most powerful recreational scuba fin, the longest fin or the widest split fin on the market, but its amazing flexibility, ease of use and unique ability to be worn during all dive phases makes it a top fin to seek out.

I'm beginning to think that I collect fins just like my wife collects shoes. I still use some of my old fins from time to time—I'll use my flip fins for excessive boat and shore duty and I pack force fins in my travel bags—but no matter how many I own, I'll still be on the lookout for the next great ones. It wouldn't surprise me if they turn out to look just like a seal's flipper, a military spec force fin or some other fluke of nature.

Dive Knives: The Cutting Edge of Dive Gear

Back when I first started diving, I bought the biggest pointy knife the dive shop sold. I intended to use it to fight off great white sharks and other denizens of the deep. Over the years I've hardly ever used that knife. I cut a piece of string with it once, and I still carry it around from time to time. The steel has never rusted, and I think the knife still looks cool. But since those early days I've learned a lot about dive knives and maybe you can use some of the following tips (pardon the pun).

If you go inside any modern, well-stocked kitchen, you'll find an assortment of knives. There's usually a serrated-edged bread knife, a paring knife to cut apples and perhaps a thick-bladed butcher knife. After diving a while you'll also end up with a random assortment of dive knives for various uses and underwater activities. A zip knife or line cutter, conveniently wrist-mounted for quickly slicing through fishing line, can come in handy. A stainless steel, EMT-style scissors placed on your right shoulder strap or tucked away in a pocket will snip through metal fabricated fishing lines too tough for some conventional dive knives to cut. A blunt-edged knife placed on a hose, waist belt or the inside portion of the leg is great for prying open oysters and rock scallops and usually comes with a serrated long edge for cutting through large ropes.

I never recommend carrying a sharp, pointed knife no matter how cool they look because that sharp point is more likely to go

Real Shark Tales

From past experience I've found that the best way to keep sharks away is to carry an underwater camera. It seems sharks would rather vacate the immediate area than pose for an informal photo shoot. At the end of a dive in Maui I was just stepping up the dive ladder when a small white tip reef shark splashed right behind me with a fish hanging halfway out of his mouth. I had just turned my camera off. Then there was the time off Grand Cayman Island when a black tip reef shark circled my assigned buddy who took off without me while I was still slowly descending from the surface because the housing of my new instamatic camera was flooding. Do you sense a pattern here?

And while diving in the Pacific Northwest I haven't fared any better. I dived at Camp Parson Boy Scout camp looking for crabs and saw nothing, while just 30 feet away from where I was diving the boys caught a three-foot spiny dogfish shark, but I didn't see a thing underwater. I know the Northwest is famous for bluntnose sixgill sharks, but I've never seen one. I once saw an emaciated dogfish down at the oil dock at Edmonds hovering between the wooden piles. I think the only reason he let me take pictures was because he was too old, too emaciated and too tired to swim away. The only time I saw more than one shark at a time in the Pacific Northwest was when my friends and I deliberately chummed the water up in Canadian waters and attracted over a hundred dogfish in various sizes and aggressive states.

I guess the bottom line is that if you want to see a shark, chum the water like they did on the movie *Jaws* and almost any response is possible. If you prefer not to see a shark, just dive with a camera loaded with film in a dry, waterproof housing. Sharks can sense an exuberant photographer on the prowl over a mile away, but even on a good day, an armed photographer can only see less than 100 feet with one eye glued to his camera lens.

through your wetsuit than ever poke a hole in an unsuspecting fish. But I've seen countless certified divers enter a dive shop, pick up a large pointed knife and proclaim, "This should keep the sharks away." The truth is, it's to your advantage to fend off a shark with a flat-edged knife or, better yet, to tap the shark with the handle of the knife. Thrusting a sharp point into the skin of a shark draws blood, and that can only make matters worse. Sharks operate on millions of years of refined instinct after blood is spilled in the water, no matter whose blood it is. The scent is so powerful that some species of shark just take a bite out of anything close by, including members of their own species. That's why a blunt-edged knife works so well—it just rubs the shark the wrong way and he tends to move on to other things. I've never been bothered by sharks unless I chummed the water on purpose, but if for some reason you are being bothered, it's probably a good time to leave the water and forget about the Kung Fu knife scenes.

In reality, dive knives can be a lifesaver, but it's usually when they have to be used to disentangle a diver from a man-made obstruction. Strapping a knife on the inside of your leg to avoid catching on anything and attaching another knife on your lower chest or shoulder region leaves at least one knife accessible at all times, even when your range of mobility is temporarily restricted. (Personally I don't feel comfortable on a dive unless I'm also carrying my zip knife and my scissors.) With a minimum of two knives strategically placed, you'll most likely never encounter a situation where you have to use them, but the day you dive without a knife may be the day you really need one most. Safe diving, in this case, includes a tool that can ultimately do more than just look cool.

Dive Lights

When driving your car, you use the right lights for the right driving conditions—high beams for dark country roads, low beams at dusk and fog lamps in low visibility conditions. You also have half a dozen lights inside the car to read gauges and maps or to see what you misplaced in your glove compartment. Underwater you'll want the right light for the right diving conditions too.

First, let's go through a two-second introduction and summary on the size and power of batteries, and then we'll go right into real world applications, which as divers we care about most. A battery's power is typically 1.5 volts whether it is a "C" sized cell or a "D" sized cell, although a D cell is bigger than a C cell and the power of a D cell lasts about twice as long as the power of a C cell battery. In addition, the larger the number of batteries used the longer the power lasts. Rechargeable nickel-metal-hydride batteries may last half as long as conventional batteries, but over the life of a dive light it is easier to carry a battery charger around than 400 alkaline batteries. In addition, some rechargeable battery kits can double the wattage output on some models of dive lights.

One of the first things a new diver will ask is how many dive lights he needs. If you're only doing daylight dives, then I suggest at least one flashlight with four to eight watts of power. You'll need it to peek inside crevices to spot the tentacles of the giant Pacific octopus, and on bright sunny reefs you'll need it to peer between coral ledges for signs of rare shells, spiny lobsters and gold pieces of eight. On summer days in Seattle I used to carry a predecessor to the Princeton Tec Torrent light. The eight watts of power used eight AA cell batteries so it was small but packed a lot of power for a three- to five-hour dive. It came in handy when the plankton concentration was so thick that it blocked out the sun's rays so that at 80 feet it was pitch black. The dual internal o-rings were also a great leakage safety factor. The UK Sunlight SL6 at eight watts, although slightly larger, also works well for daylight four- to five-hour excursions, and this model usually comes in standard kits or is readily available as a stand-alone product.

On night dives you can never carry enough lights. I recommend three plus a cyalume glow stick or a light beacon or similar device attached to your tank. You'll want your primary light to have at least 12 watts of power. The rechargeable UK Sunlight D8 has 30 watts for 1.25 to 3 hours or you can switch to 14 watts for 7 to 10 hours. This wid-beam light is big and heavy and can almost double as a weight belt, but it is built to last and, until recent advances in LED technology were made, this was by far my favorite night-light. I once found one that had been submerged for over six months; it was all banged up and covered with barnacles, but it still held a full battery charge and lit right up.

The UK HID Light Cannon 100 has 25 (equivalent) watts of power and, because the light output is closer to that of the sun, its blue rays penetrate far in the water column; however, it doesn't light up the entire reef like the rechargeable D8 light. When you turn on the various lights in the dive store, the HID 100 may shine the brightest on the far wall in one concentrated area, but it may not be the best light for you. The Light Cannon is smaller and easier to carry, but because you have to turn it on and wait a few seconds before the high intensity discharge illuminates, you might find it frustrating. It works best when turned on before you get into the water and left on until the dive is over. It also breaks easily if you are not careful where you set it down or what you bang it against. It's a high-tech light for high-tech, responsible divers.

The Princeton Tec Shockwave II rechargeable with 15 watts for 4 to 6 hours or 7.5 watts for 8 to 10 hours is lighter and easier to carry; I take it along in one capacity or the other on almost every dive. Other notable primary lights include the Sunlight C8 rechargeable with 20 watts for 1.5 to 2.5 hours, the Sunlight D4 rechargeable with 18 watts for 1.25 to 3 hours and the Pelican Nemo with 13.8 watts for 3 to 4 hours.

You might recall from your basic dive class that they recommend a primary and a secondary backup light on night dives. If one of the lights goes out, use the backup light to guide you back to shore and end the dive. On night dives I want my backup light to have at least eight watts of power, and, although I probably go overboard, I carry a third light just in case my buddy or I have a faulty light and need extra backup. By carrying a tertiary light—or technically two primary lights—you won't ever have to end a dive early due to a dive light malfunction. If you are traveling and only carrying two lights, make sure one of them has the most wattage power you can get your hands on. You pay thousands to get to a dive destination, so you deserve the best illuminated views possible, and it's always better to have other divers swimming close to you to see what you're viewing than to be following the other divers to get a glimpse of what they are looking at.

Comparing LED lights to incandescent (bulb) lights used to be easy because these practically indestructible lights are great for locations where electricity is scarce, but the light-emitting diodes with their lumens of bright white light power just couldn't compete with their higher watt (bulb) cousins. With advances such as the UK Aqua Sun rechargeable with a water-cooled heat sink embedded right in the center of the lens, you get 825 lumens of power. The Big Blue BB1X30 by Bossk USA emits 1,000 lumens. So what is a lumen? It's a measure of brightness. Measuring the light output of LEDs by watts is rather like an American measuring miles on a Canadian road where all the signs are in kilometres. But it's even trickier than that because in some cases you can't convert them. For example: on some lights 1 watt = 6 lumens while on other lights 1 watt = 41 lumens, with the average being between 1 watt = 14–25 lumens. In addition, a UK C8 xenon bulb light may emit 367 lumens while a C8 edge-emitting LED (ELED) will have 257 lumens, but a mini Q40 ELED will emit 67 lumens while a mini Q40 xenon bulb will emit only 50 lumens. Comparing oranges to apples is far easier, and that's why you should expect watts to disappear from the scene in the next couple of years, and lumens with their true quantitative measure of light-emitting brightness to inherit the world—just like kilometres versus miles. In the meantime getting 10 to 20 dives out of one LED dive light compared to only an hour's burn time on some bulb/watt models may be the deciding factor for many traveling as well as local divers for years to come.

If you're a photographer, you may find the UK Mini Q40 light handy. It straps onto the side of your mask and comes in handy when you are trying to keep your subject in sight while using all available hands on your camera and strobe system. There are other fancy headgear light systems, but this one is a quick and inexpensive fix for recreational diving needs.

One light that every diver should have for safety is a Coast Guard-approved, low-profile strobe light like the ACR Firefly II or III (manual). I have one of these permanently attached to my buoyancy compensator. People can see this strobe on the surface three miles away, and underwater it makes a great beacon to swiftly attract your buddy's attention. The strobe can last hours and the batteries up to five years if not used. It's the ultimate night strobe and anti-lost-at-sea night device. The Princeton Tec ECO Flare is another recent contender that can emit 6 lumens for up to 500 hours. The

Aqua Strobe with 70 flashes per minute and 8 hours of burn time is another good safety option.

As for tank lights and beacons, you've got a wide variety to choose from. The color of the tank light or pulse of the strobe can make it easier for your dive buddy to distinguish you from others in a group of divers. Most of the batteries are small disks that don't last long, so if you are going on multiple night dives or you dislike changing batteries, I suggest getting a UK light beacon with 0.1 watts of power for 24 hours on two AAA batteries or the Aquatec Mini LED light stick (the strobe model lasts for 50 hours and is impressively bright for such a small sturdy device) or the Sports Flare with 4 lumens and 8 hours of burn time. There are other great lights with non-standard battery sizes, but I stick to A, C or D ratings as the other lights burn out and tend to sit in my closet for years before I can find replacement batteries. I've been able to find AA Kirkland brand batteries on small islands where standard household electricity isn't even an option. (How does Costco of Kirkland, Washington, do this?)

To sum it up, your primary night dive light should have the highest watt output you can afford—at least 15 watts or 400 lumens. Try the UK Aqua Sun ELED rechargeable at 825 lumens before you make your final decision, that is, if you don't mind carrying a bit bigger light. Your secondary light should have 4 to 8 watts or 100 lumens for daylight exploration. A strobe light for safety and location purposes should be attached to your BC. Unless you want to hand-pick each light, the UK Fathom 4 box set may be a good entrance choice for you. It includes the Sunlight C8, Sunlight SL4, Mini Q40 and the Dive Beacon. The Princeton Tec ultimate dive set includes a Shockwave LED at 400 lumens, a Torrent LED and an Eco Flare. The Princeton LED Pack is a great travel and energy-conscious set and includes the Shockwave LED, Impact XL, Eco Flare, a coil lanyard and a mini-retractor. Oh, and just as a reminder—don't forget to take a night diver course, get a big shore lantern and/or better yet, use a lighthouse near the shoreline to light your way back to your dive entry point.

Signaling Devices

What always amazes me is the number of people who scuba dive without the proper emergency essentials. Chances are you will spend your entire diving career having a great time exploring reefs, wrecks and other relics and never have to give a thought about something as inconspicuous as a signaling device. You may even have done a thousand buddy checks before entering the water, but on your last dive do you recall seeing a whistle attached to your buddy's buoyancy compensator?

How can I possibly stress the importance of signaling devices? Perhaps by taking the position that by wearing or carrying signaling devices on every dive, you'll never find yourself lost for alternatives when accidentally lost at sea. Blowing three short blasts SOS-style on your whistle and inflating your six-foot-long orange tube may get your buddy's attention if he is just nearby on the surface. A blast horn connected to your inflator valve may be heard up to a mile away, but what would you do if you were out at sea, just like in the movies, and all you could see was empty horizon?

Airlines, during emergency training, say that the first 24 to 72 hours are the most critical for someone lost at sea. This is the time when the greatest numbers of search efforts are made and the period during which you need to be doing the most to get noticed and to keep your face in the spotlight. Unfortunately, the best item to signal for help while at sea is not typically carried by most divers. An inexpensive signal mirror like the ones issued by the military and found at most surplus stores can fit into the pocket of just about any BC and when pointed correctly can be seen up to 25 miles away in direct sunlight. A silver knife blade, the glass plate of a dive mask, a CD or anything shiny might be seen a few miles away, but nothing signals farther and comes complete with a built-in, cross-hair view finder for directing the sun's rays at potential targets than a small hand-held signal mirror. If you don't want to put together your own kit, the Divers Alert Network (DAN) signal sausage comes with a storage pouch that contains a windstorm whistle, small signaling mirror and a chemical light stick. At night, in addition to dive lights and glow sticks, I recommend wearing a Coast Guard-approved strobe light. I have one permanently mounted on the upper right side of my BC. Some models can be seen as far away as 5 miles while flashing, the batteries typically last years when not in use and the strobe may work up to 39 hours while continuously flashing.

Other things you can do to make sure that your chance of being spotted is the culmination of preparedness and not just dumb luck should include waving fins or yellow weight pouches in the air—provided you are in calm waters. Yellow bicycle tape on the undersides of black fins helps overall visibility above as well as below the surface. Last but not least, and especially if you are wearing a drysuit, place a cellphone in a waterproof case or bag and place it inside your drysuit in an easily accessible location. You won't get cell coverage during the dive, but you may be able to order a pizza or call for help once back on the surface. Provided that you are wearing a hood, while you are waiting to be discovered by a boat, plane or a talent agent from Hollywood, remove your weights and float flat on your back. This way you will have minimal contact with the water and the amount of heat transferred

Sea Marshall Dive Alert. MARINE RESCUE TECHNOLOGIES

from your body to the water will be reduced. If you are not wearing a hood (10 percent of heat is lost through the head) and you happen to be with others, huddling together may be the best way to prevent heat loss.

And if you really want to go overboard with lost-diver-locating devices, carry a Sea Marshall™ alert unit. Its neoprene carry-pouch can clip anywhere. When activated, this unit broadcasts a signal of 121.5 MHz, which is the international search and rescue homing frequency. The EL light antenna can be easily placed over a mask and hood and glows like a chemical stick necklace. Not recommended for pool parties. It's rated down to 300 feet.

As a dive instructor I've been using both the original Dive Alert surface and subsurface signaling devices for close to 10 years. It's easy to gain undivided attention with one quick tap on the button, and the walrus-like noise travels quickly across any size pool. With tank bangers and similar devices, you can really only indicate relative position or the *need* to communicate, but with my trusty submersible Dive Alert in the H_2O/subsurface mode I can designate one tap for attracting attention, two taps for regrouping and three taps for stop, look out, or even that it's time to end the dive. The endless sequence possibilities between long and short pneumatic blasts are up to you and your dive buddies to devise. In the past I've used two short taps and a hand on my head in the shape of a fin to point out sharks to a buddy. Once I actually used one long tap to warn a diver who was about to ascend that he was going to hit his head on the bottom of the dive boat; I guess it's easy to get engrossed in the beauty of a Cayman reef and forget to look where you are going.

As for my original Dive Alert surface model, I've kept it permanently connected between my power inflator on my cold-water BC and my low-pressure hose. The high-pitched sound it makes is one that I would never use unless in an emergency and definitely not near anyone else's ear or my own. It's probably one of the best emergency devices you can own because, no matter how out of breath you are or how thick the fog is, that sound is likely to penetrate nearby docks, harbors and major shipping lanes.

The new Dive Alert Plus combines the former Dive Alert surface and subsurface models in one ultimate unit that connects or disconnects quickly to just about any model of BC inflator hose. It is smaller than the old submersible model, and the new pneumatic dolphin noise it emits in the "H_2O" mode is a little more pleasing to the ears. In the air mode the sound still carries long distances across the water's surface, but it is now more like a conventional whistle being blown.

For safety, I highly recommend wearing the Dive Alert Plus on every dive. For best results keep the unit in the "H_2O" mode and ready to use while exploring underwater. You and your buddies can make up your own pneumatic signals and morse code signs. After-dive care is simple: just rinse as suggested. And if you ever encounter an emergency situation on the surface or want to get the attention of a boat captain, simply rotate the switch to "AIR" and blast away. Keep in mind that, as corny as it sounds, sometimes being a hero is just a by-product of having the right equipment on hand at the right time. The Dive Alert Plus is great for signal communications underwater, but it's a serious signal device on the surface that's easy to use, easily accessible and ready when time is of the essence.

Remember, if you carry the right gear, becoming lost at sea will be a minor and temporary inconvenience. However, diving without the right signaling tools and not having the ability to use them when needed could leave you with nothing but a breathtaking view of the distant horizon.

> **For more information about signaling devices:**
> www.diversalertnetwork.org
> www.seamarshall-us.com

Why You Need a Lift Bag

While diving, you spot what looks like it could be a black weight belt with faded Velcro-lined side pockets lying on the sandy bottom. (You'll be surprised how grungy things can look underwater and how new they look after a little cleaning up at home!) You race over to it before your buddy has a chance to grab it, but when you try to pick it up, you realize it must weigh close to 40 pounds. What do you do? If you choose to hold it in your arms and drag it back to shore, the extra 40 pounds will put you almost face down on the seabed. If you fill your buoyancy compensating device (BC) to compensate for the weight, you could be putting yourself at serious risk. If you inflate your BC and for some reason accidentally let go of the extra weight belt, you're likely to be on a one-way uncontrollable jet-speed trip right up to the surface. Even if you somehow hold onto your prize, its Velcro compartments could open up and spill their contents at any time, and you won't know how good the Velcro is until you get a chance to examine the belt at the end of the dive. Maybe the Velcro will hold well, but what if inside each of the compartments the former owner has placed old socks filled with lead pellets? (Don't laugh; I've found such systems.) The problem is that if the pellets fall out a little at a time, at what point will you realize that you're getting lighter and ascending faster and faster toward the surface?

Now you are coming to the end of the dive and your buddy signals for you to surface. Do you have enough lift to get you and your new treasure up there? You'll have to hope your buddy doesn't need a hand because all five of yours will be busy holding the weight belt, inflating your BC, switching to your snorkel, adjusting your mask and checking your compass and pressure gauge. Oh, did I mention pressure gauge? Pulling, tugging and dragging on your new find could have caused you to suck down an extra 500 to 1,000 pounds of air. Unless you had extra reserves in the beginning, you could be in trouble.

Now let's try this same scenario with a 50-pound lift bag. You tie your lift bag to the newly found weight belt and, using your secondary regulator, you put enough air inside the lift bag to make the weight belt just barely negative. Now you can easily lift it with one hand with little physical exertion. Next, while holding onto the belt, you add just a touch more air to the lift bag until the bag and belt are neutrally buoyant in the water column. Now the belt can hover anywhere you like all day long. You can swim around while guiding it with two fingers. There is little risk for you, and it only took a small amount of air from your tank.

So now you're into treasure hunting. How big a lift bag should you get? I recommend a 50-pound lift bag or less for most recreational activities. At this size you might be able to fit it into a spare

BC pocket. As a tech diver I like to carry a 100-pound lift bag tucked between my twin tanks and the small of my back, and I keep it in place with bungee cords. A bag any bigger than that and your buddies will think you're planning to bring back the *Titanic*.

Lift bags come in many sizes and types of material, but whatever material you choose, rinse it thoroughly after every dive because nothing seems to cut better than dried salt crystals. As it's hard to turn a bag upside down and empty out a large volume of air underwater, if you choose a large bag, get one with a dump valve. You'll find it easy to pull the knob connected by a string to the dump valve near the top of the lift bag. Once enough air has trickled out of this opening, you can turn the lift bag upside down to let the rest of the unwanted air escape.

You might see tech divers sporting one or two lift bags because they use them in conjunction with reels and lines as location markers on the surface to let others know where they are doing their decompression stops and sometimes to send up messages. Divers also use lift bags when they are building subsurface structures such as underwater park enhancements. There are a lot of reasons why you should own a lift bag too. For example, it could save you a lot of time and energy, but it also might pay for itself the very first time you use it to bring something reusable back to the surface.

Underwater Cameras

I first saw Pioneer Research's SeaLife DC500 underwater camera at the Dog Day Rally put on by Diving Unlimited International, Inc. (DUI) at Owens Beach State Park in Tacoma, Washington, in September 2008, and I had the opportunity to speak with the company's North American director. I was really intrigued by all the advances they had made since the introduction in 1993 of their DC100 digital camera, which I still carry everywhere. Then a month later at the DEMA convention in Las Vegas I got my hands on a DC500 of my very own. Right out of the box and with no more preparation than a scan of their two-sided, quick-start, fold-out instruction sheet, I took the DC500 on a dive in the pool at the Riviera Hotel and Casino. This was when a group of us were attempting to set a world record for the largest underwater conference, and I noticed right away that I was the only one of the 15 journalists present with an underwater camera. Some of them had years of experience as photojournalists and routinely used cameras worth thousands and thousands of dollars, but the day of the conference I had the only underwater camera at hand.

The DC500 system is so compact that it's easy to keep this camera with you at all times and be ready to shoot anywhere and anytime. The built-in capability to zoom from telephoto to macro lens settings allows you to take a wide variety of shots without carrying a lot of accessory equipment. I did use an extra-wide-angle lens for the pool, but it attached easily and quickly to the rugged metal- and rubber-coated housing. The built-in 10 megabytes of memory allowed me to take quite a few lower resolution shots of the event and since they were the only ones taken, they got printed around the world. Since that debut I've added a 256-megabyte SD memory card, and superfine resolution is the new limit. At 5 megapixels I can get 79 shots; at 3 megapixels and normal resolution someone not bent on trying to get the Pulitzer Prize can get 370 shots.

Besides being able to change the quality and quantity of shots during a dive, you can also change external flash modes if using the SL960 or SL960dx strobes from normal flash, macro flash and far flash. The buttons on the underwater housing are easy to use during the course of a dive, and after reading the short instruction manual, even an adult can use all the camera's features. It took me about 15 seconds to change shot size, quality and flash settings even though I was wearing gloves under pressure, but I'm sure with more practice I could reprogram the camera while doing fin kicks and holding onto a lobster.

Time magazine wrote up the DC500 as "one of the most amazing inventions of 2005." In my opinion the best part of the camera has to be the shark or quick shoot mode. Previously I carried a separate film camera just to photograph sharks, seals and other fast-moving subjects because digital cameras are notorious for the long delay between pushing the shutter button and the shutter actually opening to record the shot. With the DC500 this lag can be reduced to a mere 0.17 of a second, which is almost non-existent. You just press the "OK" button, a shark icon appears on the viewfinder and auto focus and exposure control are set. Then as long as you want the same background scene, you just click away at your subject. When you're ready to change scenes or reset to auto focus and exposure, press the "OK" button again to discontinue shark mode. This feature would have really come in handy on one of my previous trips to British Columbia when we were feeding spiny dogfish sharks. It's hard to keep a slow-lag digital camera focused on target when your target is a group of five-foot-long sharks that are bumping into your shoulders and swimming between your legs, and between the time we pressed the shutter buttons on our old digital cameras and the shutters actually opened, the sharks were long gone. I'm actually surprised I got any shots at all on that dive, but with the new DC500 digital camera I can't wait to try it again . . . though perhaps with less aggressive seals or even fun-loving dolphins.

The DC500 system is so light that I was even able to hold it in my hand while operating an underwater scooter to zip myself from one photo session to the next. The special features can be set up in seconds, and the continuous shooting mode, video clip mode and audio mode to listen to voice or sound recordings are just a few additional features that make this a powerful camera on land too. The docking station where you can recharge the lithium battery, connect to a TV or instantaneously download shots to your computer via a USB port just put this camera over the top on the charts. I can't promise that with all this might and tech power your pictures will end up on the cover of *Time* or *National Geographic*, but I can predict that with a little practice you'll get pictures that you'll be proud to show anyone.

The SeaLife DC500 digital camera, however, was just a step in the Pioneer Research team's quest to revolutionize the world of underwater photography. They took their 2005 invention of the year, added more features, repositioned a few buttons, made the camera easier to program and turned it into a brand new work of art called the DC600. A six- megapixel digital camera elite set with enhanced land and sea exposure modes, it comes with a digital strobe, an additional macro lens and a travel-friendly carrying case. I tested the DC600 at Sund Rock, a marine preserve near Hoodsport, Washington. The first fish I encountered was a buffalo sculpin, and my first shot at maximum strobe output strength highlighted the fish as well as its nest of pinkish eggs mere inches away on the side of

You're very likely to be photographed while trying to photograph when diving with the crew of the *Nautilus Explorer.* MIKE LEVER

a rock. Pressing halfway down on the shutter button informs the camera to get all the settings ready. When you press all the way down, the camera immediately flashes and sends a signal via an optical cable to the strobe to fire at precisely the same moment the camera records the shot. The lag time between shutter pressed and shot recorded is virtually non-existent. A picture forms on an enhanced 2.5-inch viewing screen so you can see exactly what you shot and you can decide whether you like the setting and light conditions. You can delete the picture at this point if you want; to keep it, just get ready to take the next shot. You can reposition the camera or the strobe or change the strobe output level during the brief eight or nine seconds it takes the strobe to recharge for the next shot. The strobe recharge time depends on the type of batteries you use. SeaLife recommends 2300 mAh AA batteries, but I was using 1500 mAh batteries and still got 90 shots before the recharge time began to show signs of slowing down.

I took several shots at various settings of the sculpin before I moved on to a large wolf-eel tucked under a boulder. It was hard to get any light directed on it except from straight on, but by simply turning a knob and reducing the strobe light output, it was easy to get the best possible shot. A lingcod helped me test the macro lens that I had attached by a quick release tray just under the strobe frame where the camera is mounted. All I had to do was slide out the wide-angle lens and pop it right into place over the camera housing. It's really a sweet and easy-to-use locking system.

At a sunken boat I changed the exposure value using the buttons on the camera housing. You can make the shot brighter by +2.0 exposure value (ev) or darker by –2.0 ev in .3-ev increments by just tapping a button or two in rapid succession. Without changing the ev, everything on the boat appeared dark, but by changing to +1.7, the plumose anemones on the boat were not only visible but became bright orange or white when the strobe fired and recorded the shot. I had not really appreciated the ev feature until that moment, and I'm convinced that if the photos look this good in dark, cold Northwest waters, I should expect to get a Pulitzer Prize for every shot I take in clear tropical waters.

The maker recommends using a 1GB SD storage card that should give you 292 shots at the 6-MB fine quality setting. I took my 90 pictures in the space of a 50-minute dive, which means I used up the strobe batteries at approximately the same rate as the 3.7-volt lithium battery inside the camera. On land the camera battery lasts a little more than an hour when in constant use, so expect to recharge both camera and strobe batteries after every dive. In the tropics where you go on one-tank dives followed by lunch and sunshine, battery recharging is an easy task; in the Northwest where you spend hours on board a boat and do at least two dives before returning to shore, I recommend taking an extra towel, an extra 3.7-volt lithium camera battery, extra strobe batteries and a bottle of fresh water to rinse off the camera between dives before exchanging batteries. It's a small price to pay for having such a compact, easy-to-carry system.

Oh, I almost forgot to mention new features such as sunset, sunrise and fireworks scene mode. If you're shooting pictures on land at sunset—you guessed it—just press a few buttons and the camera sets it up for you, displays it on the screen and makes you look like a photographic genius. The new spy mode could come in handy if you're trying to photograph skittish wildlife: hit this mode and take a shot every 30 seconds or up to every 5 minutes while you stay downwind of your photo subject. You can also join your photo subject by using the timer setting to take two sequential shots instead of the typical one shot.

Sure, the DC600 is a great land camera with lots of new options and it comes with a great pedigree, but it's also an awesome underwater system that is just waiting to record all your underwater adventures. After my first dive with it, I hooked it up to my TV via a cable that comes with the kit and within seconds my daughter was spellbound by the photos of fish appearing on the screen.

Pioneer Research's latest contender is the DC800 8-megapixel digital camera, a masterful addition to its line of underwater cameras that comes with a larger, 2.7-inch view screen, which makes it easy to set up a picture before you click. This model also has a larger battery, so you can easily get two dives out of one battery charge. A wide triangular space-age shutter button makes it easier to use while wearing even the thickest cold-water gloves. The enhanced 4X optics zoom lets you take close and wide-angle shots without the need for a separate wide-angle lens. The DC800 boasts 24 picture selection modes including "spy mode," and the five sea modes include new distinct light settings for blue seas, emerald-green seas and plankton-filled rivers and lakes. I find that using a 2-mg SD card allows for 534 photo images at the finest setting (more images at lower settings), but with a 4-mg card you can double this number or use the available space to store up to 28 minutes of 640 by 480 video when you toggle from picture to film mode.

With so many image possibilities, I keep this camera on continuous setting for land shots. That way every time I press the shutter, I get three shots in a row. When you're snapping shots of fast-moving subjects like beluga whales, walruses or fidgety daughters, this mode can be a lifesaver. In the space of a few minutes I got plenty of images of a beluga whale surfacing, blowing out air and diving back down underwater. I couldn't have got these shots even if I'd spent a whole weekend shooting at single frame mode. The AEB setting, on the other hand, allows for taking one shot but gives you three images—that is, one image at three different light level settings. This gives you more creative freedom when you're taking quick shots and you don't have time to set the exposure value by hand. You can do all this plus set the system in manual mode and

Underwater Video Basics

As an instructor of some 16 dive-related specialties, I have to tell you that Steve Miller's *Underwater Video Basics* is one of the best instructional videos I've ever had the pleasure to view. It was so good, in fact, that I didn't think I was being instructed, but rather that I was just sitting forward in my seat anticipating the next insight into the world of videography.

Steve Miller and his professional team at 24FPS Productions make videography look fun and easy. They take you from selecting a camcorder, caring for your equipment, framing shots, setting up story lines and dive shots, to underwater communication and interaction with marine life, and they do it all by telling you what you'll *enjoy* doing next.

My only complaint was that at 47 minutes the DVD was too short. In fact, the video shots taken at Captain Don's Habitat in Curacao were so spectacular that I could have watched them for hours, so I guess I'll just have to keep pressing the replay button. Caution: this video will make you want to film underwater. For more information: www.underwatervideobasics.com.

choose your own aperture/shutter priorities just like the old school SLR film cameras some of us enthusiasts remember fondly. Perhaps the best mode of all is the automatic mode, which means that regardless of your experience level, a few magazine-quality images can be brought to life on almost every dive.

The buttons are simple, clearly marked and easy to use on both the camera and the rubber-armored housing. If you use thick Northwest cold-water gloves, I suggest using a Velcro-attached stylus or eraser-tipped pencil to adjust the diamond-shaped cluster of four buttons, but the other buttons, including those for close-up and telephoto, are easy to use no matter what dive apparel you're wearing.

For brighter, lighter tropical dives you may get by with just the camera and housing, but for cold-water dives I recommend the DC800 Pro set, which includes one Pro Flash strobe. The flash output level is adjustable and at half setting it instantly recharges to take the next shot. Start out at half level and then view your image results to see if you need more or less flash before you take the next shot. How easy is that? For those who want the ultimate control of lighting, similar to some $9,000 SLR housed system but for way less in price, the DC800 Maxx system comes complete with two Pro Flash strobes and a hard case, making it the ultimate affordable digital kit.

The only downside to any DC800 camera system is maintaining possession and use of it apart from family and friends. Fortunately, its affordable price should help resolve most domestic rights and sharing issues all the way from high in the mountains down to 200 feet underwater.

> **For more information:**
> www.sealife-cameras.com

Women's Drysuits: What Makes Them Different?

Most people who dive more than a few times a year in the Northwest quickly come to the conclusion that wearing a drysuit is the only way to go. A drysuit will keep you dry and toasty warm year-round, and for multiple dives it will give you more maneuverability than a wetsuit and you can wear anything you want under it. So I encourage anyone—but especially women—who repeatedly dives in water between 30° and 50°F to wear a drysuit. One reason is that on average, the onset of vasoconstriction—the process where the body tries to conserve warm blood by pulling blood away from the skin and extremities—appears earlier and faster in women. Halfway through a dive, a male diver may be still warm and comfortable, but his female dive buddy may already be feeling the effects of vasoconstriction. The first sensations are usually cold fingers that soon lose their dexterity and the increasingly urgent need to find a restroom. A vasoconstricted diver may eventually begin to shiver, a clear signal to end the dive early. To avoid hypothermia a good rule to follow is "once you are cold from exposure, the dive is over."

The second reason is that women on average have more fatty tissue than men; men on average have more muscle mass than women. While the fatty tissue may initially help conserve heat loss, it's the work done by the muscles that uses energy and as a by-product gives off heat that keeps the diver warm in the long run. As a result, a muscular diver swimming vigorously will be the most likely diver to reduce or even replace heat lost during a dive.

Third, because the average woman is smaller than a man, the surface to mass ratio is higher. The greater the surface to mass ratio, the quicker heat is lost and the sooner one becomes cold, and as we all know, friends don't let friends dive cold.

With these three factors working against women, it's no wonder that women on average get chilled faster than men during a dive. It's also clear why a woman's need for insulation and warmth is more critical than the exposure suit needs of a male diver. One British company claims they make drysuits for the "discerning lady diver," and some drysuit manufacturers say that their drysuits are unisex, but I think we need a little room here for clarification. Women in general may need more room around the hips and chest region, but they require smaller sizes in almost all other areas including shoulders, waist, arms, leg length and shoe size. So how can any drysuit be unisex? One way modern dive shops solve this problem is by offering several brands of off-the-rack drysuits in multiple sizes and colors. A tall woman may fit into a brand of drysuit that runs on the skinny/tall side, while a shorter woman with more curves might find another brand of drysuit just right. It's a process of selecting the closest fit possible. In the end a female diver should expect a drysuit that's comfortable but not too bulky. One that is too large in some areas may increase drag while swimming. Extra bulk will also require the diver to carry extra lead weight for water displacement. A drysuit with too much unused volume may also drastically change volume according to depth and undergarment compressibility. As the volume decreases with depth, the more air the diver will need to purge into her drysuit to keep it from pressing against her body—what is known as "drysuit squeeze." At depth, she might also have the perception that the majority of her tank air is going right into the bulky drysuit while she is trying to achieve neutral buoyancy.

The ultimate fit is achieved by wearing a custom-made drysuit—provided you have some discretionary funds. You will need to provide 21 personal measurements to get your own streamlined drysuit with all the colors, materials, zippers and other features you most want.

Drysuit Undergarments: The Inside Story

When I was a scoutmaster, before we left on a hike we reminded all our new boys that "cotton chills" because it is amazing how little perspiration it takes to turn a cotton shirt into a one-way system that sucks the heat right out of your body. You start feeling cold and your body reduces blood flow to your extremities, a situation that causes your blood pressure to rise and could lead to chest and heart problems in some people. To compensate for this rise in fluid pressure, you get a great urge to relieve yourself of excess fluids. You start to shiver—controllably at first then uncontrollably—as you turn down the road toward hypothermia. Some of the other symptoms include: feeling numbed, fatigued, anxious, confused or irritable or losing coordination or consciousness. At this point the solution is simple: take immediate steps to get warmed up; if you don't get warmed immediately, the situation can become critical. If you ever see another diver starting to shiver, stop the dive and warm him up as soon as possible.

Getting cold while diving is more likely to happen to a wetsuit diver. If it happens to a drysuit diver, there's a good chance that under his drysuit he is wearing a cotton T-shirt, cotton underclothes or even a cotton sweatshirt and pants. Only once in my life did I dive with a cotton sweatshirt and pants under a drysuit. I was teaching a rescue diver class and I had to borrow a drysuit from another instructor because mine had somehow been left at home. I stayed on the surface as much as possible, but for those moments when I had to go underwater I was so cold that I could barely contain my enthusiasm while the students practised rescuing me.

My first drysuit was a little big on me and it came with an undergarment (DSU) that looked so much like a ski outfit that when I went into stores wearing it, people would ask me how the skiing was today; the dive patches on my shoulders didn't fool them a bit. That DSU was thick and bulky, but I wore it for four years everywhere I went, dive sites and classrooms included. The only problem with it was that the deeper I dived, the more the fabric compressed and the easier it was to lose my body heat. In addition, I had to use more air than I wanted just to keep layers of air between my drysuit, my DSU and me. This trapped air is what stops the drysuit from conducting all the heat into the outside ocean. Without it, the drysuit squeezes against the DSU and the DSU squeezes against the body, and this accordion effect will allow your body heat to be conducted away faster than you can find a lavatory at the end of a cold dive. This loss of warmth isn't good for you or the nearby milling plankton.

So what makes a good DSU? Northwest waterways are usually somewhere between 40° and 60°F, so a DSU rated around these extremes should keep you nice and toasty on most local dives. If you plan on diving in colder water, you can add polyester long johns under your DSU or over your polyester T-shirt and underwear; they don't add as much volume to one of the new form-fitting DSU systems as an extra layer of fleece might.

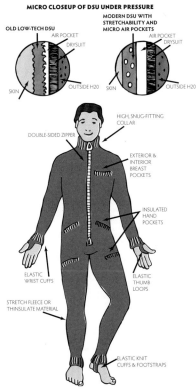

Once you get a state-of-the-art drysuit undergarment (DSU), you won't want to take it off until the end of the dive trip. ILLUSTRATION BY T. KARBASHEWSKI

Thinsulate and fleece are two of the most common materials used in the manufacture of DSUs. (In fact, this is one of those times where getting fleeced is a good thing!) The new micro-condensed fleece material is a really good choice because it already comes compressed and the volume changes little with depth. I also like its ability to stretch in most conceivable directions.

This brings us to a very good point: when wearing your new DSU, you should be able to stretch your arms behind your back just like a monkey at the zoo. You should be able to do yoga, rotate and crouch too, because once you get a new DSU, you won't want to take it off until the end of the dive trip because state-of-the-art DSUs are just that comfortable. The new DSUs also dry quickly and whisk moisture away from the wearer quickly and without effort. That's why you see divers standing with their drysuits half-zipped up or with the top part hanging around their waists while they are drying out and exposing their DSUs for all the world to see.

Your next DSU needs lots of pockets. Pockets to put your hands in to keep them warm, pockets to put your car keys in for quick access and an inside pocket where you can put a cellphone wrapped in a waterproof bag. Oh yes, and pockets to let people know that you really are wearing a dive-related garment and not just thick holiday-colored pajamas. While you're at it, if you plan on spending a lot of time gearing up in windy conditions or lounging on boat decks, you may want windproof material on the outside of your DSU. And a high collar will keep you warmer both above and below the water's surface. However, the most important feature of your DSU should be a bi-directional or double-sided zipper that allows you to zip down from the top or zip open upwards from below the hip line. I don't know how many times I've come back from a long tech dive and been ever so thankful for a fast, small opening to the outside world.

What if you already have a DSU? You might want to check it for rips and thinned or spread-out fabric areas due to wear and tear or old age, because an old suit is a prime candidate for losing its effective thermo rating. If you feel some cold spots around your chest, legs or arms, you might want to upgrade to a new DSU. But don't throw away your old one. Tests have proven that drysuit divers with backup DSUs never seem to have leaky drysuit problems. I've had a trickle of water run down inside my neck seal from time to time while trying to keep an eye on my students, but my drysuit has only had a major leak on two occasions, and both times it was due to pilot error. The ironic thing about a small drysuit leak is that when it does leak, a good fitting DSU will keep the cold water from hitting your body as fast as the water would sweep through a typical wetsuit. Things seem to warm up a little before your body signals you something's not right. A slow leak can even lull you into thinking you can head back to shore in a leisurely fashion before you get too cold—that is, unless you forgot to take off your favorite cotton dive-logo T-shirt prior to putting on your DSU. In that case, you'll have to drag your baffled buddy back to shore faster than a seal chasing a salmon in the middle of a pod of killer whales. The good news is that by the time you reach shore, you'll be too cold to care if any Boy Scouts witnessed your ordeal.

Dry Gloves: Warm Hands, Longer Dives

No matter how warm your drysuit is, unless your hands are dry, heat is going to be conducted out of your fingers, and your hands are going to grow cold. Most Northwest divers already know this, but what surprises me is the number of drysuit divers who still wear wetsuit gloves. Sure, there are some great brands of wetsuit gloves, but none of them will keep you as warm a pair of dry gloves, especially between dives, because water conducts heat 20 times faster than air.

Dry gloves are generally composed of dual layers. The outer shell is usually made of rubber, latex or neoprene and the inner layer of polyester, fleece or other non-cotton, man-made materials. By increasing the material thickness of the underlining gloves you can increase the amount of heat your hands retain during a dive and keep them from ever becoming cold. The dry gloves are attached to the wrists of your drysuit with a series of o-rings and/or collar rings.

The biggest obstacle to divers switching to dry gloves is that their initial cost is three times that of wetsuit gloves, although most of the price is for the o-rings and the plastic or rubber collar sleeves. The actual gloves may be less than a pair of wetsuit gloves. The way I look at it, though, is that if you value finger dexterity, want to extend your bottom time or reduce your rate of air consumption, then you have to stay warm and that means especially your fingers. I mention dexterity because divers practising emergency scenarios with cold, wet hands are less likely to be able to perform simple safety tasks such as disconnecting air hoses or unlatching clips and buckles. A wet glove diver may get cold and perform these skills poorly after less than an hour of diving in cold Northwest winter waters, but a dry glove diver may perform these same simple yet critical safety tasks on multiple dives with no problem. And if you plan on future technical dives for hours on end with instructors such as Ron Akeson of Adventures Down Under in Bellingham or Don Kinney of Edmonds Technical Diving Service, you'll definitely need dry gloves.

So which particular style and configuration of glove is best for you? First, it depends on what type of drysuit you plan to use in conjunction with your dry gloves. For instance, ring seal setups similar to the old and reliable Viking dry glove system work well with latex wrist seals, but according to Brett Taylor, a technician at Capital Diver and Aquatics in Olympia, the multiple o-ring systems hold on better to drysuits manufactured with thick neoprene wrist seals. Diving Concepts, OS Systems and OMS all make multiple o-ring seal systems that work well with both latex and neoprene wrist seals, provided that the neoprene wrist areas do not have stitches running down the length of the forearms. According to Ron Ault of

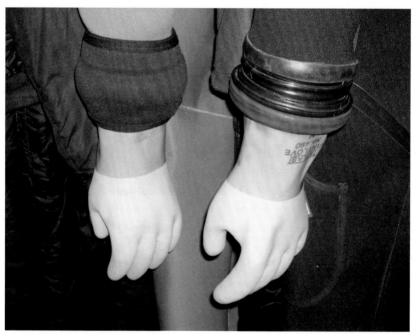

Not only do some dry gloves fit any drysuit, but some drysuits come custom-made to fit most dry gloves.

Hood Sport 'n Dive, it is hard to keep o-ring seal connection points from leaking around this type of stitching.

With the Viking system you place a rubberized collar ring inside the latex wrist seal of the drysuit, and then place another rubber collar ring over the outside of the wrist seal, making sure it overlaps the inner rubber collar. That's about as technical as it gets. You just put on your rubber or latex gloves over the exposed outer rubber wrist collar ring and—for the first few times only—pull like a possessed Scandinavian demon. Fortunately, once the gloves are stretched, they are easier to put on. The rubber gloves that come with the Viking system look like oversized, heavy-duty Norwegian bovine milking gloves, but you can choose the thickness of your underlining gloves and a more suitable outer-layer latex glove. I prefer a thinner fleece inner glove, and for $5 I bought a pair of thin latex gloves at a marine supply store to use as my outer glove. The latex gloves look like unlined dishwashing gloves, and they are much easier to pull over the exposed rubber wrist collar ring. What I like about this system is the maximum finger dexterity it gives; I can operate tank valves and camera equipment almost as easily as I can barehanded. The down side is that if the inner glove lining is too thin, I might get cold quicker than expected. Sheer or thin gloves also mean a greater chance of rips and leaks, but in my book, wet dry gloves are still as good as or better than wetsuit gloves any day. Besides, I always carry backup gloves and liners in case my latex outer glove gets torn; after all, with this system glove replacements cost not much more than an air fill.

To keep from getting a mild headache trying to figure out how to put together the multiple o-ring systems manufactured by Diving Concepts, OS Systems, OMS and similar brands, it's easier to just look at the pictures. Big o-rings go everywhere on both the gloves and wrist seals of the drysuit. It takes longer to set up, but everything holds together firmly, and this is especially important in regards to neoprene drysuits. Once together, all you have to do in most cases is twist an outer ring and the gloves pop on or off the wrist connection ring. It's a very slick design that has recently been perfected so as not to pop apart unexpectedly—as was the case with a few earlier models. Another benefit of this system is that it allows you to take almost any type of glove and incorporate it into your own dry glove system. Most experienced divers use heavy duty lined or unlined big blue gloves that can grab onto anything and take serious abrasive activity before they will ever leak. You can also insert thick underlining gloves inside the blue outer gloves to keep your fingers warm as toast, the only trade-off being that you lose a slight amount of dexterity. Some divers take out the pre-sewn underlining that comes with most packaged models of the ubiquitous blue gloves and use their own underlining fleece gloves instead. The benefit to this configuration is that if for some reason water does seep inside your glove, you don't have wet gloves all day; you only have a wet fleece inside glove that you can change for a spare dry one between dives.

Glove set-ups such as the Diving Concepts system also allow you to use neoprene gloves in a dry glove configuration. Bob Scarzafava of Anacortes Diving and Supply likes to use neoprene gloves because he enjoys having warm, dry hands, but if he sees a giant Pacific octopus, he's likely to take a glove off so he can touch the octopus with his bare hand. This way it's not as abrasive as touching with a glove, and it's a very tactile way of bonding with such a magnificent sea creature. After the visit he pops his neoprene glove back in place and continues on his adventure as a neoprene wet glove diver.

So now that you know some of the benefits of the dry glove system and some of the choices that are available to you, I hope you will put a pair to use on your next dive. For others, I hope you use this information as a justification for purchasing a drysuit. No matter which style of dry gloves you choose, you will end up staying warmer on and between dives, your fingers will remain nimble and every dive will feel undeniably more comfortable, slightly more enjoyable and overwhelmingly more fun.

Diving with the Sea-Doo Seascooter VS Supercharged

Two weeks before Halloween last year my buddy and I got a chance to test the DAKA Sea-Doo Seascooter™ VS Supercharged. We put them into the water on the Hood Canal in a spot I had always wanted to explore but never thought I could ever swim the entire distance to in less than a day using my own two fins. We made the round trip in just over an hour and our legs were still rested, we had plenty of air left in our tanks and if we had brought extra batteries, we would most likely have gone out for a second ride. We had a blast zipping around, turning every which way and practically stopping on a dime. I felt like the cowboy who just learned how to ride a horse instead of walking everywhere, but in my case, I'm a diver who can now make any future dive a self-induced drift dive. In addition, underwater distances just became shorter, and my air consumption rate has been significantly reduced as I leisurely scoot along beneath the waves.

To divers who don't like long swims, want increased air time or want to drift dive without first flying down to Cozumel, I say the time has come, the technology has improved and the price is now right to try an underwater scooter. The Sea-Doo Seascooter VS Supercharged is rated down to 100 feet and has two speeds. At the slow speed (using the right index finger on the trigger) you'll glide along just slightly faster than by fin-kicking. At the fast speed—around three miles an hour—(using both right and left index fingers slightly pressed against the triggers) you'll be moving faster than the quickest diver ever could but still slow enough to take in all the scenic beauty around you.

For our test flight we entered the water right behind the old location of Hood Sport 'n Dive on the Hood Canal. In the distance I could see Sund Rock Marine Preserve, which is home to giant Pacific octopuses and wolf-eels. Most divers travel there by kayak or boat or drive over and park for a small fee. Dive instructor Mike Philbrook is the only one I know who is brave enough to routinely swim the round trip distance, but with a Seascooter on high speed I was able to go there and back in 45

The Sea-Doo Seascooter is light and easy to carry around on dry land, but definitely more exciting to use underwater. RON AULT minutes. I had to jet around for another 22 minutes before the battery finally gave out, so on our next trip my buddy and I are planning to visit Sund Rock's south wall. Total battery life on high speed was 107 minutes, which means that even at high speed it could last longer than tanks holding 80 cubic feet of air.

On the return portion of our trip I held my digital camera in my left hand and kept only my left index finger lightly pressing down on the second speed lever. Although I was moving faster than a diver using fins could move through the water, I was still going slow enough to hang onto my camera, the left scooter handle and a line that connected my hand to my trailing dive flag float on the surface, and the camera felt stable in my hand with little water resistance. I pulled right up to a nudibranch perched on a rock, let go of the engine thrust levers, and the scooter quickly came to a stop. I composed and snapped off a picture and was on my way again in less than a few seconds. I could really get used to this style of self-controlled drift diving.

At the end of the dive I had more air in reserve than I normally do due to the lack of physical effort during the dive. At 18 pounds the Sea-Doo VS Supercharged is so light that it was easy to carry out of the water. (My kids used to carry around cats that were heavier!) The new heavy-duty Explorer model, which is rated down to 160 feet, has three speeds, goes slightly faster and weighs 32 pounds. Both scooters are relatively easy to recharge, taking eight and ten hours respectively. These scooters may not be as fast as snowmobiles, but you'll see lots of underwater terrain and creatures, move faster than the swiftest crab and be able to swim circles around your dive buddies—just like an inquisitive harbor seal out to have a good time and a great dive.

> **For more information:**
> www.seadooseascooter.com

Travel Gear 101

Having spent some 28 years in the airline industry, I have learned the hard way always to pack my suitcase defensively. I plan for a worst-case scenario so there won't be any overwhelming or disappointing setbacks or unfortunate surprises while I am getting to or from my dive destination. So here are some travel tips I've accumulated over the years that you might find useful for your next great diving adventure:

First, it's all about the destination.

Second, it's not so much what you bring but how you pack it or, better yet, where you pack it according to level of priority.

Third, it's all about what you pack.

Sound confusing? Not really when you break it down and start with the destination. For local car trips I like to carry every piece of dive gear I've ever owned. I keep it in giant plastic containers with lockable sealed lids, the kind you get at hardware chain stores. If you have a big truck and lots of room, then I recommend the heavy-duty plastic containers with built-in wheels and extendable long metal handles to roll your gear around. These mega-sized plastic bins and containers will keep the water out of your vehicle after a dive, but most boat owners will ask you not to board with them as they take up a lot of space and you can't fold them or stow them when empty. So on a boat, big mesh bags with shoulder straps and foldable roller bags decorated with dive emblems and extra pockets come in handy. IST makes a sturdy mesh bag that will carry everything except your air tanks. It has extra rugged handles, padded shoulder straps, an outer dry compartment, one long inner compartment and two small inner pockets for keys, wallets and such. On international trips I like to take just the bare necessities and the more remote the destination, the less I take with me. I mean, if it doesn't have 24-hour electricity, who needs a battery charger or, for that matter, rechargeable batteries?

My second rule is the biggest in my book. I organize everything by how important it is to my trip and pack accordingly. I pack most of my camera gear in one of those fishing/photography/hunting vests. I use clothing to wrap around certain items to cushion them inside the pockets, a swimming suit being a good example, because if nothing else makes it to my destination, I can at least get in the water and take pictures. I can take my fully filled vest through airport security and wear it on the plane if I want. It doesn't count as part of the airline's one- or two-piece limit of carry-on items, yet I can put almost as much in its pockets as I can in a roller bag, and this way the items are guaranteed to stay with me at all times. Of course, I look a little bulky, but the airlines go to great lengths to avoid discriminating against fat people. They might say "sorry about the wait," but they rarely say "sorry about your weight." Once on the plane I can take the vest off and stow it in the overhead or under the seat in front of me.

Most airlines will let you take one roller bag and one smaller object on board, so make the smaller one a small daypack or bush backpack. You can use it for essentials such as regulators, computers, masks and the other gear you would never want to rent or be without on a dive trip. This is also a good place to stow in-flight food and entertainment supplies. You might even get away with something like the new TSA-friendly Travel Bag by divecaddy.net, which is designed to take the majority of your gear onboard with you; along with the accompanying mini gear bag you are set for any trip.

That brings us to the world of roller bags. For some reason, manufacturers have a rule that says that the bigger the roller bag the cheaper the price. Or they make roller bags according to airline specifications then as an afterthought add three-inch-long wheels and a handle that doesn't rest flush with the top of the bag. Or to further entice people to buy their products, they make expandable roller bags that won't close once opened at a low pressure/high altitude. These big cheap bags take up half the overhead space of a bin that was designed to hold the sacred artifacts of six frequent fliers. They can only fit in sideways while regular-sized roller bags can fit wheels first, three next to each other. So don't expect there to be any space in the overhead bin for your roller bag after Mr. and Mrs. Tourist take up all the overhead room with the two super duper roller bags they got on sale just last night around midnight at Stuff Mart. And if you don't think those bags were cheap, just look at the sales tags. They'll be hanging out of the overhead bin like signs warning you not to try putting anything else up there.

A standard 757 can accommodate some 60 roller bags in its overhead bins but unfortunately it carries a load of 156 people. No one wants to put anything under the seat in front of him or her unless the overhead spaces are filled. If you are one of the last to board the plane, you'll have the choice of setting your roller bag underneath the seat in front of you, if you wisely bought the right size, or checking it in as cargo. Notice that the cargo baggage claim tag comes complete with tiny print at the bottom to tell you what to do if the bag associated with the tag is stolen or never seen on this planet again. Things hardly ever get lost as checked baggage unless you really need them.

This brings us to checked luggage. If you're to be gone for a week and plan on wearing more than a swimsuit and what you were wearing when you boarded the plane, you will need a big suitcase. I like the big plastic or fiberglass hard shell cases as they don't rip and tear open like those made of soft materials so conveniently do. But remember that even a potential thief who can't read can understand the significance of a bag with dive destination stickers on it. It just shouts out, "Expensive dive gear! Please help yourself!" A big black bag with big yellow initials on it works best. When you arrive at your destination why tear open every non-descript black bag on the carousel when you can spot your dive gear bag a mile away? An initialed suitcase with all personal information tucked away inside it should make it to the baggage claim area—unless it gets misplaced for three hours on its way to Customs as one small airline once did to me.

Don't put anything in checked luggage that's very expensive or that you can't live without. You may be going to Hawaii, but the checked luggage may be going to Jamaica. If people who are supposedly intelligent can get on the wrong flights, why can't non-sentient luggage? Checked bags are a good place to put extra contact lens fluid, extra dive gear and extra clothes, but the key word here is "extra." If one of these items doesn't make the trip, you can shop for replacements between dives.

How to use an expandable vest, a back pack, the right-sized, 22-inch or less roller bag and checked luggage grouped according to your preferred airline's weight, height and width specifications may not sound like the most exciting topic, but without these tips, you could spend a week tanning on a sandy beach and looking at fish on colorful plates instead of looking at colorful fish in the water.

DIVE DESTINATIONS

British Columbia

PORT HARDY

It's no coincidence that the top end of Highway 19 on Vancouver Island in British Columbia is also the pinnacle Northwest dive trip destination. Reaching Port Hardy at the end of the road is the signal that you are mere miles by boat from some of the best cold-water diving in the entire world. These waters are filled with thousands of species of invertebrates, hundreds of species of aquatic birds and mammals, colorful species of fish smaller than minnows and others bigger than the ubiquitous salmon that the local populations of killer whales, dolphins and seals covet so dearly.

While other dive sites may have a Puget Sound king crab, a wolf-eel or a giant Pacific octopus or two, up here it's not uncommon to see half a dozen of one or all of these species on a single dive. It's all about the abundance of food. Here all a sea creature needs is a piece of substrate to call home, and the food will be delivered by the currents faster, more easily and more plentifully than a Las Vegas high-roller-style buffet. In turn, the substrate can house more species per square inch so that the patches of strawberry anemones are redder, the plumose anemones whiter and the orange peel nudibranchs brighter.

But don't take my word for this abundance. Just dive the famous Browning Wall and somewhere down the first 200 feet-plus of wall you'll come to the same conclusion. And if you think the Browning Wall is impressive, then you have to visit Dillon Rock and explore its wolf-eel condos. Don't be surprised by how many wolf-eels you encounter at this rock pinnacle that goes down to 60 feet and barely crests the surface. It doesn't take much to coax these gentle giants out of their dens—a prickly purple or red giant sea urchin will do the trick. The wolf-eel's big gummy lips and powerful jaws were made for crushing sea urchins and gobbling down the inner contents, the roe, which is also prized by the people of Japan and China. Wolf-eel condos are open 24–7, and I highly recommend a night dive with these creatures as they are less shy about showing off their dance moves after the sun sets. Oh, there are several species of rockfish, swimming scallops and giant Pacific octopuses found here too, but it's the animated and playful wolf-eels that steal the

The boat ramp at the Quarterdeck Marina in Port Hardy leads to some of the best diving in all the world.

135

Nautilus Explorer at Shushartie Bay off Vancouver Island, BC. Taking a photo this good may require a very long swim. BERNARD P. HANBY

show at Dillon Rock. I dived this site three times on one trip just because I enjoyed the wolf-eels' company so much.

Dive Sites

There are over two dozen world-class dive sites just northeast of Port Hardy, but Nigei Island seems to be the epicenter. Seven-Tree Island, Browning Passage, Browning Wall and the wreck of the *Themis* at Croker Rock are all dive sites located close to the sheltered waters of Clam Cove on Nigei Island. Basket stars, glove sponges, finger sponges, gorgonian and soft corals go out of their way to eat up battery life and fill film and digital storage cards on every dive. Keep in mind that the water can be 42° to 50°F with visibility occasionally down to 35 feet, although it typically exceeds 100 feet.

Dive Resorts and Guides

You can enjoy Port Hardy and its great diving by staying at one of the many bed and breakfasts located around the town. You can also stay at the Quarterdeck Inn located above the Quarterdeck Marina and watch what's going on in the marina from your room, the pub

The *Nautilus Explorer* tender; now boarding for sights down under. BERNARD P. HANBY

or the local marina store. The Glen Lyon Inn next to the Quarter-deck Marina is within walking distance of the many independent dive charters who rent out for the day or by the hour and call this area home year-round.

But if Port Hardy is the Mount Everest of Northwest diving, then the best way to experience this area is with a good guide. Captain John deBoeck has spent over 27 years guiding and exploring in these waters. From his resort, Browning Pass Hideaway, in Clam Cove on Nigei Island you can experience three or more awesome dives a day. The cabins and lodge float gently mere feet above these enchanted waters. You'll hear birds and seals, breathe in fresh sea breezes and gaze down at the busy sea life below the surface. How much closer to nature can you get than this? John's vast knowledge of the marine life and local dive destinations encourage divers to return year after year to dive with him and his operation. John gets high praise from everyone who meets him.

Coming in next with 18 years of host and guide experience is Bill Weeks, who works out of God's Pocket Diving Resort on Hurst Island. This resort is based on land and surrounded by God's Pocket

Provincial Marine Park, which is comprised of a whole group of small islands and islets at the entrance to Queen Charlotte Strait. Here, Bill and Annie Ceschi have worked to build a labor-of-love dive destination. They have two main cabins, each with four side-by-side rooms for guests. Besides plenty of sunbathing deck space and a dining room, there is a clubhouse with one wall dedicated to charging cameras and other dive gear. With so much wildlife in this area, expect to reload and recharge your camera even after a 60-foot end-of-the-dock dive, let alone after diving from their 40-foot-long, heated cabin boat.

With 16 years of instructing and local diving experience is the amiable Bavarian Marcus Kronwitter, host of Malei Island Resort, which is on a little island off the northern end of Nigei. Marcus and his wife, Cecelia, have built their own modern island lodge with four double guest rooms, a hot tub overlooking the waterway, a self-contained wind and solar energy supply system and their own water processing system. You can dive right into the water, dive from the Malei Island's cabin cruiser or with one of the many other local dive charter services. Marcus can make arrangements for just about any dive adventure you desire. The Malei Island dive resort is the perfect place for a group of eight divers or just you and your favorite someone. If Robinson Crusoe or any other castaway could have lived in relative luxury yet had an island to himself, this is where he would have wanted to be.

Dive Charters

There are at least two live-aboard vessels that circle these waters. The MV *Songhee,* built in 1944, is a 95-foot-long, wooden-hulled, former Canadian naval supply ship that was converted into a touring/dive vessel in 1990. It is Transport Canada-approved to carry 49 people on its 24-foot-wide deck for a day of sightseeing, but it also has six double-occupancy guest rooms and can easily accommodate 12 divers and their gear. This ship has a nautical range of 4,000 miles, so you could theoretically go out to sea for quite some time. Divers are picked up by water taxi at the Quarterdeck Inn and Marina in Port Hardy and transported out to Clam Harbour to rendezvous with the ship. Customers can also be picked up in Port McNeill and other agreed-on locations.

The second vessel that frequently tours these waters is the 116-foot *Nautilus Explorer*. This high-tech ship, built in 2000, is owned and operated by Mike and Mary Anne Lever. It departs from the little fishing village of Steveston in Richmond for its Port Hardy trips, which makes it easy for most US citizens as you just have to cross the Canadian border and drive an hour or so north—no ferries and no hours-long drives up Highway 19, the Vancouver Island Highway. You can board in the evening and wake up the next morning in front of some of the best dive sites in British Columbia.

While the scenery above and below the water is breathtaking, onboard the *Nautilus Explorer* it's how you get there that makes this journey so great. The nine lower air-conditioned staterooms come complete with private washrooms with showers. The two upper deck executive staterooms have a little more room and large windows for more expansive views, but you may not spend a lot of time in your quarters because there are just so many other things to do onboard. You'll find guests hanging out in the main salon, on the main deck or in the Jacuzzi on the upper deck. The dining room when not in use for fresh treats and meals is also a favored hangout to look at the day's photo shots, play card games or just relax and unwind with a good book.

If you have camera or video gear you might spend some time on the dive deck where there is plenty of table space and outlets to get your equipment ready for the next great dive. At the center of the dive deck is a slanted ramp where the 38-foot dive skiff is stowed when the ship is in port or underway between dive sites. At dive sites the skiff is lowered into the water, ready to take divers out to the sites and to pick them up at the end of their dive. What makes this skiff operation so smooth and

With a plethora of exposed rocks, islands, and rocky shorelines, the Port Hardy area is a boat diver's paradise. BERNARD P. HANBY

refined is that when you first board the *Nautilus Explorer,* you stow your gear—BCs, tanks, weights, regulators—in your own designated spot on the skiff and you leave it all there for the rest of your stay. When it's time to dive, you don your wetsuit or drysuit, walk to the stern of the dive deck, step aboard the skiff, go to your designated sitting area to don your gear, sit down until the skiff reaches your diving destination and take turns jumping in the water and seeing the underwater sites. When you re-board the skiff, you remove your gear as you make your way back to the mother ship, then leave your gear in place as you disembark the skiff and rinse off before changing out of your suit and making your way up to the dining room for another scrumptious meal or to the main salon. And while you download photos, discuss the last dive with others or fine dine, the crew of the *Nautilus* refills your scuba tanks with air or Nitrox (for a slight extra charge and worth it), and you are ready to go on the next dive. How cool is that? It doesn't take very long to feel like you're the most pampered diver in the world.

If I were King Triton, I would make it mandatory for every diver to take a five-to-nine-day cruise on the *Nautilus Explorer* to Port Hardy or beyond. You'll stop at wrecks like the HMCS *Saskatchewan* and the HMCS *Columbia,* wall dives such as Browning Wall, pinnacles such as Dillon Rock, macro dives like Butternut, fast-paced drift dives such as Rock 'n Roll or night dives at some of these as well. From the main deck of the *Nautilus Explorer* you might see dolphins riding alongside the bow and crossing back and forth as they jockey for position to ride the bow waves. While they enjoy themselves, they turn on their sides to peer up at the divers looking down on the show. You may also see whales spouting in the distance, eagles soaring overhead and bears standing on the nearby shoreline—everything that the *National Geographic's* crews come to film on a routine basis. Below the waters you'll encounter the familiar wolf-eels, giant octopuses, king crabs and tons and tons of fish species. But here it's more than just seeing a scallop or two; it's being in the middle of a thousand scallops or thousands of strawberry anemones or multitudes of other species in a setting few other humans have ever explored and where the local inhabitants rarely or never encounter our species.

I should add that once you've had the pleasure of discovering

If you are looking for North Island Dive and Charter in Port Hardy, don't look for a little posted sign, just look for the side of the building.

the world of the *Nautilus Explorer* in Canada, you may want to venture out even farther. *Nautilus Explorer* destinations also include Alaska, Mexico and beyond. As Captain Mike Lever says, "If there is a cool place that needs exploring, I want to be the guy." Currently, the crew of the *Nautilus Explorer* has been working diligently on shark conservation. "Sharks are clearly in peril of extinction so that people can have shark fin soup," Mike says. "It's a terrible thing to feel that one might be watching the final extinction of a number of species." The *Nautilus* crew invites individuals and organizations to support the Guadalupe Conservation Fund, which finances the study of great white sharks. They are also involved in a program aimed at aerial surveillance of the Revillagigedo Islands marine reserve in order to discourage illegal fishing practices there. One of their latest projects includes encouraging children, such as Mike's own young son, to view through the shark cages and see for themselves that sharks are cool and beautiful rather than scary, and that they are worth protecting.

Dive Shops
Marcus Kronwitter and Kevin McIntyre own and operate North Island Dive and Charter, the first and oldest dive shop in Port

Hardy. The shop is easily visible as you drive down the main street because of the large scene painted on the side of the building. Port Hardy is a small town, even though it's the largest on the north end of Vancouver Island, so everyone knows everyone here, and things are just a bit more laid-back, especially during the winter months. That's why when the

For more information:
www.getawaybc.com
www.vancouverislanddive.com
www.godspocket.com
www.malei-island.com
www.northislanddiver.com
www.quarterdeckresort.net
www.glenlyoninn.com
www.songhee.ca
www.nautilusexplorer.com

dive shop is closed, there's a sign on the door that reads: "This is a one-man dive operation." It then goes on to give you telephone numbers to call if you need assistance. I called and both Marcus and Kevin were down at the shop in minutes, but it's probably better to call in advance just in case they are teaching, chartering or helping with someone's boat. Besides doing last-minute repairs, the shop carries a wide assortment of items that are handy on offshore excursions. They are also a great source of information on local charters, accommodations and other dive-related topics. Groups from the Seattle area such as the Boeing Seahorses have used their services for years.

I haven't talked about the town of Port Hardy much less the deer, elk and other wildlife one sees on the way up Highway19. The problem is that the adjacent world-class dive sites overshadow the beauty of this pristine area. Like any other good diver, I only wish I could go there more often and explore even more of the world-class dive sites and overwhelming abundance of natural scenic beauty.

QUADRA ISLAND

The first time I took a group of divers to Quadra Island, which is off the east coast of Vancouver Island near Campbell River, we pulled up to the lodge and saw deer running across the yard. Mike Richmond, who owned Abyssal Dive Charters at that time, called these four-legged creatures "lawn salmon"—yes, you might say that his view of the world has been slightly skewed by his love of under-water exploration. As a guide, Mike's wit and humor were only surpassed by his knowledge and experience of the local marine environment. His 30 years of local dive experience has left a heavy fin print on the local dive sites as most were either named by him or for him; this explains such names as "Row and Be Damned" and "Richmond's Reef." After he sold Abyssal Dive Charters to Earl Lowe and Deb Seymour, Mike built another dive lodge, and for a while he escorted everyone from the plateau down to the boat dock in a truck with a military-style or lumberjack crew compart-ment attached. On the back end just above the doorway he had painted the words "PADI Wagon" and a slogan that read "If you didn't dive with us, then we both lost money." The wagon made for a fun four-minute ride down to his 26-foot aluminum boat tied up at the dock.

The diving here is spectacular and people come from around the world to dive. I remember once sharing a boat and lodge with three young Germans. In order to help out with international rela-tions, I gave them a boat diver specialty course for the non-profit price of the course/picture card. It was just one more thing besides

Cracks and crevices are the preferred habitat of white stiff-footed sea cucumbers.
BERNARD P. HANBY

the fantastic diving that these guys would have to talk about when they got home. We all had a great time together just as on all my trips to this island. Oh, and the Germans were good divers too. Mike, his lodge and the boat combined to make an experience I'll never forget.

Dive Sites

The diving is so good off Quadra that when, as an active dive instructor, I offered the trip to dive shop employees and customers, it filled up with divemasters and instructors before I even had a chance to hang up posters and offer the trip to the general public. Now you would think that after a few dive trips we would have seen everything the island had to offer, but there are so many dive sites there that on every trip we had at least one new dive site to try out as well as revisiting some of our old favorites. Some of my favorite sites so far include:

Row and Be Damned: a drift dive where you see lots of urchins and other invertebrates during the first part of the dive then rocks, boulders and barren substrate towards the end of the drift dive. We found a baby giant octopus just hanging out in the open as we first descended.

Steep Island: a beautiful wall dive. Giant tubeworms grouped together under an overhang are separated into decoratively spaced patches by strawberry anemones. Local nudibranchs like to hang out above 40 feet. The currents seemed to switch directions every 10 feet or so of depth.

Quart-a-whisky or Quathiaski Cove: the site of the old ferry dock. On the sandy bottom you will find sturgeon poacher, old bottles, giant dendronotids, foot-long-plus nudibranchs, coffee pots, giant Pacific octopuses and just about anything else you can name. It's a potpourri of dive life and discarded artifacts and a great spot for both day and/or night dives.

Seymour Channel: a great spot for viewing white sea cucumbers and large abalone, cruising dolphins and whales. Sea lions play close by.

HMCS *Columbia*: a decommissioned *Restigouche*-class, 366-foot Canadian Navy destroyer that was sunk on June 22, 1996. The top of its superstructure and wheelhouse are at approximately 60 feet. At roughly 94 feet we swam across its starboard side, which sits at 40 degrees to port.

Dogfish: a secret spot where, if it's the right time of year, you can see hundreds of spiny dogfish. Back in August 2002 I went on my first cold-water shark dive here with Dyna Mike's Dive Charters. Equipped with salmon heads and tails, we jumped into the water and soon found ourselves surrounded by at least 80 sharks of the kind known locally as spiny dogfish. Most were between three and four feet long with the larger ones usually moving slowly and the smaller ones zipping around like short-fused rockets. Normally they swim away from divers, but during a feeding frenzy they are as likely to bump into you as they are to glide between your legs or swim around you. The big ones can bump into you and leave a small bruise, but that's about as bad as it gets, provided you don't tease them or do something stupid like pull on their tails. Even though they look like cute and cuddly mini-sharks, they do have sharp teeth and appear menacingly impressive when captured on digital. Between August and September they hang out in schools and don't mind having their pictures taken if you move fast enough. I found this experience to be a great entry plunge into the world of North-west shark dives.

Gorge Harbour: a small bay on Cortes Island where Native

Purple sea stars are naturally born groupies who can't resist collecting in mosh pits.

petroglyphs mark the rock walls above the surface. The average depth is only 38 feet. From the mid-point of the channel the visibility is at least a 100 feet in either direction and you can see the subsurface inhabitants clinging to the channel walls. Although the surface was 55°F, at the bottom it was 50°. We saw over 20 species of crabs here including butterfly and baby king crabs. There are tons of anemones here as well as small fish.

Other notable dive sites are Copper Cliffs, April Point and Whiskey Point.

Resorts and Guides

Currently Earl Lowe and Deb Seymour operate the aluminum sister ship to Mike Richmond's boat at Abyssal Dive Charters, and I have heard nothing but good reviews. I got my first opportunity to meet them at the DEMA convention in Las Vegas in 2008. Both Earl (captain and Nitrox blender) and Deb are professional chefs, and I'm told that the meals and desserts they serve are worthy of their reviews. The staff of Adventures Down Under, the dive shop where I used to instruct in Bellingham, goes up to Quadra to stay with Earl and Deb at least once every year.

Spiny dogfish, like most sharks, are only aggressive after you pull on their tails.
BERNARD P. HANBY

Getting There

To do a trip properly to Quadra and Cortes islands, I recommend you be experienced or at least advanced diver certified, so you'll be comfortable with some of the area's ever changing currents. I also recommend that you bring an underwater camera plus your passport. If you go up to British Columbia on a Friday, try to catch the Tsawwassen–Duke Point ferry around noontime or earlier. Once you get over to Nanaimo, drive north for about two hours to Campbell River then take a ten-minute ferry over to Quathiaski Cove on Quadra Island. By leaving early, you will have time to stop at the local pub at Quathiaski Cove for hot wings and chilled beverages before settling in at Abyssal Dive Charters. Ask anyone who's been to Quadra Island and they will say that the journey was definitely worthwhile and the diving spectacular.

For more information:
www.abyssal.com

THE COMOX VALLEY

Eighty million years ago the Comox Valley on Vancouver Island was part of a sea teeming with bizarre and gigantic marine life. Forty-foot-long swimming reptile-like creatures glided through the water in search of prey. The small head of an elasmosaur snaked through the water some 15 feet in front of its body, catching its prey by surprise. Mosasaurs and giant sharks roamed the seas full of bony-plated fish, giant turtles, ammonites and species similar to the present-day nautilus. When these creatures vanished, many of them left their imprints in the shale; the mineralized skeletons of others turn up periodically on the banks of the nearby Puntledge River. The seas receded and the mountains lifted, then were chiseled into their present forms by hundreds of thousands of years of glacier activity. The ancestors of the Salish people would later come and inhabit a valley rich in elk, deer and bear—the word *comox* means plenty—beside seas with an abundance of shellfish, salmon, seals and whales.

The modern nearby seas are still teeming with life, though on a smaller scale both in the variety and size of species than during earlier times. But today people come from all over to take part in the region's abundance of recreational opportunities—hiking, biking, surfing with wind and sail, fishing and skiing, but especially some of the most spectacular scuba diving in the world. Few locations have so many activities available within a 30-minute driving radius. Within the space of a few hours you could, if you wanted to, ski down Mount Washington then go on a boat dive with sea lions. People are serious about their outdoor activities here in the Comox Valley. Even those who prefer more casual leisure activities such as beachcombing end up collecting large amounts of flotsam and jetsam, and you may see their collections proudly displayed on the sides of garages or decorating houses within walking distance of the beaches.

There are three main cities located in the Comox Valley. Cumberland is built right on top of old coal-mine tunnels. Around 1914 over 3,000 Chinese immigrants came to work the mines, forming the second-largest Chinese population on the West Coast (San Francisco had the largest). The last mine closed in the 1960s, but a museum still displays what life was like when coal was king here. Today Cumberland is a quiet bedroom community with a main street that sports several youth hostels for mountain bike riders, rock climbers, hikers and skiers on tight budgets or for those who just want to be close to the mountains and a short distance from Lake Comox.

Courtenay, the largest of the three cities with a population estimated at 70,000, lies at the southeast end of Comox Harbour. Fifth Street is the site of small businesses, boutique shops and restaurants. At the south end of town is a modern shopping and parking complex complete with a Wal-Mart and Future Shop. The Coast Westerly Hotel adjacent to the Puntlege River is a short walk to many of the local attractions and seems to be a well-regarded gathering place for local residents especially during holiday occasions and for international tourists throughout the rest of the year. Half a mile from the hotel and just one block behind Fifth Street is a museum that houses a varied collection of well-preserved prehistoric fossils. On the second floor of the museum is an exhibit of the First Nations people.

Legend has it that world traveler Sir Francis Drake entered Comox Harbour in 1579 on the *Golden Hinde*, although for political reasons this adventure remained secret for hundreds of years on the orders of Queen Elizabeth I. The Royal Navy established a training

Steller sea lions don't have the luxury of time and additional energy required to resolve all personal space issues. BERNARD P. HANBY

station in the harbor in the middle of the 19th century, and it was Captain George Courtenay of the Royal Navy who became probably the most famous fisherman in these waters. Around 1848 he would take the *Constance*, a 50-gun frigate, up and down the nearby rivers in search of good fishing grounds, possibly making him the most heavily armed fisherman of his day.

Within 25 years of his fishing expeditions so many steamships were taking shelter in Comox Harbour that the government decided to build an appropriate sized dock. There is now a large, three-sectioned marina and a pub and bistro that overlook the boats. Peering back at the marina from the main jetty walkway, I was reminded of one of those 10,000-piece jigsaw puzzles where masts of sailing boats form an endless sea of white poles and give little clue which mast belongs to which boat. For those who enjoy sailing and fishing this is the place to be. The main Comox townsite lies directly up the hill from the harbor. The few blocks of shops are freshly painted with artfully arranged flowers, and there is at least one exceptionally good restaurant where everyone seems to meet on the weekends. Comox is also home to an air force museum and the Filberg Heritage Lodge and Park.

All three of these towns have something unique to offer the visitor, but most importantly each town has a population of very friendly people who enjoy a slower pace of life. There always seems to be time to strike up a conversation, meet new people or just share a smile. The only time you'll ever see a local frustrated is when you bring up the metric system. Apparently Canadians in this area still prefer to measure distances in feet, but on the roads all the signs are in government-approved kilometres. Thus, they generally explain how far point A is from point B in relation to time. "You go down the road about ten minutes, eh?"

Dive Sites

One of my favorite dives in this area is the 125-foot cargo steamship SS *Capilano,* launched in 1891, which sank in October 1915 after striking a submerged object off Texada Island. It lay upright and undisturbed on Grant Reef until 1971 when a fisherman snagged the hull. The top of the wreck can be reached around 120 feet. The rusted metal hull is mostly still intact, but the wooden decks have all but rotted away. Plumose anemones form a white outline of the ship's perimeter. Huge rockfish, some of them over two feet

Giant plumose sea anemones group like a forest of trees on submerged structures. BERNARD P. HANBY

in length and between 40 and 100 years old, vigilantly patrol the heavily corroded remnants. On good days you can expect to see the entire length of the wreck and may not even need to use your dive light. Any way you look at it, though, the wreck is an awesome sight to behold.

Another popular site is called Singing Sands where a 34-foot–long, cement-hulled sailboat rests in 65 feet of water. Who could have foreseen that such a vessel would ever sink? Three giant resident octopuses don't seem to mind its fatal design flaw.

Although bluntnosed sixgill sharks usually haunts waters at depths down to 4,500 feet, between April and September this ancient species of shark may be seen frequenting waters as shallow as 60 to100 feet near Hornby Island. It's a rare treat to see one of these 9- to 15-foot leviathans, and although they have sometimes been spotted all the way down to Seattle in shallow waters, your best hope of seeing one close up and personal is right here off Hornby close to where the sea lions play. Sixgills are curious by nature and may swim close to you—my friend had his video camera nudged by one—but there has never been a substantiated report of one attacking a diver at these shallow depths. Since these giants have the ability to hover perpendicularly above an object with their heads pointing straight down, it could be inferred that they prefer their meals aged, decaying and not going anywhere anytime soon.

Charter Vessels

Bill Coltart, the owner of Pacific Pro Dive and Surf in Courtenay, is a big believer in diversification and multiple capabilities. He has been running charters since 1994 along with teaching scuba, tech diving and rebreathers while working as a paramedic on the side. You might say he prefers a busy lifestyle. In 2004 he launched a new 32-foot, high-speed boat, the *Ata-tude*, specially designed for eco-marine tours, taxi service for people with bikes who are on their way to spend the day on Hornby Island and, of course, great scuba diving-related charters. Pacific Pro Dive also has an exclusive five-day package that includes two days of diving near Hornby Island where large sixgill sharks visit in the summer and sea lions frolic in the winter. Add two days of diving near Campbell River where you'll see tons of small colorful invertebrates, and this package

This is the headquarters of Pacific Pro Dive & Surf. The boat *Ata-tude* is in the nearby marina.

becomes a major macro/micro extravaganza. Other dive shops can book the *Ata-tude* directly, or individuals can arrange everything through the dive shop.

Where to Stay

Recently Pacific Pro Dive teamed up with the Coast Westerly Hotel in Courtenay to offer an outstanding hotel and dive package. Besides large rooms, comfortable beds and great food, this hotel has a drying room for scuba gear and their indoor swimming pool has hand-painted scuba-related murals on its walls. This is a four-star hotel and a great place to stay if you have a significant other who prefers non-dive activities. Your non-diving partner can relax with room service, go shopping or visit nearby tourist attractions while you dive your heart out.

The Comox Valley also has a wide array of astonishingly good cuisine. Somehow they have been able to save and separate different ethnic recipes to the point where Indian, Chinese and British traditional entrees can be ordered in the same restaurant, yet the cooks have been able to maintain the individual distinct flavors and tastes. In fact, the British-style cuisine in the Comox Valley tastes just as good if not better than the same meals I've been served in

Imagine a shrimp resting on its back and using its feet to collect food while being protected by armoured calcareous plates and you have envisioned the structural design of a common barnacle.

London, England. You may also notice that whether your fish and chips are being served on elaborate platter-sized dishes with your colas in daiquiri glasses or just on paper plates and cups, they take great pride in their secret beer-batter recipes, and you will be hard pressed to find fish and chips fresher and tastier anywhere else. And they even offer you a choice of gravy, vinegar or ketchup on them. South of Courtenay on the road to Royston there are multiple locations to picnic. Just 15 minutes down the road you will come to Buckley Bay where you can take a ferry to Denman and Hornby islands. Both offer co-operative craft stores featuring the work of local artists, and both are great spots to spend the day exploring, biking or observing the wildlife. Denman Village has a turn-of-the-century general store and a museum, while Hornby offers two Hawaiian-style sandy beaches and breathtaking views over Helliwell Bluffs.

NANAIMO

For a dive instructor, the town of Nanaimo on the east coast of Vancouver Island has to be one of the best places to bring a group. It's the perfect spot to finish up advanced, deep or wreck diver certification.

Dive sites

The main deck of the 366-foot-long *Mackenzie*-class destroyer escort HMCS *Saskatchewan* rests at 110 feet and the bridge tower reaches up some 65 feet, making this wreck an ideal spot for so many activities. Now with the 442-foot-long, Victory-class HMCS *Cape Breton* about a hundred feet away, this "boat access" only dive area is even more popular with divers as well as dive instructors. Yet despite the popularity of these two former warships, what I look forward to most is what we do following our first spectacular dive.

Once everyone is back on board the boat and the winds and waves are favorable, I like to visit the windward side of Snake Island where there is a small half-moon cove and a gravel beach complete with a sunbathing seal colony that usually numbers between 30 and 150 members. This exclusive club looks us over nonchalantly as we make our approach to anchor nearby, although if the boat comes in too fast or too close, many of the seals will take off into the water. Once the boat is anchored and you are wearing a warm drysuit, mask and fins, you can float in the water and watch the seals on shore or the inquisitive ones that glide in the water just below you. Seals are very curious, so once they've determined that

View of Nanaimo from Newcastle Island. The residents of this town love to sink former military ships in their spare time. ISTOCKPHOTO

There are no snakes on Snake Island, a short boat ride from Nanaimo, but there are plenty of seals.

you are not a threat, they will come right up to you. When you are this close to nature, time between dive intervals slips right through your dry gloves.

On the leeward side of Snake Island, you can do a wall dive not far from shore. It's an okay wall dive, but that's not why my friends and I like this site. As you swim close to shore, you'll notice several large, low-lying rocks separated from Snake Island by a 10- to 15-foot-wide channel where the water runs 3 to 9 feet deep, and you'll see half a dozen or so harbor seals sunbathing/resting on the exposed rocks. At the end of the wall dive you can ascend the slopes to these exposed rocks or, if you prefer, you can swim right over to them. Either way, you'll see seals swimming under you and around you as you make your way there. Swimming through a particular 3-foot-deep gap between the rocks you can enter a small channel and come face to face with these playful creatures. You'll notice right away that they love to sense their world with their mouths, especially

Harbor seals love to play tag, especially with divers wearing bright fins.

by nibbling and pulling on fins when you're not looking. If you have a camera, they'll not only put on an underwater swimming show but will also stick their whiskers right against the camera lens. One of the more

For more information:
www.divingbc.com
www.divemaster.ca
www.cedar-beach.com

aggressive individuals left a slight tooth mark on my camera lens as he tried to figure out if it was edible. He quickly moved on to other things, which was fortunate, because I don't need blurry close-ups of whiskers. The seals are fast and graceful as they swim constantly around you, and they must think we are the most awkward creatures ever to enter the water world.

It's a rare treat to be able to interact with wildlife on such a large scale and this is one reason to tell your friends why it's so much fun to dive here. So next time you visit Nanaimo, by all means visit the great wrecks, but save a tank of air to interact with the locals. And remember to take along a camera as all good photos should be choreographed with at least one seal of approval.

VICTORIA

Take the scenic Northwest coastline, add tourist and waterfront attractions similar to those found on San Francisco's Fisherman's Wharf or the harbors of Baltimore or Sydney, Australia, mix with San Diego's weather, sprinkle with English architecture and local charm, and you've got one of the most interesting and picturesque cities in the greater Pacific Northwest—Victoria, British Columbia.

A lot has changed since the Hudson's Bay Company first set up shop here around 1843. Today, it's much more than displays of beaver pelts, clay pipes and wishbone china giving way to designer T-shirts, decorated shot glasses and maple-flavored cookies. Now people come from around the world to enjoy the flavor of this city. Half a dozen languages can be heard as you wait to cross a street or browse one of the many gift shops. On weekends the city teems with tourists who have come by commercial land or sea airlines, cruise ships, ferry boats or conventional highways to see all the sights packed so conveniently around the main lively inner harbor section. They come prepared to see every sight on their lists in one short weekend, but to be honest with you, even with the aid of double-decker tour buses, horse-drawn carriages and zippy little harbor taxis, it could take several trips to see all of the sights this city has to offer.

The key to taking in as much as possible seems to be staying centrally located. On my last trip to Victoria we stayed at the Executive House Hotel, just a block away from the waterfront. From our room I could see the Royal BC Museum a block and a half away with its impressive First Nations exhibit, Northwest dioramas and six-storey-tall gray whales splashing on the screen of the National Geographic IMAX Theatre. From the left side of our patio/lanai I could see the chimneys of Craigdarroch Castle, an 1890s mansion-turned-museum, a good 40-minute walk from where I stood. If you like intricately carved wood and don't mind ascending some 87 stairs, then this museum is a must-see.

Straight out from the lanai I spied the tops of the trees in Beacon Hill Park, which is the home of the largest heronry (blue heron nesting site) on the West Coast. I snapped a few pictures of the herons while my daughter fed the ducks in the pond. This centrally located park, besides being a playground for human activities, is also a well-groomed wildlife sanctuary, and contains a zoo where people

The inner harbor area of beautiful Victoria, BC. ISTOCKPHOTO

of all ages enjoy petting baby goats, watching piglets play tug-o-war and listening to peacocks endlessly calling out to one another.

Toward my far right off my lanai I looked straight out at the sailboat and yacht-filled inner harbor and the Pacific Undersea Gardens aquarium where land-locked people can descend a short flight of stairs to look out at the local fish and sea creatures in a semi-enclosed, natural-looking environment. The harbor's stone banks and walkways are also home to street vendors, artists displaying goods and a colorful, wide variety of entertainment entrepreneurs. The region around Victoria offers great hiking, golfing, eco-touring, kayaking and fishing. In fact, the day before our first dive trip out of Victoria, a lucky fisherman at nearby Pedder Bay Marina caught a 34-pound chinook salmon.

The final reason for visiting Victoria has to be the shopping. Sure, if you need a pair of boxers with a red maple leaf on the front, Victoria is the place to go, but besides all the typical souvenirs you may want to plan a trip here around Easter when all the heavy winter items are marked down to make way for the skimpy summer fashions. (Note: there's almost always something on sale on Government Street.) One quick note about the exchange rate: many shops will accept U.S. dollars at par; only a handful of places accept Canadian dollars only. But credit cards are more expensive to use than almost any other method of payment because a foreign exchange service fee is added on. I know because I've got the credit card bills to prove it.

Dive Sites

Have you ever visited a dive shop that has tons of marine life and great shore dive access right behind the shop? How about one that has its own boat charter operation and regularly takes people out to some very popular, if not world-class, dive sites? What if I mentioned that they are ready to lead or teach most levels of diving right up to and including technical diving and that they have a long-standing good relationship with other dive shop operators? You might think I'm talking about a dive operation based in tropical waters or the Caribbean, but Erin Bradley, owner and manager of the Ogden Point Dive Centre (OPDC), offers this and so much more just a mile or so away from downtown Victoria.

I first came across the OPDC a few years back when my wife and I were driving along the water's edge of scenic Juan de Fuca Strait and stopped to have lunch at the Ogden Point Café, located directly above the dive shop. We enjoyed the food and the view of the breakwater where people go snorkeling and scuba diving on a regular basis, but at the time I had no idea how close I was to one of the most popular shore dive sites in all of Victoria. Lingcod, giant octopuses, wolf-eels and rockfish put on a daily show for locals and tourists alike. For

Erin Bradley of Ogden Point Dive Centre keeps busy between dives.

those who like boat dives, the OPDC has the 26-foot *Juan de Fuca Warrior,* a custom-designed aluminum boat built for swift currents and high maneuverability around such places as Race Rocks. The *Cape Able,* a 42-foot cabin cruiser, which is docked in Sydney, is used for larger groups and more distant destinations. The OPDC has weekend trips, away trips, in fact, all different types of packages. A few of their more popular wreck dive destinations include the *G.B. Church,* a 175-foot-long coastal freighter; HMCS *Mackenzie,* a 366-foot-long destroyer escort; and Xihwu Reef, the site of possibly the fastest flying underwater 737 airliner in the world. Well, no, it doesn't really fly, but with the current occasionally moving strips of kelp over the wings, you may encounter a slight sensation of flight.

On my first trip out on the *Warrior,* we met at the shop, stowed our gear on the trailered boat then walked a few minutes down the street to where they slipped the *Warrior* into the water next to a small dock. The short walk gave us divers a chance to get to know one another, and I must say I was with some very experienced divers that day. It seems people come from all over the world to dive Race Rocks as well as other known local dive sites. In fact, it takes a book by Greg Dombowsky called *Divers Guide to Vancouver Island South* to help cover all the dive sites in this region.

The *Warrior* zipped across the waves like a race team hydrofoil. On this particular trip we dived the Albert Head Wall, which has large plumose anemones and colorful sea stars and tons of zooplankton gliding by on a soft current. Our second dive was Brochie Ledge, a pinnacle close to the Ogden Point breakwater where a wrecked and abandoned ship, the *San Pedro*, was blown to bits to supposedly enhance the view of the waterway. On our dive we encountered ceramic artifacts, shards of porcelain cups and saucers, steel turned to reef structures and tons of assorted rockfish and scallops.

After returning to the boat ramp, we walked to the shop while our dive gear was escorted ahead of us via trailered boat. Back at the OPDC some divers took advantage of the hot showers and changing rooms while others rinsed off their gear. The center also has an on-site repair facility and a rather extensive line of scuba equipment.

While on a whale watching tour a few years back, our guide took us around Race Rocks. This sanctuary is under constant study and you can see the results on several excellent web sites, including one with an underwater web cam that displays the flora and fauna of this area around the clock. From the confines of our giant Zodiac-style rubber craft I could look some 20 feet below the surface at what appeared to be a breathtaking dive site. At that moment I knew I would return and dive the area.

Pacific pink scallops are beautiful to view, both underwater and in a light garlic butter sauce.

Where to Stay

You can book a package deal with the Days Inn (across the street from the ferry terminal) and the *Coho* ferry for a reasonable price. However, if you are looking for a room with a view, I would recommend the Executive House Hotel. If it's nightlife you are after, you might check out the Strathcona Hotel just a few blocks up Douglas Street. One word of advice, though: no matter where you stay, in Canada lager is light beer and pale ale is dark beer. (Note: I painstakingly researched this point before submitting this dialectical opposition information for your future libation consideration.)

Getting There

Fortunately, getting to Victoria is easier now than back in the days of the Hudson's Bay Company. If you are traveling by car from Seattle, I recommend driving the 80 miles to the Anacortes ferry terminal, from which it's a three-hour boat ride over to Victoria. Along the way you'll pass the San Juan Islands. The trip is very scenic, but the best part about taking this route is the short Customs line-ups both in Canada and on the return trip to Washington. Even the last car off the Anacortes ferry seems to spend less time in Customs than the usual wait time at highway border crossings.

Always try to photograph the best facial side of a copper rockfish. BERNARD P. HANBY

If you prefer a 90-minute crossing to Victoria, the *Coho* car ferry leaves out of Port Angeles, and this route includes the scenic drive up Highway 101. However, be warned that you'll have to make the drive to Port Angeles very early in the morning, but by the time the sun is up, you will be boarding the ferry. This Port Angeles–Victoria route is seasonal, however, and because the ferry goes straight across and parallel to the wind-generated waves entering the Strait, the ride can occasionally get bumpy. Our ride over to Victoria was smooth as silk, but on the way back two days later we were all a little green around the gills and some passengers were definitely seasick. The longer inland sea rides, such as from Anacortes, seem to be a better choice for those who get a little queasy on the water.

For those who do choose the scenic Port Angeles route, there is plenty of parking for walk-on passengers in the lots across the street from the ferry terminal entrance. The price for overnight parking changes seasonally, but the weekend we were there it was $7 per day. The walk-on system is very convenient provided the bags you are schlepping have roller wheels. Customs is quick (bring your passport) and you can even change some money at a small window booth before boarding the ship. Warning: eat before you board because the *Coho* trip is so quick that they carry a very limited selection of theoretically consumable food items. My advice is to stop at the architecturally pleasing Longhouse Market located next to the Seven Cedars Casino off Highway 101 about 25 minutes short of the *Coho* ferry terminal. They have freshly made breakfast items in the deli section, and you can dine in or take everything to go. They also may have the only gas station open that early in the morning. Once the ferry has docked in Victoria, expect to take up to an hour disembarking and winding your way through Customs, but with that out of the way, expect to have a great time no matter how long you stay or what you plan to do in Victoria.

As you look at a map or browse on-line, you'll see that there are many other interesting ways to make your way to Victoria, but no matter which route

For more information:

www.tourismvictoria.com
www.executivehouse.com
www.divevictoria.com
www.royalbcmuseum.bc.ca
www.racerocks.com

you choose, if scenic views, good food, tempting beverages, bargain shopping and tons of activities are what you crave between great dives, then Victoria is the perfect place to visit. Depending on the time of the year, the local tide tables and which route you took to get to Victoria, you could arrive in time to catch a "same day" dive with Ogden Point Dive Centre out to Race Rocks, but with unknowns such as the length of time it will take to get through Customs and Immigration, it's best to arrive a day before any planned dive-related activities.

NINE WONDERFUL WRECKS AND ONE POTENTIAL WRECK IN BRITISH COLUMBIA WATERS

When it comes to quality and quantity of wrecks to explore, the waters of British Columbia have to be at the top of the list. Warships, cargo ships and wooden ships dating back to the 1800s give plenty of options and multiple adventures. It's not just the ships that are so outstanding but the quantity of marine life each ship acquires with time and the types of marine life drawn to specific regions and

Plumose anemones can thrive where other creatures would be hard-pressed to survive.

habitats. The Artificial Reef Society of British Columbia (ARSBC) has to be the most active artificial reef society in the world, so it's understandable that eight of the wrecks I mention here were sunk on purpose for divers to enjoy and explore and for fish to thrive on.

HMCS *Mackenzie* is a 366-foot, 2,900-ton destroyer escort sunk in 1995 just north of Gooch Island and four miles east of the town of Sidney. It sits at a depth of 100 feet and you can expect 25 feet of visibility. It's in an area known for strong tidal currents so it's best to explore this wreck with a knowledgeable guide or charter operation. Before it was sunk, the original forward guns were dismantled and replica gun barrels made out of sewer pipes were put in their place, but the replicas appear real because of all the hard camouflage work done by the encrusting barnacles and other small resident creatures. In addition, kelp covers the radar tower, wolf-eels patrol the hallways and all kinds of shrimp and nudibranchs man the decks and mortar well. Talk about hard-working volunteers!

The *G.B. Church* is a 175-foot-long coastal freighter sunk in 1991 off Portland Island near Sidney in Princess Margaret Marine Park. It sits at 90 feet and you can expect around 35 feet of visibility. The sinking of this ship turned the underwater sand dunes here into an oasis of marine life. Sand alone could never have supported such a thriving colony of copper rockfish, tubeworms and red algae, to name a few of the vivacious local residents. A short boat ride from the Sidney area and 17 years of marine growth have made this reef (former wreck) into a very popular dive destination.

Xihwu Reef (pronounced "key-quot") is the resting site of a Boeing 737. Sitting at a depth of 60 feet, this 100-foot-long plane sits on 11-foot-tall stands so that it looks like it's flying through the water. The added height also allows you to dive from underneath it into the cargo belly area. This may be the only plane in the world that you can board without first clearing security, even if you are carrying a dive knife. Don't expect to find any pilots here. As many of us in the airline industry already know, most commercial airline pilots can't survive in an environment where they are not fed every 20 minutes (no offence intended to pilot whales). Seriously, however, although this is the newest artificial reef site to date, it hasn't taken long to attract the initial members of a thriving marine community. The best part about diving any wreck over and over is being able to

The MV *G.B. Church* under tow and then sinking off Portland Island in August 1991. BERNARD P. HANBY

observe first-hand the changes in the local sea life community and how Mother Nature deals with her new artificial appendage.

All three of these sites can be reached by boat from dive shops as far south as Victoria. The Ogden Point Dive Centre has one boat stationed in Sidney just for these excursions, but local charters out of Sidney can be arranged with companies such as 49th Parallel Dive Charters or with nearby resorts such as Cedar Beach Lodge Resort on Thetis Island.

HMCS *Saskatchewan* is a 366-foot, 2,900-ton destroyer escort sunk in 1997 next to Snake Island. It's a classic dive where the main deck rests at about 100 feet. Advanced divers in good physical shape and good on air consumption can almost swim from one end to the other before having to come up and do a safety stop. There is a lot of life on this structure, especially invertebrates. Currents here are usually mild so it hasn't taken long for most known species of critter to have relatives living on, inside or around this ship. Don't be surprised to find juvenile Puget Sound king crabs some 65 feet up in the crow's nest area, scallops on the main deck and harbor seals off the portside.

FMG (fleet maintenance group) HMCS *Cape Breton* is a 411-foot-long, 9,500-ton victory ship sunk in 2001 off Snake Island near Nanaimo on the east side of Vancouver Island. It took over 18 months to prepare the HMCS *Cape Breton* for sinking and less than four minutes to sink it. The world's second largest diver-prepared artificial reef, the ship sits at 142 feet and, when first sunk, stretched up to within 35 feet of the surface. Because of its length and depth, it should be considered an advanced deep dive. It shouldn't take long before the marine life descends upon it as it has on the HMCS *Saskatchewan* a short distance away.

Ocean Explorers Dive Charters as well as many other local dive charters come out to these two sites several times a day. It's always a good idea to stay at the Buccaneer Inn, which caters to

The tall resting pillars allow easy access inside the belly of the Xihwu Reef 737.
ISTOCKPHOTO

divers and is conveniently located near an excellent pub. Restaurants are just a short walk across the street.

HMCS *Columbia,* another 366-foot destroyer escort, was sunk off Maude Island near Campbell River at a depth of 120 feet. This wreck is tilted on its side, and if you get less than 20 feet of visibility, your whole inner axis of vertical versus horizontal seems to get thrown off kilter, although the angle doesn't seem to bother the marine life, including the juvenile octopus living onboard in a cubbyhole at 90 feet. The relatively calm surrounding waters make this dive accessible year-round, and it is visited on a regular basis by Abyssal Dive Charters, the *Nautilus Explorer* and dive charters from nearby Comox. However, the problem with this shipwreck is that there are too many great dive sites nearby with 100-foot-plus visibility competing for your attention. It's like discovering a bar of silver in a sea of platinum and gold, though it's still an interesting dive.

HMCS *Chaudiere* or "the *Chaud"* was yet another 366-foot, 2,900-ton destroyer escort, and it was sunk in 1992 off Kunechin Point in Sechelt Inlet on the BC mainland. This wreck tilts to port with the stern sitting at 55 feet and the bow at 105 feet. Thousands of orange plumose anemones, white tubeworms, sea vase tunicates and other critters make this a spectacular dive site. Porpoise Bay Charters and Suncoast Diving dive here on a regular basis.

The SS *Vanlene* was an 8,354-ton cargo ship carrying 300 Dodge Colt cars from Nagoya, Japan, to America in 1972 without the aid of any operational navigation equipment. The 29-year-old captain found land the hard way. Eventually the ship broke into two pieces, and the bow now rests at 25 feet and the stern at a maximum of 120 feet. If you need some Dodge car parts, head out to Barkley Sound off the west coast of Vancouver Island. Rendezvous Dive Adventures can take you there and to other great sites in Barkley Sound.

The SS *Capilano,* at 125 feet and 235 tons, is small compared to the other ships, and you can't go inside it, but if you want to see how big 100-year-old rockfish truly get, then you have to visit this 1915 wreck. The main deck sits at around 120 feet, so if the fish start to look bigger than you or they speak with slightly slurred accents, ascend just a few feet to where you can take in the full outline of the ship. Bring a light with you too, as it can get

The stern of the HMCS *Chaudiere* in September 1991. BERNARD P. HANBY

cold and dark in rockfish land. Bill Coltart and his team from Pacific Pro Dive and Surf in Comox can take you out to this must-see site.

HMCS *Annapolis*, yet another 366-foot destroyer escort, which weighs in at 3,420 tons, has not yet been sunk, but I added it to the list to let you know what the ARSBC is planning next. Commissioned in 1964 for submarine warfare and carrying a Sea King CH124 helicopter, in its day this $31 million, steam-driven vessel could generate enough electricity to light 18,000 homes. The ship, which has been to foreign ports such as Vladivostok, Guam and Hawaii, is spending its last days above water moored at Gambier Island for reclamation and environmental cleanup. Removing its homing torpedoes is easy, but cleaning up paint, removing toxic waste, cutting out diver safety exits and in general making the ship safe for fish and divers alike takes thousands of hours. The final resting site for the *Annapolis* was slated for Howe Sound, the most southern fjord in BC and a short, easy drive north from Vancouver. But locations have a way of changing due to unforeseen circumstances, such as avoiding currents and accommodating Coast Guard and Fisheries and Oceans regulations. I have photos of the 737 in Comox where it waited for months and months before the final word came down that it would be sunk near Chemainus. The *Breton* was at one time also scheduled for a shallower location before assuming its final resting spot.

The ARSBC doesn't just sink ships; it provides each artificial reef with guardians for life, continually monitoring these sunken habitats to make sure they remain safe for divers. Volunteers also track fish numbers and the resettlement activities of other marine species.

There may be an activity sponsored by the ARSBC that might even interest you.

I haven't mentioned all the minesweepers, battle-class trawlers and hundreds of wooden fishing boats, towboats and side-wheel steamers strewn around the bottom off British Columbia's shoreline, but there are books that specifically detail many of these local wrecks. Those I have listed are just some of the more prominent, if not the best, wreck dives to consider on your next expedition to British Columbia. And just like your mileage, your opinion on what are the best wrecks of BC may vary, but ultimately you'll come to the overwhelming conclusion that thanks to the hard work and dedication of devoted volunteers, sponsors, dive shops and other members of the non-profit ARSBC, wreck diving in BC is truly in a league of its own.

The Dive Industry Association of BC (DIABC) is the non-profit blanket organization that represents virtually all of the players in the province's dive industry. Check the web site, www.diveindustrybc.com, for articles and up-to-date information on diving in BC

For more information:
www.artificialreef.bc.ca

Washington State

NEAH BAY:
COLD AND BOLD TROPICAL COLORS

Talk to anyone about diving at Neah Bay and the first thing they'll mention is the beautiful colors. In fact, with all the diversity of colors there you feel as if you are somewhere in the tropics. If you set a finger down on a rock, chances are you will brush up against a strawberry anemone, a white plumose anemone or a lemon nudibranch. Rock scallops are colored and camouflaged by green algae, dark purple bryozoans or yellow sponges in never-ending art deco patterns. Young Puget Sound king crabs glow bright orange against living white backdrops, while the adults with their burgundy tops and light yellow and iridescent undercarriages move

Neah Bay, Olympic Peninsula. BERNARD P. HANBY

along the rocks like squat armored tanks. And these are just the colors of the life on the substratum. Octopuses, wolf-eels and rockfish swimming in the open provide another layer of vibrant color. Add to this seals and whales, up to 80 feet of visibility and an underwater landscape formed by rock and lava flows way before Starbucks ever brewed their first cup of tall mocha decaf, and you have a spectacular scuba dive destination right at the northwesterly tip of Washington State.

Dive Sites

The truth is that you barely leave Neah Bay before you come to the first dive site: Whadda Island. There are three main areas to dive here, and "the fingers" section is one of the bay's top-rated dive sites. Although you'll see tons of kelp and rockfish around the island, at the fingers you'll also see large lingcod and kelp greenling perched on the sides of sloping ridges that extend out from the surface near the shore and down to a depth of some 100 feet. As they extend out and away from each other, these ridges flow northward and form wide canyons. The currents in one of these 40-foot-deep walled canyons can quickly sweep you out into deeper water, or you can be brought swiftly back to shore while exploring an adjacent canyon. It's a good place to have the tides and their divine force on your side.

The top of Duncan Rock, a popular site at high tide, is poised barely feet above the surface; below the surface the rock is cut into V-shaped slopes with a wall on one side of the slopes. Small creatures cover every inch of them down to 120 feet or so, but because of navigational and weather considerations, this site gets fewer visitors than other sites, so don't be surprised if the marine life emerges to check you out.

Not far from Duncan Rock is Tatoosh Island, a wildlife sanctuary with interesting cutouts and rock formations and lots of life under the waves. Steller sea lions are known to join dive groups in this area. From Tatoosh Island you can look over to Mushroom Rock, another area with interesting water-sculptured formations.

As far as shore dives go, there's the wreck of the *Andalusia* in about 50 feet of water in front of Snow Creek Resort. Sail and Seal rocks are located in a partially protected bay, and First, Second and Third beaches are also notable shore dive sites. In fact, if you start from the Olson's Marina at the Sekiu jetty and work your way west,

Kelp greenling are easy to spot, as they appear to be covered with chicken pox.
BERNARD P. HANBY

you are going to need another weekend or two just to fit in all the local dive sites. On all of these dives keep a lookout for orcas, humpback whales and gray whales, and be prepared to see plenty of 100-year-old rockfish and a litter of white shells on the substratum, especially near octopus dens.

Neah Bay is a long way to go just to be turned back by bad weather and uncooperative currents, but May, June, July and August are the best months of the boat dive season, and during this time the currents are best every other weekend. While many of the local sites may be approached by boat, diving at Duncan Rock should only be attempted with a skilled captain who has previous experience there; even then the shifting currents or a sudden fog may change your dive plans. At present Porthole Dive is the only outfit I know that you can charter to Duncan Rock, and they only dive there during the prime dive season and only when the currents are favorable. For this trip they use their new 41-foot *Mark V* that accommodates 14 divers.

Getting There

Now before you set this book down and rush out the door, here are a few things you might find helpful. Neah Bay is approximately

Mushroom Rock, Olympic Peninsula. It makes you wonder how many divers it took to carve this fun guy? BERNARD P. HANBY

170 miles and one ferry trip from Seattle. Since it takes so long to get there, and there are so many sights to see and places to dive, it's best to devote an entire weekend to this adventure.

Where to Stay

Snow Creek Resort has camping five miles from Neah Bay. Curley's Resort and Dive Center, 20 minutes away in Sekiu, is not only one of the better-known motels in this vicinity but also the closest place to get air fills and last minute dive-related items. On their web site you will also find a list of half a dozen local shore dives. One non-diving activity that's a must while you are here is a short hike up the newly renovated Cape Flattery Trail. It takes 20 to 30 minutes, but from its scenic points you can look out at the nearby shoreline and sea caves, observe the puffins, sea otters, migrating whales then gaze out to Tatoosh Island, Vancouver Island and the Pacific Ocean.

Okay, so now's a good time to tell your friends about all the

For divers, Curley's Resort is the local place to stay when visiting Neah Bay. BERNARD P. HANBY

Cape Flattery, Tatoosh Island, and Seven Sisters. If you can't make it here for the great diving, at least come here for the sheer natural scenic beauty. BERNARD P. HANBY

colors and wildlife, grab your dive gear and head up to Neah Bay. You can even tell your dive buddies it was all your idea. They might complain about the initial distance, but after their first dive they'll be wondering why didn't you talk them into going to Neah Bay years before.

PORT TOWNSEND AND PORT ANGELES

Port Townsend is a picturesque town featuring the unique architecture of the late 1800s and early 1900s. Its buildings house modern-day shops, galleries and blues bands and it has strolling areas and docks where you can peer down into the water and watch sea stars glide across the sandy substrate. In essence, Port Townsend is a charming town that just happens to double as a great dive destination.

Dive Sites
Hudson Point, one of the best dives, is right off the end of Water Street. It is one of the favorites here for advanced divers because, if you hit the tides right at slack, there's a large variety of wildlife located in a small area that was a submarine tender site in the first and second world wars. On a typical dive you may encounter one of the three resident giant Pacific octopuses living in tubes or hanging

out along the jetty walls. Kelp crabs, plumose anemones and nudi-branchs are the usual suspects here. Fish of assorted species come and go with the currents and harbor seals peer out of the water to see what's happening on shore. It's a great place to dive as attested to by the many professional photographers who visit on a regular basis.

If you look at the map on the Admiralty Dive Center web site, you will see three separate color-coded dive routes in the general vicinity of Hudson Point. In addition, there is one route starting at Hudson Point and drifting south adjacent to the shore where div-ers can go on an old bottle collection dive. Beneath the downtown piers is another great place for those who like to collect old bottles, though I find it ironic that a bottle has to roll around for over 80 years, get sandblasted and filled with debris before it's worthy of a collection. The local divers don't mind if you collect these turn-of-the-century bottles, but just make sure that they are empty of contents, such as not-so-turn-of-the-century juvenile octopuses. I always find it hard to believe that the eight-legged inhabitant of

Antique bottles are found in the waters near this old section of Port Townsend.

a tiny medicine bottle could grow to 20 feet in length in just five years.

Nearby Fort Worden is another interesting dive site to visit and you can stay the night at the former military quarters. You'll find lots of crabs in less than 45 feet around the cement pipes, tires and eelgrass, but after a dive here, expect to spend extra time cleaning sand out of inconceivable places.

Port Angeles is less picturesque than Port Townsend. The route along Highway 101 passes grassy fields and elk crossings and culminates in a paved arterial way filled with shops and fast food restaurants, but it's hard to tell where the suburbs end and the city limits begin. Down on the waterfront next to the Marine Life Center is a small sandy beach where on any given weekend you'll see groups of divers heading—almost in shifts—in or out of the water. The depth in this part of the harbor rounds out to 50 feet with sunken logs providing crevices for fish and shrimp to call home. The weekend we were here a group of divers from nearby Peninsula Community College were doing navigational training for their advanced diver certification. It's a nice half-moon bay beach, but what's really great about this site is that if you don't happen to see some specific

Northern kelp crabs have skinny legs and small claws, but what they lack in stature they make up for with a bad, aggressive attitude. BERNARD P. HANBY

creature on your dive, you can enter the adjacent Marine Life Center and see if it is on display in one of the saltwater tanks.

So I didn't paint a pretty picture or dazzle you with praising prose about Port Angeles? The fact is I didn't have to because, if you drive through town past half the harbor and turn left on the truck route that redirects you to Highway 101 west and follow this route until you turn off on Highway 112 then continue to Camp Hayden Road—a total of 11 miles—you will arrive at one of the best and most beautiful dive sites in the whole state of Washington: Salt Creek County Park. During the first and second world wars this area was known as Fort Hayden. Near the top of the highest hill where now sits an empty, heavily constructed lookout site and turnaround road for tourists, two 16-inch cannons were mounted. Below on the hill, yet some 30 feet above the Strait of Juan de Fuca's cold, salty waters, sits a large visual-sighting pillbox and a concrete staircase that leads down to the black basalt rock formations on the shore. This basalt terrain reminds me of dive sites in Hawaii, but be warned: unlike Hawaii, this rock formation is steep, smooth and slippery when wet. You'll also need more than just advanced certification to dive here. This dive is for the person who dives often, is in

The west side of Tongue Point near Port Angeles offers sandy beaches and a small offshore island; all that's missing are coconut trees.

Many small fish and invertebrates make bull kelp forests their exclusive homes.
BERNARD P. HANBY

top physical shape, is ready for the possibility of a strenuous swim and has excellent navigation skills in order to locate entrance and exit points away from breaking waves.

There are three main trails leading down to the basalt shoreline. The trail that starts beside the visitor information board and leads down past the pillbox has the best gravel beach access. At the other end of the beachfront across from Campsite 5 is another information board, but the trail here is steep. The middle stairway leads down to some small tide pools. A fourth stairway located by Campsite 60 leads to a breathtaking view of the Tongue Point Marine Life Sanctuary, the main tide pools, Crescent Bay and a small uninhabited island in the bay. Depending on water clarity, you can also look right through the water at the passing sea creatures.

The underwater marine sanctuary is accessible to shoreline diving, but before venturing out, you would be wise to verify slack tide times and durations, set something large, colorful and very visible next to your entrance point and get a good bearing on your compass. Once in the water you'll think you are in the kelp forests of Monterey. You'll meet sea creatures of every sort and size, but you will have to move extra slowly and have a few knives on hand in case the currents make you play tag in the kelp forest—which is another reason to dive slack tides. On the fun side, keep a lookout for playful seals and river otters.

I might add that 500 yards offshore from Tongue Point lies the wreck of the *Diamond Knott*, a 360-foot cargo vessel that sank in 1946. According to Mike Kesl, the ship was under tow, but, when they reached Tongue Point, the currents were so bad that the most the tugboats could do was to hold on until the mortally wounded vessel slipped beneath the waves. The shallow end of the wreck is a 100-foot-deep dive at best, and the 140-foot end is considered a technical dive only. In recent years wave action has taken its toll on the hull, and parts of the bridge, railing and mid-section have disintegrated. Needless to say, the typical strong currents here make this Holy Grail of wrecks accessible only by boat and only when the currents permit. Among the very few charter boats that go out to it on a regular basis is Porthole Dive Charters, and their preferred months seem to be June and July. You have to be in good physical shape for this dive as Mike Kesl has seen divers go through a tank of air while just descending to the wreck.

Dive Shops

The Admiralty Dive Center in Port Townsend is probably the largest dive shop on the northern end of the Olympic Peninsula. Sudie Parker, who owns and operates the business, opened the shop about two and a half years ago. Sudie is also the captain of many vessels and a journalist who has covered a number of sailboat-related topics. (You can view some of her stories on the web.) Currently she uses her captain skills to go out twice a year to dive the *Diamond Knott* and Neah Bay. Closer to home she's led dive teams out near Protection Island to dive the crane whose raised arm lies 60 feet below the surface. In the shop her main dive instructor is Joey Johnson, who has over 25 years of dive experience and is now a NAUI instructor-trainer. In addition to all the typical dive shop services and features, they do Nitrox and other gas mixtures fills, but please call ahead if you need special gas blends or to arrange for argon gas fills. Sudie is very happy with the number of women not just becoming divers but dive instructors and dive shop owners. She is currently diving once every three months with groups of female dive professionals, following it up with lunch to discuss women and diving as well as to promote diving in general.

In Port Angeles, the headquarters for Scuba Supplies, owned and operated by Mike Kesl, is Sound Kayak and Bikes, located about two walking blocks from the beach. Mike opened his first dive shop in 1969 and has been in this present location since 2002. With so many years of recreational diving, teaching at Peninsula Community College and continuous work as a commercial diver, he is a great source of information, but I've found that it's best to call in advance if you want to meet him because he keeps himself busy with both recreational and commercial underwater projects.

Getting There

The best way to save on gas and see both Port Townsend and Port Angeles in a single weekend is to drive to one destination then over to the other site the next day. You can camp at Salt Creek County Park and have access to coin-operated showers, but if you prefer an upgrade, you may consider one of the many hotels in Port Angeles such as the Red Lion Hotel, which is adjacent to the beach. If you want dining, music and walkways near the shoreline, a hotel in Port Townsend might be your best bet to stay the night.

From Olympia, Port Townsend is just over two hours by car and Port Angeles two and three-quarter hours, but both take less time to reach via ferry from Seattle. If it's truly a scenic, pleasure-filled trip you are after, then you have to take the ferry from Keystone on Whidbey Island over to Port Townsend. Since it's hard not to stop for a dive at Keystone along the way, if you have three days to make the trip, it's even better. However, any of the mentioned dive sites are worth a single-day trip one at a time, and even if your dive gear is in for repair and your sinuses are blocked, standing at the viewpoint and looking out over the Tongue Point Marine Life Sanctuary is a must-do pilgrimage for any respectable cold-water diver.

For more information:
www.admiralty-dive.com
Scuba Supplies 360-457-3190
www.portholedivecharters.com

ANACORTES AND THE SAN JUAN ISLANDS

If you are looking for a town with beautiful views, plenty of parks and a natural gateway to great diving among the San Juans and beyond, Anacortes has to be at the top of your list. It's surprising how many people think that this town is on the mainland, but it is actually on the northern tip of Fidalgo Island, and accessed by three main bridges. The Deception Pass bridge with its majestic height and spectacular scenery has turnouts on both sides where tourists can gawk at and take pictures of the sheer cliffs and raging torrents of water passing through the narrow passage between Fidalgo and Whidbey islands, although the power and force depend on the phase of the moon. Over half of Fidalgo Island seems to be anointed with parks and lakes. Washington Park, the biggest one, boasts 220 acres of trails as well as campsites and lookout points where you can peer down on dolphins or killer whales swimming through Burrows Pass. You can view eagles soaring overhead or by

The northern channel at Deception Pass. The view is spectacular, but the currents can be unforgiving.

Cap Sante Marina is located right in the heart of the boat haven.

using binoculars spot them feeding their young in their great nests high in the trees or dotted along the shoreline of nearby Burrows Island.

During the 1890s when it was anticipated that Anacortes would become the terminus of the transcontinental railroad and the Manhattan of the west, land prices soared from $50 an acre to $3,000 for a corner lot. People rushed to build brick buildings, but they built them all inland, and Anacortes became known as the waterfront town with no waterfront. When the railway failed to arrive, the area became depressed and was not revitalized until lumber mills, fishing fleets and canneries came in. Now the mills and canneries have moved on, but the fishing fleets are still in port, and they help to fill in the picturesque and panoramic view at Cap Sante Boat Haven when you look down from the nearby park.

The Anacortes History Museum and the sternwheeler *W. T. Preston* are two historical sites that you may wish to visit while in town. It is also claimed that the local marine hardware store is the oldest on the West Coast—although all the merchandise I saw appeared to be relatively new. The old brick downtown area of Anacortes is currently the site of specialty stores and gift shops. The nearest mall is across a bridge and 20 minutes away in Burlington.

Anacortes restaurants boast great island food including Hawaiian, Greek and more traditional local island seafood. Stop by the Rockfish Grill and Anacortes Brewery for local seafood and, more importantly, for local home-brewed beer. Fresh-from-the-tap beer is also available in liter-plus-sized brown glass jugs so you can share your libation experiences with your less traveled friends back home.

Anacortes is one of those small towns that everyone wants to move to, provided they either telecommute to a six- or seven-figure occupation or they just unloaded a former property after it quadrupled in value and they can now move into modest peek-a-boo-view homes as "equity refugees." Fortunately for the rest of us, everyone qualifies to enjoy all the parks, lakes, shopping and great diving this area has to offer as Anacortes is just over an hour away from the Seattle area.

Dive Sites

Some of the dive sites close to Anacortes include Cone Island, Sares Head, Strawberry Wall and Williamson Rocks, but there are more than 40 other dive sites around the 15 public and accessible islands and too-numerous-to-mention pinnacles. Harbor seals, Dall's porpoises, white-sided dolphins, killer whales, wolf-eels and giant Pacific octopuses are the main underwater attractions here, but while one site may host a large variety of nudibranchs, another will be primarily home to swimming scallops, schools of assorted rockfish or giant sea urchins and Puget Sound king crabs. And while the underwater sites may vary, circling beneath the Deception Pass Bridge is always a hit with everyone between dives.

Juvenile Puget Sound king crabs live a solitary life, but as adults they may be seen hanging out with solitary cabezon fish. BERNARD P. HANBY

There are some shore dives along Fidalgo Island too. Rosario Beach and Deception Pass are both well-known sites, but strong currents, especially at Deception Pass, necessitate an advanced diver background and a good working knowledge of currents and tide flows. Slack tides are few and far between around Deception Pass, if you catch my drift, and you will need to be wary of the boat traffic off Rosario Beach.

But Anacortes is also the gateway to diving the San Juans and beyond, and like any other seasoned Northwest diver I will jump at the chance to dive the San Juan Islands. I don't really care what the destination is, what time of year it is or even who else is going. I already know that the trip will be fun as some of the best diving in the northwestern part of the hemisphere is right off the 450 peaks that rise above the high-tide line in the San Juan Archipelago. It's no wonder that the K, L and M killer whale pods all call these waters home. Tons of marine life both above and below the waterline—seals by the hundreds, swimming scallops by the thousands and strawberry anemones by the millions—can be counted during a single day of diving. What's more amazing is that at one dive site an unlimited number of rockfish species will swim around you and at the next there may be only a handful of rockfish but several wolf-eels or octopuses may be the main local residents.

Anacortes Diving & Supply on Commercial Avenue is just a few short blocks from Cap Sante Boat Haven.

Although only about 170 islands in the San Juans are actually named, already 50 to 100 dive sites have been named. And I wouldn't be surprised if eventually there will be more named dive sites than islands as each new or rediscovered site adds a new adventure and a new insight on the local aquatic slice of life. Some of the trendy sites include: Dawn's Bottom, a 176-foot wall dive; Jenn's Jungle, a 70-foot vertical wall dive; Christmas Crack; and Rick's Rump. Okay, so these handles didn't exactly come from the Vatican's list of preferred dive site names, but the sites are fun and they do have tons of marine life that until recently few divers have ever seen. That's why you'll want to write them up in your dive logbook along with the more traditional site names such as Bird Rocks, Spieden Island, Peapod, Long, and Bell and Strawberry islands. I won't try to name all the other dive sites, the 60 inhabited islands or the 13 islands open to the general public; it's best to find out the local names one dive trip at a time.

There are several ways to explore the San Juan Islands. You can ask the people at a local dive shop if they have a trip lined up for the near future or check the activities section of *Northwest Dive News* to see who is putting together a San Juan adventure. Anacortes Diving and Supply and Adventures Down Under in Bellingham are just two of many local stores that dive the San Juans on a regular basis. Ron Akeson of Adventures Down Under also plans technical dives around the islands; one of these is Randy's Surprise, a 175-foot wall dive off Henry Island. Unfortunately, if you are into wrecks, Ron says that the closest is the *Bunker Hill* in the middle of Rosario Strait. This ship's bow is on its side at 285 feet, and even a quick look will require long decompression stops for qualified technical divers. I should add that the ambient light here might reach down to 150 feet on a good day in May/June or September/October.

One thing to remember about the San Juan Islands is the "rain shadow effect." As Dave Patterson explained it to me, it means that it's typical for moisture-bearing clouds to diverge as they pass around the Olympic mountain range and let down their rain north and south of the Islands. So, while it may be raining or drizzling around Seattle, there's a good chance that it's only overcast or possibly even clear around the San Juans.

Dive Charters

Deep Sea Charters based at Cap Sante Marina and Diver's Dream Charters based at the Skyline Marina take divers out of Anacortes for the day or weekend, depending on current conditions, group desires or prearranged itineraries.

Unofficially, springtime starts the minute you depart Anacortes from Cap Sante Marina aboard the *Deep Sea* operated by Deep Sea Charters. A 46-foot-long former whale watching charter boat, it has been navigating the San Juan Islands for over three years now. Its former captain and owner, Dave Patterson, spent billions of dollars (plus or minus) in renovations to make it diver friendly, added new electronic equipment and installed an onboard air compressor that pumps up to 3,500 psi. The boat's registered capacity is currently 36 passengers or 18 divers, but the number of divers is typically kept down between 14 and 16, depending on the time of year.

The main deck is 15 feet wide, one of the widest decks of any single-day dive excursion boat that I've been on in the Northwest, giving divers plenty of space to stow gear, pass by other divers and

The *Deep Sea* has a large covered deck with plenty of viewing windows.

gear up without stepping on each other's fins. This deck is covered but plastic see-through windows allow divers to view the scenery at all times. A head is conveniently located beside the cabin's main entrance. Inside the cabin is a raised table and bench seats and a kitchen area complete with assorted hot drink mixes and snacks. The captain's control quarters and a passageway leading to the four-person bunk room/dry room/changing area complete the forward section of the enclosed area. On the stern is a camera-rinsing station, a mask-rinsing station, extra tanks in a rack and a fresh-water rinsing area where you could theoretically rinse off all your gear with up to 140 gallons of fresh water.

Mark King is the current president of Deep Sea Charters, although the last time I was on board the *Deep Sea*, Dave Patterson was still the owner and captain. Before we left the dock, Dave gave us a quick briefing on the ship so we'd feel right at home. By 7:30 a.m. the sun was already bright, so he went up to the second (observation) deck to operate the boat controls for the day. A few of us went up the ladder to watch him move out of the harbor and take in the picture-perfect view of the boats in the marina. You can't

The upper deck of *Deep Sea* is perfect for whale watching, sun bathing and reviewing technical decompression tables while your eyes are closed.

beat a former whale watching boat when it comes to finding a spot to take scenic pictures. Blue skies and panoramic views of islands and rocky shorelines led us right to our first dive site.

The divemaster that day was Tom Jacobs. He briefed us on a dive site called Sares Head, a wall dive that could go down to 180 feet, although he advised us to stay above 130 feet. He said we would find basket stars around 110 feet, but my dive buddies and I were content to photograph nudibranchs and anemones between 65 and 80 feet and scallops at 40 feet. The wall was filled with invertebrates and teemed with life everywhere the tiny creatures could manage to hold on. A slight current moved us along from one creature colony to the next. Visibility seemed to be between 10 and 20 feet but below 60 feet it was never any more than the length of my dive light's beam. It makes a great day or night dive, depending on your depth.

Once back on the boat we exchanged tanks and then we were invited to help ourselves to hot clam chowder or ravioli. Dave said they usually have two varieties of hot soup during the wintertime, but in the summer they can accommodate just about any group's menu request including a picnic of fried chicken, potato salad and rolls. While some of us dined on hot soup, others looked through the ship's library to find information on the creatures they had seen underwater. The boat carries a good supply of creature books, including one on birds that's the size of a spare tire. Jim Badgley, who was hosting a group of divers from the Silent World dive shop in Bellevue, went up to the upper deck with a few others and stretched out on the benches to catch some sunrays. They had driven up from Bellevue that morning. Others came from as far as Gig Harbor, a three-hour early morning drive.

For the second dive Dave took us to Williamson Rocks. You can only dive here in the winter months when the plankton level is low, and on this day the visibility was 20 to 40 feet. In the summertime these rocks are a haven for seals that don't really seem to care if the visibility is next to nothing. They just use their whiskers to navigate through the broadleaf kelp forest. Last summer Fred, the gray whale, could also be spotted near this area, but on this day we only saw two harbor seals playing in the water on the other side of the island and a juvenile bald eagle peering down at us from the top of the rocks. We swam near shore and took pictures of thousands of scallops swimming and dancing in the water column. A few good-sized lingcod passed by us as we moved from 85 feet up to 40 feet. This was a cool dive, literally, not only because of the amount of undisturbed wildlife, but because my drysuit leaked and became a collection site for plankton-rich, cold water samples. On the way back to port Tom passed out little "Deep Sea Charters" stickers that we could place in our logbooks.

After Dave Patterson was strong-armed by an aerospace firm with a big checkbook and plenty of ink to give up his captaincy and go back to the real world, Mark King became the owner of Deep Sea Charters. You may see him working as first mate and/or dive-master on the *Deep Sea* while Captain Gene or one of the other familiar captains is at the helm. Mark has been diving since 1991 and you can tell from his purchase of the Deep Sea Charters operation that he loves the sport. In fact, weather and waves are the only things that can keep him from going out for the day. The *Deep Sea* now travels around the San Juans hitting hot spots such as Black Rocks, the larger two of the four islands in the Cone Islands group, a new dive site at Revolution Point and the ever-popular Strawberry Island.

One of my good friends and fellow instructors has been diving regularly with Phil and Judy Jensen since they took ownership five years ago of Diver's Dream Charters and the 42-foot *Lu Jac's Quest,* which they base at the Skyline Marina. The boat has been used for chartering out of Anacortes since 1998 and Phil has been diving the San Juans since 1990. He now has just over 32 years of diving experience, but I wouldn't hold that against him. Phil will be glad to take you diving almost anywhere, depending on tides and currents, and this is a man who really knows some good locations where you can go overboard. He says that even during the winter months there are some great dive sites at wind-secluded locations such as Broken Point and Rosario Wall. His favorite sites, however, have to be along the southern end of Lopez Island or up at Sutia or Matia islands. Phil and Judy also do sightseeing and wildlife tours, kayak shuttles, special wedding and/or funeral service charters and will even pick up and drop off divers at Friday Harbor on prior arrangement. The last time I saw their boat they had just dropped a group of kayakers off on the other side of Deception Pass. The group

Phil and Judy Jensen aboard *Lu Jac's Quest*, taking divers on a scenic tour between dives.

looked like they were having a lot of fun navigating around Pass Island State Park.

Mike and Dawn Hillard have sold their dive shop operation at Friday Harbor, and Rick Myers and his team from Bandito Charters have formed the current dive operation there, using the name Naknek Charters/Bandito Charters. The operation takes its name from the 43-foot boat *Naknek*, which has a heated cabin with a good-sized deck for gearing up. Kurt and Peggy Long captain the boat and run the operation out of Friday Harbor, but the big dive shop there is gone. It's all about the charter operations and dive trips now, although they still carry plenty of rental gear and an air supply to accommodate any diver's request, provided you give them a little advance notice. Rick and his team have worked hard and have come a long way over the years to get to this new pinnacle point of charter expansion. Their web site is up and running and lists more dive sites than I've already mentioned.

Dive Shops
Kelly or Bob Scarzafava of Anacortes Diving and Supply will be happy to answer any questions you have concerning local diving, gear

rental or repair, drysuit supplies, camera needs or other last minute purchases before your next great dive. They have owned and operated their dive shop, located right on Commercial Avenue, for the last 10 years.

Now I happen to feel that it's important to visit every dive store in the universe. After all, how do you know what you really need unless you can find it at the end of an aisle? Isn't acquiring the latest and greatest dive gear the best and greatest use of time between dives? So even if you already own two of every single piece of dive gear ever invented and would just like to hook up with a knowledgeable group of local divers, I suggest you check out their web site or give Bob and Kelly a call.

Where to Stay

One option for visiting the Anacortes/San Juan Islands area is to take a five-minute ferry ride from the north end of Commercial Avenue in Anacortes and stay at Guemes Island Resort. This way you can shop and dine downtown and then retire to a 17-acre park-like setting on the northern end of Guemes Island for a few nights or a fortnight. Whether you stay in the Guemes house, Mount Baker House or one of the six cabins, you'll find it a very relaxing experience with rustic charm and panoramic views. Most dive charters

This is a cute little Inn serving a continental breakfast a few blocks away from Cap Sante Boat Haven.

will pick you up from here for day diving trips and drop you back off with your film depleted, digital cards filled to capacity and logbooks in desperate need of updates. However, you can shore-dive right in front of the resort, although the gravel substrate is best viewed at night when the sea pens and a local giant Pacific octopus come out to play. There is a wall dive at Square Harbor that goes down to 150 feet, but it's a hearty five-block downhill hike to get to this site, which helps make boat diving so appealing. The island boasts 350 residents and one store where they will be glad to tell you how to get by without anything they don't have in stock. A few days of relaxing here and your whole perspective on the rest of the world could ebb along with the tides.

Two other places where you might consider staying while visiting the Anacortes area include the Anacortes Inn and the Anaco Inn. The Anacortes Inn offers 44 units, most with queen beds but some with a king and a kitchen or a king and a Jacuzzi, and the rates include a continental breakfast. The Anaco Inn, just up the road and slightly closer to Cap Sante Marina, offers suites with a jetted tub or a fireplace or even a three-bedroom unit that feels more like a home than a hotel. It has a dining room for complimentary continental breakfasts as well as wireless internet service. The room I last stayed in had a full kitchen, but with the Greek Island restaurant just 50 feet behind the Inn, that kitchen could remain untouched for years.

Now if you really want to sample true island life, you have to stay at one of the inns, bed and breakfasts or county parks on one of the other outer islands, or perhaps at a more central location such as Friday Harbor. Don't be surprised to see a group from a dive club spending a few days relaxing on the outer islands, having crab and shellfish feasts and, of course, diving.

For more information:

www.deepseacruise.com
www.lujacsquest.com
www.guemesislandresort.com
www.anacortesdiving.com
www.anacortesinn.com
www.anacoinn.com
www.cityofanacortes.org/parks.asp
www.anacortesrockfish.com
www.islandcam.com
www.adventuresdownunder.com
www.naknekcharters.com

If you go to the San Juans during the summer months, you had better make reservations as early as possible, as accommodations and dive operations fill up fast, especially with repeat business. You'll know why once you dive the islands. Oh, and before I forget, anytime someone says that the diving is better up in Canada, I'd just like you to point out to them that although the San Juan Islands are southeast of Bellingham, Washington, they are actually northeast of Victoria, British Columbia, and almost directly across from Sidney, BC. But personally, I find the diving great anywhere along these latitudes and I think you will too.

WHIDBEY AND CAMANO ISLANDS

North of Seattle are two islands that were shaped, scoured and carved into their present forms by thousands of years of glacial activity. All those tons of ice depressed the land, but after the glaciers retreated, the land rose up again. This is why to this day it's possible to find remnants of sea creatures at the higher elevations of these islands.

Whidbey is the larger of the two islands. For years I've been

Easy shore access makes Keystone Park a very popular dive site.

taking groups of divers to Fort Casey State Park and to the most popular shore entry on the island known locally to divers as Keystone. Changing rooms, coin-operated showers, plenty of parking and tons of marine life make it a great dive site. This is a marine preserve whose main feature is the jetty wall constructed of large boulders to protect the green and white-lined Klickitat Ferry as it pulls in from Port Townsend and docks at the sparse Keystone terminal. I didn't find this dive site on my own. This is where my instructor took his students, and it's where his instructor took his students. The underwater park is where I came mask-to-eyeball with my first giant Pacific octopus. Depending on the time of year, you can see wolf-eels, octopuses or egg-guarding lingcod peering out between the boulders. For best viewing results bring the biggest dive light you can afford because it's the only way to see suction cups larger than your light lens receding into the crevices. The giant Pacific octopus is an amazing creature to view, and its great size is second in interest only to its innate elusiveness and incredible shyness.

For this dive, once you get geared up, follow the path leading to the top of the jetty then descend the narrow trail to the beach

A giant Pacific octopus is very intelligent and can easily perform an eight-legged moon walk. BERNARD P. HANBY

to enter the water. Follow the jetty out, exploring along the way to about 55 feet of depth, which should be reached when you are close to the end of the jetty, but don't forget to look behind you to see all the schooling fish. Don't go past the end where it dips down past 85 feet because the currents pick up quickly. In other words, don't go past the end of the jetty unless you are carrying a current and valid passport.

Be sure and bring a knife and scissors on this dive to take care of unwanted fishing line. Although this is a marine protected area, to my amazement, on one dive here with my wife a fishing lure descended and wrapped around her arm. Then we watched in disbelief as the lure whipped back around her arm and headed for the surface again. By the time we surfaced, the suspected poacher was long gone with said fishing lure in tow.

Another great dive site is the nearby abandoned pilings. I'm not sure how long they will be out there because they are slated to be removed by the State, but as long as they are standing, it's worth the walk down the shoreline and the swim out there. Generations of plumose anemones and smaller invertebrates hang onto their vertical surfaces and you may find an octopus out in the open here engorging on the abundant supply of crabs. Farther down Admiralty Beach are sandy areas great for collecting old bottles. You'll need a permit to dive here at night.

On the south end of Whidbey Island on the edge of the picturesque town of Langley is the Langley tire reef. If looking around old tires for sea life is your idea of a good time, then you won't find a better site than right on the exposed side of the Langley marina. You will actually dive around the outer wall that shields and protects the inner harbor. As fishermen may be casting from the overhead marina walkways, when you are heading out to the dive site, you should give a wide berth until you round the first corner. Straight out past the tire reef you'll find nothing but soft sand and salmon bones tossed over the sides of passing fishing boats, but inside and around the tires you'll find a vast and rich number of colorful invertebrates.

Other great dive sites await you off the shores of Whidbey Island, but you will need a boat or kayak to reach them. Deception Pass on the north end of the island can be done from shore by advanced

At Deception Pass, waters flow deceptively fast during tidal exchanges; hence the name. BERNARD P. HANBY

divers at slack tide, but the dive is made a lot easier when there is a boat nearby and ready to do live (not anchored) pickups. Possession Point Fingers, Possession Point Ferry and the Habitat are all excellent dives on the south end of Whidbey. In fact, the Fingers may be one of the best wall dives south of Canada. The metal structures of the Habitat and the ferry wreck are both good locations for encounters with lingcod and rockfish.

Whidbey Island is one of those places where there are many more great dive sites waiting to be discovered. I once went out on a Zodiac with a team from Emerald Sea Dive Club to collect creatures for college students to study at Fort Casey. We jumped in the water right in front of the flag field at Fort Casey, and as I came to rest on the eelgrass bed, I found to my disbelief that one of my knees was resting on an arm of an octopus. Needless to say, that young eight-armed male spent the summer in school before returning to the ocean.

On Camano Island you can do a shore dive at the State park. Pat Ocean, the owner of Whidbey Island Dive Center in Oak Harbor, also recommends diving Onomac Point if you have access to a boat. This artificial reef is a good spot to view plumose anemones and small invertebrates or hunt for lingcod.

On the other side of Camano Island, sharing the same waters as Port Susan and almost at the same latitude as Camano State Park is Kayak State Park. This is a shallow dive where you'll find an abundance of crab and other small invertebrates moving through the eelgrass. Underneath the dock at less than 30 feet you'll sometimes find brand new crab rings lying on the substrate because the park personnel routinely cut the lines attached to crab rings left

Short plumose anemones never seem to get the respect that their cousins, giant plumose anemones, receive. BERNARD P. HANBY

tied to the dock overnight. The posted warning signs don't seem to discourage some people. Besides crab rings, I once recovered a ring for someone off the end of the dock; it just goes to show you that you never know what you'll find sitting under the dock of the bay.

Dive Shops
The Whidbey Island Dive Center is right next to the Taco Bell in Oak Harbor. This is the closest place to get air fills, last minute scuba gear or kayaks. They also sell an informative booklet on local shore, boat and kayak dives called *The Whidbey Island Dive Guide*. Not only does Pat and his team at the dive center have knowledge about the local dive sites, but they also have a large push-pin map on the wall showing where they have dived around the world.

Getting There
You can cross over to Whidbey via the Mukilteo ferry, or for the panoramic view of Keystone Park take the Port Townsend ferry over to Whidbey. To get to Whidbey by road take the I-5 up to exit 230 then follow Highway 20 south through Oak Harbor. Camano Island can be reached by road by taking exit 212 and heading west via

Whidbey Island Dive Center. While diving on the island, you'll get to know this dive shop well.

Highway 532. To get to Kayak State Park, take exit 156 off the I-5 and head west.

It's well worth the effort to cross over on a ferry or pass over a bridge to see the abundant wildlife around Whidbey and Camano Islands. Although it's easy to drive up for the day, you can spend the weekend at the Coachman Inn in Oak Harbor or in one of the many bed and breakfasts located on the south end of Whidbey near the Langley tire reef and all the shops and restaurants along First Street. Come to think of it, since the glaciers have receded, there isn't a better time than right now to visit and dive Whidbey and Camano islands.

> **For more information:**
> www.whidbeydive.com
> www.thecoachmaninn.com

EVERETT, MUKILTEO AND HAT (GEDNEY) ISLAND

When someone mentions diving in Everett, they are usually talking about diving down the hill by the ferry terminal in Mukilteo. The three distinct dive sites on the point of land jutting out into Possession Sound make this one of the top three dive training sites in the

Seattle area. From Seattle to Bellingham, students and instructors converge here to take advantage of the easy access to open water, above-average visibility, large range of depths and tremendous diversity of sea life.

Dive Sites

The Mukilteo T-dock is the most popular of the three sites. There is a sea wall on the right side of the Silver Cloud Inn and adjacent to the Marine Biological Research Facility. Sand has recently filled in the remodeled stairway so it's an easy walk down to the beach. Stepping into the water you have plenty of room to gear up before descending a gravel slope that gives way to a steep, sloping sand embankment. At 20 feet you may come across a guide rope running parallel to shore—this is where a lot of dive classes complete their skills before touring the local area. Past this rope line you'll find tons of juvenile crabs with only their antennas sticking out of the sand. Down at 130 feet the steep slope smoothes out and two-foot-wide sandy ripples lead to a long, air-consuming path past 175 feet and beyond. You can go deep here for training purposes or better yet, stay around 35 feet and check out some underwater

The west view of the dive site right in front of the Mukilteo Silver Cloud Inn.

pilings, a geodesic dome and other man-made artifacts located near the T-dock. If you go to your right past the T–dock, you'll find two consecutive shallow bowls of desolated sand. However, around the perimeter of these areas you'll encounter kelp greenling, lingcod, cabezon, stubby squid, sole and flounder. After swimming what seems like a half-mile or so, you'll arrive at the oil dock, and around it in less than 35 feet of water you'll find a plethora—perhaps even thousands—of oversized crabs. You have to stay a few feet off the substrate here because the fine silt whips up easily, but you can max out on your crab limit very quickly. Some divers used to dive the other side of the government compound then walk back along the restricted shoreline to the oil dock, but the area has been closed off due to remodeling and dismantling of the old oil storage containers. So now the only option is a long swim down to the oil dock, but as you'll find out, the swim is worth it if you truly love fresh crabmeat.

At the Mukilteo State Park located to the left of the ferry terminal and adjacent to the picturesque postage stamp-sized lighthouse, you'll come across a variety of dive sites. After a short walk from the beachfront restrooms into the water you'll find a clay embankment

At low tide the beach at Mukilteo extends some 20 feet; at high tide, not so much.

at 30 feet of depth and a second embankment at 70 feet. Empty holes bored in the clay by former rough piddock clam residents give refuge to myriads of small invertebrates. This area is a good spot to see lingcod and octopuses too. Near the public boat ramp it's a steep, sandy drop-off past 150 feet with nothing to see except artifacts discarded or lost overboard from passing boats, but for technical divers it's a great location to do decompression stops. It is especially important at the park to plan your dives according to slack tides in order to avoid strong currents.

In the winter sea lions patrol all these dive site areas in search of salmon. They never bother groups of divers, but I have heard directly from a solo diver that they harassed him when he was diving alone, bumping into him and pulling on his fins. This lends additional positive support for the buddy system.

If you have access to a boat, you'll soon discover that just across the waterway via the boat ramp at Mukilteo State Park there are two other hot spots in Possession Sound. The first is the Possession Point Ferry. Take a 200-foot ferry boat and burn it down to the waterline, then sink it 80 feet deep, shake and stir with currents and salt water, and you have one fantastic artificial reef quickly filled

You never know what you'll find scuttled by boaters near the Mukilteo launch ramp. BERNARD P. HANBY

The Three Gs of Crab-Catching

After years of pinched fingers, Acme kits and coyote-style crab-stalking tactics, I've learned to beat those little roadrunners at their own cartoon-like antic game. When you see antennas sticking out of the sand and a light shade of sifted sand about the same size as a crab, it's easy to scoop out the sand and catch the little guy, but if the crab is on the move, you are going to need the three Gs to assure categorical, crafty, crab-catching success.

With a thumb on top and the other fingers on the bottom, it's easy to turn a Dungeness crab over and determine the sex without getting pinched. KRISTINA HUGHES

THE GEAR: Any net, bag or hand will work for one crab, but if you want to bring home the daily limit, I recommend a goody bag that has a spring-loaded stainless steel opening and can be operated with one hand (you will be holding the crab with your other hand). The first few inches of the bag inside the opening should be smooth, so that after you measure the crab you can shove it in the bag and shut it as quickly as possible. The rest of the bag can be made out of mesh for drainage and water resistance reasons. Just a warning here: crabs have evolved an uncanny ability to get tangled in mesh bags; I think they learned this from transient slipper lobsters from Hawaii. So unless your bag has a metal-rimmed mouth and a few inches of smooth surface on the inside, you can spend an eternity trying to put one crab into it. I've watched hundreds of crabs run for cover while I fought with one mesh-bag-savvy crab. I got the feeling that it somehow knew how to slowly sacrifice its own life and at the same time deplete my precious reserve of air in wasted frustration so that others of its kind would have ample time to run away and hide.

THE GRACE OF THE CHASE: Female crabs tend to sit still and snicker as you approach them because they know that if you pick them up, you'll just have to set them back down again, so why bother to run? They have slightly more rounded top shells and their abdomens measure approximately two or more fingers wide, whereas a male's abdomen is only about one finger wide.

Male crabs of any size are very wary of divers. The best way to get close to one is to swim with your arms close to the sides of your body because they seem to view divers as slow, lumbering fish. It's best to swim only fast enough to reduce the distance between you and the crab until you are less than an arm's reach away. Once the crab is within striking distance or in the grab zone, strike like a praying mantis. The thing to remember is that a crab can rarely increase its speed enough to counter this praying mantis maneuver, but it can outrun an outstretched hand all day.

THE GRAB: When within range, turn your hand so that when you sweep it behind the crab your thumb will come to rest on the top of the shell. Next, pivot your hand a little more and slide your fingers or glove under its belly. The bottom-side of the crab should now be resting in the palm of your hand. By applying a little pressure, you can lift the now-docile crab without getting pinched. Next turn your wrist to check the crab's sex and then, if it's a male, measure it with your free hand to make sure it exceeds the minimum size limits. Practice can help preclude future accidental glove tears and abrasions.

U.S. fishery regulations allow only male crabs to be taken. In Canada the minimum size limit is 6.5 inches for the Dungeness crab. The Department of Fisheries' rationale is that any crab bigger than that is almost certainly a male. The red rock crab has its own restrictions.

Okay, so you've encountered an extremely wary male crab. He's big and tasty. You know it, and he knows it too. You have over 15 feet of clear visibility and he won't let you get within 5 feet from him. Arms folded at your sides and the praying mantis maneuver just won't cut it today. This is when you enlist the aid of your dive buddy. Crabs tend to gravitate towards shadows and logs, so you hover motionless a foot above the substratum while your buddy circles around the crab and chases it toward you. It's like the old cowboy cattle roundup. You might even feel a little dry in the throat, but it's not from dust on the trail. It's from breathing too hard through your regulator as you hover motionless and wait patiently. Your buddy is now driving the crab straight towards you. As it enters the grab zone, you spring into action and grab the mad crab.

with tons of fish and plumose anemones. Dive site two is the Possession Point Fingers, one of the best wall dives in the area. The first section of the wall's ledge is at 30 feet, the second juts out at 50 feet and a third section cascades out in spots at about 70 feet. The wall contains serrated horizontal mini-ledges honeycombed with openings and small holes, which an enormous number of small fish and invertebrates call home. Parts of this wall are nothing but shrimp villages and high-rises. At about 25 feet the sandy embankment is home to some spectacular large orange sea pens and a few Dungeness crabs buried in the sand. Along the wall there are holes and caverns big enough to reach in and shine a light around, which makes this site a very unique dive destination. The last time I was here we saw one octopus garden, but the Pacific giant was "out for lunch." Visibility and currents can be a problem if the local rivers are running high with sediment or if you try to dive anytime other than slack tide. In February the visibility was around 20 to 30 feet. Use Nitrox or enriched air for this dive as you'll want to spend most of your time at 80 feet of depth. Although the wall only lies some 60 feet offshore, the sheer cliffs on adjacent Whidbey Island make this spot a boat dive only. Aluminator Water Taxi Service out of

The ultimate method is the wolf-pack approach, for groups of four or more divers. Two divers swim between pilings or pier poles. Two or more other divers swim outside and adjacent to the pilings or on a slope just below the pilings. The pile divers flush the crabs out into the open; the other divers gather the scampering crabs.

No matter which technique you use—praying mantis, cowboy roundup or wolf pack—the crabs will all taste great when they are cooked. A few good methods for preparing crabs and cooking them are found on the following internet sites. Now where did I put my shellfish license?

www.dungeness.com/crab/cooking.htm
www.welovefish.com/dungeness5.htm
www.crabfestival.org/recipes.html

Elliot Bay in Seattle and Porthole Dive Charters out of Tacoma both come to this site on a regular basis.

Hat Island, also known as Gedney Island, is just a few nautical miles from Everett. Some 13,000 years ago a land bridge connected this island to Camano Island but as the glaciers subsided and Puget Sound filled with water, Hat Island was reduced in size and became shaped on the south side—you guessed it—like the brim of a hat. From Everett you can visit by local ferry service, chartered dive boat or you can put a Zodiac in the water at Mukilteo and run over to the island very quickly, provided the winds are with you.

A small island, used seasonally for eons by Native Americans, it was homesteaded by Peter Goutrie, a French fur trader working for the Hudson's Bay Company. Back around World War I a dance hall was built on the north end of Hat Island, but during World War II the Navy bombed that end of it. I assume they had nothing against dancing but just needed the bombing practice before deploying overseas. So why do I mention this information in a dive article? Because you never know what you might come across while diving around this island. A P-38 Lighting fighter once officially crashed off the south end of the island and was later moved out to deeper

A sea pen is an anthozoa coral colony that looks like a single life form.
An entire field of sea pens can be decimated by striped nudibranchs in mere days.

water; it is more than 500 feet deep on the side facing Everett. What else unofficially rests beneath the waves is anyone's guess. If you are into tech diving the barges sunk near the mouth of the marina, between 50 and 150 feet, are a good place to find Dungeness crabs and rockfish.

Without a boat, the next best diving is right from the Mukilteo shoreline. I've been diving and dive instructing in front of the Silver Cloud Inn for the past 10 years. You will see lots of animal life by diving less than 50 feet, especially if you go straight towards the underwater pilings. During crab season I like to surface-swim over towards the oil tanker dock where the sand beds at 30 feet are filled with Dungeness crabs visible only by their antennas and the ring of disturbed sand that surrounds their bodies. Just in front of the Silver Cloud Inn the sandbanks start at 5 feet and run sharply down a slope to 130 feet where the sand forms embankments that roll gently downhill past 175 feet of depth. I've been out to the shallower depths here hundreds of times, but I've never been past the 175-foot point, and I'm sure this area is better left to passing military submarines. I've seen the man-made geodesic dome, a toilet, car parts, a boat ice cooler and other artifacts at this site, and I thought I had seen it all. Then I talked with fellow dive instructor Bob Helton from Seattle Underwater Sports. He told me that if you go slightly to the left of the guide rope that lies in about 20 feet of water, you'll come across a bottle field at around 80 to 90 feet, a troll statue at 110 feet and a 16-foot boat at 130 feet. There is usually a resident giant Pacific octopus living under the boat and another bed of bottles and a radar dish close by. The site is not that far to the left, so getting too close to the ferry terminal shouldn't be an issue, but the depths are so great that divers should have deep diver training or, better yet, technical dive training.

On the other side of the waterfront at the far end of the State park is another area waiting to be explored when the tides are slack. At less than 70 feet you can find clay embankments filled with small invertebrate life. Closer to the lighthouse, the shoreline goes straight down to 130 feet and there's really not much to see here except swift currents and whatever boaters using the nearby boating ramp have tossed or lost overboard. Winter visibility can range from 40 to 80 feet. In the summer it can drop to what you can see rubbing up against your mask, but when you descend past the thermocline, which is usually around 20 or 35 feet, the visibility opens up, typically between 15 and 40 feet. The fish here are accustomed to neoprene-clad monsters blowing loud bubbles at excessively fast rates while swirling up tons of sand and silt with every beat of their bicycle-style fin kicks. All of the creatures here—from the small, stubby squid all the way up to the large, lethargic lingcod—are excellent photo models with quite experienced resumes. Finally, it

The Mukilteo Lighthouse is the only place I know of where you can catch crabs, do a deep dive, and get married all near the same location.

goes without saying that it's best to dive this area at slack unless you're in training to join a seal team—fur, harbor or Navy.

Dive Shops

The nearest dive shop is Underwater Sports of Everett, about five miles from the dive sites. To find it, take the Evergreen exit on 526 then take a right on Casino Road. You'll see the dive shop in a small shopping complex directly across the street from the Fred Meyer Super Store. John Jensen, the current manager at Underwater Sports, has remodeled it and it looks impressive. He and his staff are ready to assist you with all your nearby and faraway diving needs. John knows recreational diving inside out and was instrumental in honing my own instructor/leadership skills when I first became an instructor working at the Underwater Sports store in Edmonds. I can never thank him enough for his insight and advice, or say enough good things about him in general. So if you need last-minute dive supplies for your Mukilteo/Hat Island expedition, tell John I said, "Hello." I'll be back up there soon myself, as I want to take a few photos of the new to me but old to the site resident giant Pacific octopus.

Getting There

To get to Mukilteo through Everett via Interstate 5, take the Mukilteo–Whidbey Island exit, number 188. On Highway 526 follow the signs and drive past the largest one-story structure in the world, which is painted with enormous scenes of Boeing plane interiors and exteriors. Take the shortcut and turn right on 84th Street, then right on 525, and follow the road straight down the hill towards the ferry terminal.

Where to Stay

If you need overnight accommodation, you can't get any closer to the waterfront than the Silver Cloud Inn. With 70 rooms, continental breakfasts and complimentary high-speed internet service, they usually fill up quickly during the week with business executives and aviation clientele, but on the weekends they have more availability. Be sure to call ahead for reservations. The Hilton Garden Inn is located three miles up the hill next to the Field of Flight and the Aviation Center and Boeing Tour.

For more information:

www.scinns.com

www.underwatersports.com

www.aluminatorwatertaxi.com

www.portholedivecharters.com

www.arniesrestaurant.com

The Buzz Inn Steakhouse is the place to go for a hearty breakfast; it's right across the street from the Silver Cloud Inn. For a hot bowl of clam chowder between dives, Ivar's is right next to the ferry terminal and a short walk from wherever you park. At the end of your diving day if you still desire some of the best seafood in town, Arnie's is just a block or so up the hill, and besides the fine food, it features a great view of the Mukilteo basin, ferry terminal and adjacent shoreline.

No two dives are ever the same here. You might see an octopus on one dive, a squid on the next, a collectible bottle or even a seal chasing a salmon on the dive after that. Dive groups and instructors with their classes come here from Bellingham, Bothell and Seattle. Dive charters can take you out to Hat Island, and during crab season the sands near the oil tanker dock is a mecca for the 10-legged, succulent creatures. I always have a good time diving here whether I'm with students or salty seasoned professionals. I think you will too.

EDMONDS AND THE BRUCE HIGGINS UNDERWATER TRAILS

Twenty-five minutes north of Seattle is the sleepy little town of Edmonds. It's filled with senior citizens getting their daily exercise by strolling the floral-decorated sidewalks, motorists forming lines in anticipation of the next ferry going over to Kingston, fishermen trying their luck at catching salmon from the town pier and beachcombers collecting shells and driftwood, as well as some 20-plus thousand divers a year descending on Brackett's Landing, or what is more commonly known as the Bruce Higgins Underwater Trails, formerly the Edmonds Underwater Park.

This 27-acre park has been one of the top dive destinations in the Pacific Northwest for the past 20-some years. The reason is simple: this site was designated one of the first marine reserves in the nation, and it is now home to some of the largest lingcod and

From up on the hill, you get a great view of the jetty and Bruce Higgins Underwater Trails.

cabezon in Puget Sound. But it takes more than just a national designation to make a great dive destination. This park is a constant work-in-progress. Over the past 20 years, volunteer crews under the direction of Bruce Higgins have met every Saturday morning to sink everything from dinghies to tugboats in designated locations, only to watch them slowly be pummeled by currents and wave action until all that is left is a few remnants and it is time for a replacement vessel. They have also laid trails and placed artifacts—everything from 15-foot-tall cement structures to foot-long cinder blocks—and each has become a home for underwater residents, the real reason that so much wildlife resides in such a confined area. Food was plentiful here but habitats scarce on the barren sandy substrate, so the work done by Bruce's volunteers has given untold generations of everything from shrimp to lingcod a chance to thrive in an otherwise ever-shifting piece of sandy real estate. In fact, the park has become a major breeding ground for several species of fish primarily because it is off-limits to fishermen.

Other volunteers under the direction of Kirby Johnson study

and record data on some 60-plus lingcod nest locations in the park. While most places boast three- to four-foot-long lingcod, this park has a few that would measure up to five feet. (It's said that lingcod were this big everywhere in Northwest waters over a hundred years ago before fishing took its toll on their population.) Here these huge male lingcod will fight for the right to guard their white eggs at just the right nest site. The eggs are glued to each other so that they look like molded Styrofoam, but they are not glued to adjacent objects—instead the eggs are more or less wedged between and around objects. If you see a rock with a number painted on it, you may be near a former nest site. Newer nest sites have less intrusive brass tags placed next to them. The fish don't move or turn over the tags and divers don't bother the tags as much as they did the numbered rocks. Male cabezons, some as big as bulldogs, also guard their purple or greenish egg-encased offspring on anything or any surface in the park that looks halfway defendable.

When not replacing boats or studying fish behavior, volunteers sink other structures such as suspended tubing in the shape of an abstract Stonehenge. Giant tires, huge concrete blocks, small cinder blocks, assorted rocks, welded artwork and miles of various kinds of rope have also been used to enhance the park. Crews have formed

The male lingcod guards the eggs.

Lingcod eggs look like a cross between Styrofoam and cottage cheese: not so yummy.

a grid of rope lines running north to south and east to west that divers can follow to get to a specific sunken vessel or artifact. Trails are constantly being repaired and enhanced and new ones such as Triumph Way and Erratic Way being added.

In earlier times we used to dive along the sunken dry dock where a couple of local resident five-foot lingcod patrolled, and rock scallops the size of small dinner plates clung to the sides of rusting metal beams. We would drop into the water next to a steel pole located 123 feet from the ferry dock. At that time the posted signs stated we could not dive any closer than 100 feet from the ferry terminal so we had to watch our distance closely. Occasionally an unwary diver drifted too close, but a potential fine of $1,500 kept most divers away. Post 9-11 and homeland security, however, the signs were changed and now you can't dive closer than 300 feet from the ferry terminal! This has immediately put such sites as the dry dock, Jungle Gym, the Fossil, the *Alitak* and other South Park artifacts off limits to divers. For some dive sites this ordinance change could have been a death blow to viewing underwater attractions, but not at Edmonds. The park has so much to offer just north of the jetty that it still takes several well-planned dives to see it all in one weekend. To make the most of your next dive, you can buy a laminated map of the park from John Jensen and his staff at Edmonds Underwater Sports. The proceeds from map sales are used to fund future park projects.

Now that you know why there isn't any other dive destination like Bruce Higgins Underwater Trails, it's time to plunge right into the ultimate dive profile. The park is great for new as well as advanced divers. Just remember that the city of Edmonds imposes two restrictions when you dive here: that you dive with a buddy and that you wear a buoyancy compensator.

Gear up and enter the water on the north side of the jetty just in case you encounter a southbound current. If you are good at gas consumption, you can start down right off the end of the jetty. If you feel you might need to conserve a little air, follow Jetty Way west to the first buoy then descend onto Jetty Way Trail. Follow the ropes west until you come to a spot where several small boats are strewn on the bottom on the north side of the trail line; three-foot-long lingcod will be found in this boatyard with lots of shrimp scuttling about at the base of each wrecked boat. On the south side of the rope line will be large remnants of a boat frame adorned with rows of white plumose anemones. There is usually a large cabezon lurking around the west end of this structure.

At this point, move over five feet to the north side of Jetty Way and continue swimming west. You will soon come to the *Jackson*, a white, 40-foot-long boat on the north side of the trail. Four-foot-long lingcod can be found lounging about under the stern of the boat, and large cabezon like to make their homes inside it.

Now swim a few yards northwest and you will find yourself looking at the giant cement block that forms the east end of the

At Underwater Sports in Edmonds, air fills are just a short walk from the underwater park.

Cathedrals. The rope line with milk cartons entwined in it every yard or so that runs south to north and parallel to its base is called Northern Lights. Follow the rope north or just go to the end of the block, and you will see a trail running east to west crossing Northern Lights. Turn left around the corner of the block to examine the first block formation of the Cathedrals then move a yard or two on the north side of Cathedral Way and swim west. Within 60 feet you will arrive at the 74-foot-long tugboat *Triumph*. The west side of the hull is exposed to heavy wave and current action so you'll mostly find shrimp and hearty nudibranchs on that side. Anemones, sea stars and bryozoans like the milder east side. If you swim around to the west side of the *Triumph* and then north to its bow, you should be approximately halfway into your dive. A few feet from the bow you will see the boat *Glacey II* and just northeast of it is the recently sunk *Cupid*. Now go southeast until you are on Northern Lights again or until you come to the intersection of Northern Lights and Cathedral Way, which is right next to the large block and marked with a 36-inch-diameter section of cement pipe. You can return to shore by traveling east on Cathedral Way or by going 80 feet to the south and following Jetty Way back to shore. You will have just seen half a dozen wrecks, hundreds of gilled fish and untold millions of tiny creatures and invertebrates.

Sadly, the wooden bridge of the tugboat *Triumph* in Edmonds deteriorated in just a few short years.

The bad part is that you only got a quick glimpse of each of the sites; the good part is that you'll have to come back out several more times to see it all. I've logged over 300 dives in this park and still haven't seen it all.

On your second dive I recommend that you go north past the Train Station along Glacier Way or nearby Telegraph Way. Nudibranchs and harbor seals love to hang out around the boats and other sunken objects. On dive three head out to the northwest corner of the park past Tube Henge. Along the way you will encounter sea pens, squid eggs and schools of fish such as salmon swimming above your head. And don't forget to do a night dive in the park as alternate species of life show up for the night shift, and other species change habits and behavior after the sun sets.

The general rule is that to encounter lingcod and cabezon, just head out on Jetty Way. For squid, stick to the northern end of the park. Harbor seals occasionally hang around the Hiccup or beside Slinky. Around all the sites you'll find tons of shrimp, crabs and rockfish, while schools of fish pass overhead. Shrimp are found in massive numbers at the base of sunken wrecks, while kelp crabs prefer to stand on the tops of cement pipes and ward off intruders just like in the movie *Finding Nemo*. Octopuses seem to be found in the park only at times when crabs are plentiful. Although the park is one of the most popular dive sites on the West Coast and you may see other divers while surface-swimming towards sunken boats like the *Triumph*, once underwater and clear of Jetty Way, you'll most likely feel like you have the park to yourself. Visibility may drop down to only a few feet near shore during certain spring or summer days, but typically the average visibility is 10 to 15 feet and closer to 40 feet on certain fall and winter days. Keep in mind that the park may never get deeper than 45 feet even at the far north end on a high tide and the temperature will range from 44° to 54°F. Changing rooms are located near the jetty. Except during the winter, the park also has an outside shower.

One very good thing about the park is that if you find yourself running low on air, almost anywhere is a good place to surface, inflate, lie on your back and lazily kick back towards shore. Bruce Higgins and the band of volunteers have a map of the park you can pick up at the local Underwater Sports dive shop in Edmonds for a

The Edmonds changing rooms are available year-round. Outdoor showers are not available during the winter months; most likely because ice-skating is frowned upon while wearing dive gear.

small donation, and your contribution goes to help building more attractions and habitats at the park.

Just a mile south of the Bruce Higgins Underwater Trails is another great dive site, this time for advanced and deep divers. The oil dock on Railroad Avenue at Marina Beach is a T-shaped dock that extends out at right angles to the shore. At low tide you can walk out across the sand more than halfway to the end of it. At high tide it's a long surface-swim out before you can drop below, and the currents really move here at certain times of the lunar cycle.

What's so great about this site is the underwater surface area of the 45-foot-deep wooden dock pilings adorned with plumose anemones, assorted sea stars and kelp crab, while spotted ratfish, giant flounder and cabezon swim around them. You can spend your dive admiring the dock structure and all the wildlife attached to it, or you can descend the adjacent rocky slopes to 110 feet or eventually down to 135 feet. At 110 feet you'll encounter sea pens, nudibranchs and large congregations of shrimp, and the occasional spotted ratfish will join you and your buddy when you are using your dive light. It's easy to become low on air on this dive unless

The oil dock in Edmonds is a great deep dive destination. The adjacent park is great for family outings.

you keep a close eye on your gauges and follow the rule of thirds for air consumption.

The oil dock is slated for demolition in the near future and the creosote-soaked poles will be removed from the water. When this happens, the area will still be a great spot for practising deep dives, and the hillside that is strewn with rocks and boulders will still be a great place to find small creatures in the crevices with spotted rat-fish patrolling the perimeter.

Another spot that we used to dive is 100-Foot Rock. This spot is just north of Edmonds, but you can no longer cross the railroad tracks to gain access to it, so the best way to dive here is by boat. The last time I dived here I saw what appeared to be two 8-inch yellow nudibranchs courting on the top of the humongous rock at around 85 feet. Dungeness crabs and sea pens can be found on the adjacent sandy substratum.

Where to Stay
If you plan to spend some time in Edmonds, I recommend staying at the Edmonds Harbor Inn. It's located in the bowl a few blocks south

Didemnum Vexillum and Other Invasive Species

The European colonial tunicate *Didemnum vexillum* or one of its extremely close cousins has entered the waters of the Pacific Northwest, possibly via expelled ballast water from a cargo ship. Thousands of these tiny individuals form dense honey-yellow or brownish carpets that cover and suffocate hard substrates and the associated sessile life forms including certain clams and mussels. Population outbreaks are followed by relatively dormant periods, and no one knows why. My daughter says the mats of *Didemnum* sp. look like macaroni and cheese. I'd add the word "regurgitated" to that description.

These tunicate colonies filter water at an incredible rate in search of plankton that would normally be consumed by other species in the food chain. They are fast growing and reproduce by budding or sexually by brooded larva. If a colony is broken apart, pieces of it drift off and start a new colony wherever they settle, or the brooding larvae may drift off into the water column. When the larvae hatch, they look like microscopic tadpoles complete with all the standard chordate features—a notochord, dorsal hollow nerve

Didemnum sp. Noxious and quickly-reproducing play dough, anyone?
BERNARD P. HANBY

cord and pharyngeal clefts. However, as the larvae mature, they settle on a hard substrate with the aid of three adhesive papillae, and
the tail, notochord and neural tube are absorbed and the mouth
moves 180 degrees to become the incurrent siphon. With the aid
of cilia, the pharyngeal slits pull the water into the siphon where a
sticky mucous traps the plankton. The water then passes out of the
tunicate via the atrial siphon.

For defense, *Didemnum vexillum* have burr-like spicules de-
rived from the calcium salts inside their tissue structures, but the
tunic or body tissue consists of a cellulose material called tunicin
and protein fluids that include rare elements such as vanadium as
well as other possibly noxious compounds. If a colony is left to dry
out in a confined space, strong acidic odors will emanate from it.

On the coast of New England the common periwinkle (*Littorina
littorea*) has been observed feeding on *Didemnum* sp. colonies,
leaving circular bare patches in the middle of the colony. On the
West Coast a local sea star, the slime star (*Pteraster tesselatus*), has
also been observed predating on this invasive tunicate. In Washington State, the federal Department of Fish and Wildlife and the
State departments of Ecology, Agriculture and Natural Resources

Bruce Higgins isolates invasive tunicates in Edmonds. Working on the park,
neoprene gloves do not last long.

have joined forces to issue expedited permits to eradicate *Didemnum* sp., and recreational divers have been asked to report the location of any observed colonies. Volunteers at Bruce Higgins Underwater Trails nailed tarps on some invaded sites and covered others with cling wrap, then placed salt tablets under the wrapping. These methods killed off the exposed colonies in a very short time, although they required many diver manpower hours, but they only work well on confined surfaces within recreational diver limits. Invasive colonies of *Didemnum* sp. found in oyster and clam beds and on mussel farms require other approaches in order to destroy the colonies without affecting the associated multi-million dollar shellfish industry. For example, infected oysters and clams can be pulled out of the water for 24 hours, killing the tunicate but not the shellfish.

The problem with invasive species is that they generally have no predators in their new habitat, they don't share the habitat with other species and they don't share the existing food supplies. These problems will only increase as ships from foreign destinations

of Main Street. The inn has 91 rooms, which should be enough rooms and parking space to accommodate you and all your dive buddies. With wireless internet service, a computer off the main lobby to check emails, a guest laundry room, Athletic Club privileges (for a minimal fee), massage therapy, enhanced complimentary continental breakfast and microwaves and mini-refrigerators in the new wing, what more could you ask? A word of warning: in the summertime the parking lot above the park can become full by 9 a.m., so late risers may have to drop off their gear and/or park on nearby streets. However, the Harbor Inn is just a block and a half from the fishing pier, adjacent shoreline and so close to most restaurants that except for when dropping off dive gear at the beach, you may find yourself strolling everywhere just like the locals.

While in town you may encounter other divers at Claire's Restaurant on Main Street or at the Pancake House on Fifth Avenue. At lunchtime you'll see divers in drysuits having seafood down at continue to dump their ballast water too close to shore; recently, in addition to *Didemnum,* other invasive species such as *Ciona savignyi,* a clear tunicate with tiny yellow spots, and *Styela clava,* a warty-looking club tunicate, have been identified here. While stricter guidelines and enforcements will slow down the rate of immigrating species dispersing in local waters, the best immediate solutions to the eradication of *Didemnum* sp. are to find naturally occurring predators and the ongoing efforts of volunteer divers to reduce the rate of colonization. The toughest part to consider is that for over 360 million years tunicates have outlived and out-survived a wide diversity of predators and natural disasters, and now they seem to be thriving in new environments, thanks to the unwitting endeavors of mankind.

You can pick up information and photos of these invasive sea creatures at most dive shops, and it is in everybody's best interest to be diligent and report them immediately. After all, who wants to dive down and see nothing but mats of regurgitated macaroni and cheese and no other signs of life?

Anthony's Beach Café overlooking the local marina. For a quick bowl of hot clam chowder, divers also go to Skippers right across the street from the park. Those who want a really special experience for lunch go to the buffet at Sahib Indian Cuisine located right next to the park. (You can smell the tantalizing authentic curry aromas as you set up your dive gear.) Their Sunday buffet includes a glass of champagne and savory appetizers. After the dives you'll see people heading up the street to Rory's for burgers, beer and a place and time to fill out their logbooks. For fine dining or special occasions you must reserve a table at Giradis Osteria (Italian cuisine) on Fifth Avenue or visit Arnie's for seafood and fresh catch of the day while watching the Kingston ferries shuttle back and forth.

For more information:

www.nwcountryinns.com
www.underwatersports.com
www.ci.edmonds.wa.us

Edmonds may look small on a map, but it's filled with diving and dining experiences. Diving here may even become habit-forming, and repeated dives could lead to an overwhelming urge to do voluntary work in the park. Deep dives at the oil dock or at 100-Foot Rock just might start to consume all of your free weekends. Resistance is almost futile.

BREMERTON AND PORT ORCHARDS

The last time I went to Bremerton was 30-some years ago to see the battleship USS *Missouri*, but they moved the ship and for one reason or another I just never made it back out there again. Then recently I realized that Bremerton was only 28 miles from the Tacoma Narrows Bridge or an hour by ferry from Seattle. I couldn't believe it was so close, and when I learned about their local dive sites, I immediately started planning my next trip there. If you want an abundance of animal diversity, short swim distances and easy dive profile depths, then here are a few places in Bremerton that you have to dive.

The waters passing under the Warren Avenue Bridge appear calm between tide cycles.

The white basket star has changed relatively little in structural design over the last several hundred million years. BERNARD P. HANBY

Dive Sites

Harper's Ferry/Fishing Pier is ideal for impressing your friends with abundant animal life and easy dive conditions. Visibility is usually over 30 feet, currents are minimal and surface conditions are nice. Once you step down over a few large rocks, you just follow the pilings out to the end of the pier. You'll need a camera to take pictures of all the life on the pilings as plumose anemones, a variety of sea stars, shrimp and crabs adorn all the exposed surfaces. On the right and adjacent to the pier are old wooden pilings that have rotted away internally, but their outer layers are still preserved by the creosote chemicals. Lots of tiny creatures live in these hollowed-out posts so it's worth taking a peek inside each one. Straight out and slightly to the left of the pier is another group of pilings. One is leaning over and has a guideline attached to it. Follow this line a short distance and you will come to a 40-foot wooden wreck where rock crabs and octopuses like to hang out. If you don't want to mess with too many navigation skills, you can follow the guideline back to the group of poles then move to one of the farthest poles that's sticking straight up. This one also has a guideline attached to it and you can follow it to a small

Sound Dive Center in Bremerton: without doubt the largest dive shop on this side of the waterway.

wreck in 40 feet of water. A large octopus is currently residing on the starboard side of the wreck, but Dan Demeritt, a divemaster from the Sound Dive Center, says he's spotted up to five of them on one dive at this site. He says he's even seen wolf-eels swimming out in the open here. This site is also good for catching glimpses of harbor seals and squid, and you can't pick an easier site for night dives that are loaded with creature activity.

The town of Port Orchards is just north of this pier, giving Harper's Ferry dive site high marks for both land and sea activities. Parking is limited to the first four trucks, but off-road parking with unlimited equipment hauling privileges is available, and there's even a coffee stand nearby.

The Warren Avenue Bridge, which is about half a mile from Evergreen State Park, is an advanced dive that requires synchronized timing with the tides unless you plan on visiting Hoodsport or having an impromptu inspection of the Navy shipyards. The dive site is located right under the bridge, and you have to suit up at the end of the dead-end street (Elizabeth Avenue) and then walk down a recently built wood/gravel stairway/trail. At the bottom are a picnic table, two benches and an outdoor grill. Stepping down into the

Students gear up and wait in anticipation for an exciting day of underwater instruction soon to begin.

sand, you make your way on loose cobblestones out to the dive site. The pylons of the bridge are covered with creatures. Clay formations in the substrate offer homes for rough piddock clams, and old clam holes become new residences for smaller invertebrates. Check around the rocks and boulders for sea cucumbers, sea stars, anemones and groups of fish. The depth out at the third pylon is about

The white-crown calcareous tubeworm, just like some people I know, live their entire life in just one location. BERNARD P. HANBY

50 feet. Strong currents and the coming and going of boats make this a more difficult dive.

At Illahee State Park you can camp and dive at the same time. The animal life is right under the pier pilings or under the floating dock where it is only 33 feet deep. Tubeworms, anemones, perch, sea stars, flounder and all the rest of the regular cast of suspects await you on this dive. You can dive down 80 feet if you go out past the main sites and rub against the sandy bottom, but keep an eye out for boats and fishing line. This is a great site for dive clubs and large groups.

While you're there, go up half a mile to the old town of Illahee. Off the fishing pier is a well-established three-finger-shaped tire reef where you'll find crabs and other small creatures and huge starry flounders. Some divers also come here to collect old bottles. You'll have to use the pier ladder to get back out of the water, but who said collecting someone else's discarded objects was going to be easy?

Well, now that the catfish is out of the bag, save me a spot at the beach. And now that I know how quickly I can get there, I'll be going back very soon.

SEATTLE

Shore Dive Sites

No other dive destination is as close to Seattle as Seacrest, which has an easy shoreline walk into the water and a variety of sites in a very short span of beachfront. The first of them, Cove One, is right next to Salty's restaurant on Harbor Avenue SW. The area has a sandy

Cove One is typically calm and shallow, but more importantly, it's close to the public restrooms.

substrate and is host to bottles, glassware, plates—and small invertebrates. Most of these objects are in less than 15 feet of water. Now
I won't tell you not to remove any of the glasses and plates you find
at this site, but I will tell you that once a barnacle has made a glass
surface home, it hangs on with powerful chemical bonds that etch
into the glass and whose marks can never be completely removed.
Juvenile fish can also be found in the same sandy-bottomed area,
but for some reason the bigger fish stay clear of the adjacent popular seafood restaurant. Out at 80 feet you might find some fishing
gear resting in the soft, silted substratum. This cove is frequently
used by dive classes and by divers who want to work on their basic
diving skills or become familiarized with new gear.

Cove Two, with its easy access to great depths, makes an ideal
spot for advanced diver training. Here you can follow a rock and
gravel substratum down to 110 feet where a 12-foot-long giant Pacific octopus likes to hang out under some I-beams. On night dives
large sixgill sharks can be seen at this depth on a regular basis—provided you don't have a camera readily available. Closer to shore,
rock formations, pieces of boats and assorted man-made structures
have become the habitats of various marine creatures. Roped-off

Cove Three at Seacrest is adjacent to Salty's Seafood Restaurant: talk about fresh
seafood!

Pile perch love to hang around toxic creosote poles, so in those specific areas, perhaps they are not the best catch of the day. BERNARD P. HANBY

areas keep divers from getting too close to the fishing pier and the boating areas and also help as navigation aids.

Cove Three is an easy, entry-level dive site with a sandy substratum. A 12-foot-long boat rests in some 35 feet of water (depending on tide conditions) near the left side of the cove. Sea stars, nudibranchs and other small invertebrates inhabit this area. At the far

The alabaster nudibranch resembles a collage of flaming embers when illuminated by a bright dive light.

left end the remnants of a wooden pier stick out above the surface and other creosote poles lie across one another underwater. Kelp crabs, plumose anemones and fish such as pile perch call this area home.

Boat Dive Sites

For boat dives close to Seattle, try the China Wall at Blakely Rocks. Between 65 and 100 feet you'll see lingcod, seals and rockfish, but be sure to use a dive light to look between all the cracks and crevices to find octopuses, nudibranchs and other invertebrates. On a dive there with Teal Water Charters we saw a pair of one-foot octopuses dueling over who was king of the reef, while a group of harbor seals escorted a young pup around two of the divers in our group. We tried to swim a complete circle around the rocks, but the currents picked up as we made our way around the second bend. With little to hold on to, and not knowing where the currents wanted to take us, we decided to surface and found the boat in a holding pattern right beside us. Now that's service!

Another good site is Boeing Creek Reef, an artificial reef about 70 feet deep near Richmond Beach. The rocks here are home to wolf-eels, octopuses, scallops and various fish. The wreck at Blakely Bay rests in less than 57 feet of water and is actually a 20-foot boat resting in the middle of a 40-foot boat so that together they form a slightly skewed Templar cross. They are home to rockfish, plumose anemones and a few large lingcod. One lingcod was so large that when I came face to face with him with nothing between us but my camera, he just looked at me as if daring me to try and make him move. I turned my attention to some huge Dungeness crabs in the surrounding sand dune substrate, but they took off before I could raise my camera and snap a shot. On the way back to port we coasted by two sea lions basking in the sun on top of a two-story metal buoy, while a cormorant peered down at us from the second floor of the structure.

Charter Services

For boat dives out of Seattle you can try the Aluminator Water Taxi, Inc., the newest boat charter service in town. It's owned and operated by Howie Dickerman, who has been boating from Bainbridge to Boston for most of his life. He moved out to the West Coast in 1994 and received his commercial captain's license in 2003. Last February he had the 34-foot *Aluminator* built to haul commercial goods and taxi passengers and to rescue boats in distress. Soon a friend noted that the new 12-foot-wide boat would be great for dives, and Howie was contacted by the Moss Bay Dive Club and Exotic Aquatics Scuba and Kayaking.

A Munson Packman with two Volvo engines that can move 36 to 38 knots at maximum speed, this aluminum landing craft-style vessel is the same model used in the Swedish archipelago for surveying, and the US Coast Guard uses four of them for re-supplying. I've heard that the 52-foot model is used for certain foreign military applications, but even on the 34-foot model there is plenty of room inside and outside for a small platoon, SEAL team or a group of six divers plus a dive instructor and one or two divemasters to top it off. While it may not be as fast as the offshore boats Howie used to race off the East Coast during the early 1980s, it will get you quickly to most local dive sites. It has a heated cabin to keep you warm in any weather, as well as a galley and head to meet other vital needs. The *Aluminator* operates out of the marina at Elliot Bay where hot showers await your return to port and a bevy of restaurants are located nearby.

Ki and Seon Kang, instructors at Underwater Sports in Bellevue and members of the Moss Bay Dive Club, were the first to lead a dive team out on the *Aluminator*. While divers were still new to Howie, Ki and Seon Kang and their group were pleased with the overall experience. Howie took all their suggestions to heart and made some great overnight improvements. He now has an oxygen kit with two masks, extra drinking water, hot soup, bread, cheese and chocolates available between dives, new tank racks and more. He has also moved the anchor line to the stern doorway and refitted

For more information:
www.aluminatorwatertaxi.com
www.mossbaydiveclub.org
www.exoticaquaticsscuba.com
www.munsonboats.com

the handles to make re-entry more diver friendly. Check the Exotic Aquatics web site to see when they have booked the *Aluminator* for other dive destinations; you may want to join them.

SOUTH PUGET SOUND

There are dozens of dive destinations between Steam Boat Island at the south end of Puget Sound and Sunrise Beach, just north of Gig Harbor. The large diversity of substrates here allows for a large diversity of animal habitats, and even though you are many miles inland from the Pacific Ocean, you can still find seals, dolphins and

even the occasional gray whale frolicking in these waters. Timing
your dives to enter the water at slack is usually the key to diving the
South Sound.

Dive Sites

Sunrise Beach on Colvos Passage used to be the most popular wall
dive because of its protected marine preserve status, but in 2002
Zee's Reef on the northeast side of Fox Island also became a sanctioned reserve area and it is currently the location of a lingcod
study. It is closed to all recreational and commercial fishing except
fly-fishing for salmon. About 200 yards offshore and ranging between 35 and 60 feet down is a wall of rock and sandstone about
400 yards long, one of the few natural rocky outcroppings in the
southern Sound. When I dived this site with Porthole Dive Charters
two octopuses were in residence at one end of the wall, and at the
other end we found a large wolf-eel. Incidentally, we found two
large clusters of lingcod eggs, but the males just let us swim by as

Many great dive locations are at the base of cliffs. Below the surface the landscape
bares ledges, caves and finger-like projections filled with sea creatures of every
size and shape.

Return of the Plankton

Marine Biologist Bruce Claiborne and underwater videographer John F. Williams of Still Hope Productions have put together a great DVD on Puget Sound marine life. Although the main thrust of the video is on how the seasons affect plankton life cycles, the DVD is also loaded with scenes of other sea creatures including playful harbor seals, inquisitive octopuses, invertebrates such as the ubiquitous moonsnails and sea stars and a wide assortment of local fish. It provides the scientific names of all the species viewed plus a quiz that may be used in certain learning circles, so it's a great DVD to share with a classroom of kids although it works just as well with a group of seasoned divers.

Unfortunately, because I've seen the video over half a dozen times, I now have this irresistible urge to dive Battle Point on Bainbridge Island and drift over the sand dollar colonies. Perhaps after watching the video you'll get an urge to photograph spiny dogfish sharks, hand-feed crabs to octopuses or play fin tag with harbor seals.

Fortunately, because different locations in the Puget Sound have such unique substrates, salinities, water temperatures and seasonal variations, let alone species compositions, I look forward to viewing further Pacific Northwest videography projects by Bruce and John and the rest of the team at Still Hope Productions. The bottom line, whether you're a diver or not, is that you'll enjoy viewing these hometown aquatic neighbors. For more information: www.stillhopeproductions.com.

if they were accustomed to the slight nuisance of bubble-blowing, flashlight-wielding, mask-laden voyeurs.

Both Sunrise Beach and Zee's Reef wall dives are less than 60 feet in depth and both are home to resident wolf-eels and giant octopuses. Sunrise Beach can be reached by shore, but the neighboring hills make a boat dive preferable. Besides these two well-frequented sites, there are also Point Defiance Wall, Dalco Wall and Day Island Wall.

Usually you plan a dive in the Sound at slack to avoid drifting away, but there is nothing more fun than drifting at high speed underneath the Tacoma Narrows Bridge. You'll see sunken remnants of the old Galloping Gerdy Bridge, giant octopuses and Dungeness crab, all passing at breakneck speed. It's more of a thrill/roller coaster ride than a stop-and-view-the-local-residents kind of trip when the currents are running that fast, but you really learn to appreciate the phenomenal power of water when you're moving what seems like more than two knots per second. The Narrows is also a great boat dive at slack, but when the tides are right, it's one of the wildest rides an advanced diver could ask for south of Canada.

While you may see the occasional spiny dogfish shark off Fox Island or Steam Boat Island, the main place to catch a glimpse of one of the 200-million-year-old sixgill species is right down the hill from the Tacoma Zoo and Aquarium at Owens Beach. Here, nine-foot-plus creatures come up into the shallows during birthing season and routinely at night, but it may take you hundreds of dives to actually view one of these majestic creatures slowly swimming by. I know because, even having logged hundreds and hundreds of dives around these waters, I'm still patiently waiting to get my first glimpse. In the meantime my friends have shown me homemade videos of these sixgill giants to prove their existence.

The sixgill shark is an extremely elusive prehistoric creature. PHIL EDGELL

There are some places you just can't dive unless you go by boat. The Clay Banks is one of these. On my first dive there the visibility was over 40 feet, and my fellow instructor/buddy and I saw octopuses, crabs and shrimp sheltering in horizontal cuts in the banks. We swam past columns of clay pipe-organ walls riddled with vertical, three-foot-long, circular holes made by burrowing rough piddock clams. They eventually cause portions of the clay banks to cleave off just as efficiently as industrial strength drills separate marble slabs from cliffs of solid rock. Where some of the clay had fallen off it had exposed the white and brown flesh of clam necks and the shrimp and other invertebrates moving about in the tunnels where they had taken up residence. I had never seen anything quite like this formation until that day. It was a macro photographer's dream come true. Oh, and besides the standard clay formations, sites such as Fox Island have canyons and crevices that make great places to explore for wolf-eels and octopuses.

Easy shore access to places such as Titlow Beach and Redondo Beach make all these locations prime candidates for nighttime adventures, as bioluminescent plankton enhance almost every night dive experience. At night skittish fish such as sailfin sculpins have a personality shift and are primed to be compliant photo models. On a full moon you can find squid mating at shallow depths while shrimp mill around or group in spontaneous conga lines.

You won't find warships in south Puget Sound, but at places such as Saltwater State Park, Tolmie State Park and Maury Island you will find sunken barges in various stages of disintegration supporting numerous varieties of rockfish and plumose anemones. Other vertical structures such as creosote-covered pilings slated by the State for removal are home to sea stars and kelp crab, while above the waterline they are coveted bird nesting sites. You will have to swim out around the Fox Island Bridge pillars during slack tide to view some pillars harboring a wide variety of nudibranchs.

My favorite dive site to date has to be the KVI Tower, a 30-year-old artificial reef site just offshore from the radio station's tower on Vashon Island. Between 30 and 90 feet you'll see boulders as big as cars and octagonal pilings with cracks stuffed full of sea life. I really think someone should rename this site "Alice in Wonderland" because you never know what to expect when you peek down a hole.

Wolf-eels have a slender, elongated fish body design with a face only a mother could love. The big gummy lips help take the sting out of eating spiny sea urchins, one of their favorite food groups. BERNARD P. HANBY

On the far right end of this site you'll find lots of octopuses roaming about or resting after having crab cake snacks in their dens. Just follow the trails strewn with disarticulated clamshells and broken crab exoskeletons and you'll find their dens. I spotted a 20-foot boat at 87 feet and what looked like the outline of another boat just beyond it, but my buddy and I had already been down too deep for too long, so further investigation in that area will have to wait for my next trip.

Now, having said that the KVI Tower is my favorite, I admit that I haven't explored every possible southern dive site. Aaron Cummings, owner and manager of Tacoma Scuba, says that his favorite local dive site is Day Island Wall. This 90-foot advanced dive is typically host to between five and eight pairs of wolf-eels and numerous octopuses. You can only dive this site when the currents are just right, but from the way Aaron described it, I've put this wall at the top of my need-to-dive-next list.

Dive Charters
There are at least three dive charter companies regularly coursing

these waters. In alphabetical order there are: Aluminator Water Taxi, Bandito Charters and Porthole Dive Charters. I first had the pleasure to meet Rick Myers, the founder of Bandito Charters, in 1999 when a group of us went out with him and his crew on the 43-foot *Sampan*. I was staffing an instructor development course at the time, and although I had done hundreds of shore dives in Pacific Northwest waters, this was my first boat dive here. Our first dive site was on the south end of Puget Sound near an isolated beach with only boat access, and as soon as we jumped off of the boat, the instructor candidates practised rescue procedures. With that prerequisite business out of the way, we all dived down to about 30 feet and checked out the local aquatic inhabitants. The visibility was over 40 feet, and we could see a few large sole and a couple of Dungeness crabs that were not used to seeing divers in their remote living area. Several types of nudibranchs crawled across the sand and gravel substratum, oblivious to us divers, and a skinny, white sea star nearly two feet in diameter slowly moved across the bottom in search of its next meal. When you get to plunge into an area like this that is seldom dived by others, you feel like a true explorer, and the experience seems to last in your memory just a little bit longer.

You may notice that sea stars are slightly larger here in the Northwest. KRISTINA HUGHES

Geoff Black was the divemaster on that trip, and he has now worked his way up to the rank of captain; Rick Myers says it's the whole team that's made Bandito Charters operation work so well for so long. They use three boats—the *Sampan*, the *Naknek* and the *Ocean Quest*. The first two are sister ships and each holds 14 divers; the *Ocean Quest* holds 10 divers. I like the fact that all areas of the Bandito boats are wet and they have enclosed cabin areas where you can get warmed up between dives; you can wear your drysuit or wetsuit wherever you please. Based in Tacoma since 1997, Rick and his crew travel the southern end of Puget Sound year-round but in the spring go up to the San Juan Islands as well. Check out the Bandito web site to see pictures of the boats, dive site descriptions, photos of the animal life and more.

A few years ago I went on a boat dive with Porthole Dive Charters, which at that time was owned by paramedic Mike Ferguson and Troy Sterrenburg, although Troy, who is an Emergency Medical Technician, has now moved on to firefighting. Their boat is the 26-foot, aluminum-hulled *Dash*, and I think the name refers to how fast its jet engines can get you to a dive spot, cruising between 25 and 35 mph. The boat has every electrical gadget available except Xbox or Nintendo, but cruising from one dive spot to another as fast as they go gives little time for anything other than talking about what you just saw on the last dive and what you are about to see on the next one. Its 12-foot-long heated cabin is complete with head, hot-water shower and fresh-water sink amenities. I could see that they took safety very seriously as they had installed custom-designed rails and two comfortable custom-made folding dive benches, and all rail, bench and deck surfaces had been professionally coated with Line-X bedliner-style paint to make the boat safe, wet or dry.

They took being friendly seriously too. By only carrying six divers at a time, they offered a very personalized and comfortable level of service. Mike is an advanced Nitrox tech diver and intuitively knows how to accommodate divers who want to charter their boat for those special tech needs and specific destinations. The *Dash* can also accommodate instructors and divemasters along with up to six of their own students. You can charter it to go anywhere in the state for the day or multiple days. The boat is trailer-friendly and they have put it in at Lake Chelan and go up to Neah Bay on a regular basis. I guess you could even ask them to trailer the boat to other states. My first choice would be Hawaii, but I can wait.

On the way to my second dive site with Porthole we saw a pod of dolphins off to our right. I'd heard they did their best to please their guests, but I'll never figure out how they got those dolphins to show up on cue. You know, you think about cars going over the Tacoma Narrows Bridge, but how often do you think about synchronized dolphins swimming under it? Since that dive, Mike Ferguson has expanded Porthole Dive's operations with the addition of a new 41-foot boat, the *Mark V*.

Dive Shops

The south end of Puget Sound may be home to perhaps the greatest concentration of dives shops in close proximity to great dive sites in the entire Northwest. Fresh air fills, rentals and last-minute dive necessities are never very far away, which means you'll have more time to dive per day. Also, the staff of the local dive shops know the area well, so you can get last-minute details on particular dive sites. Local divemasters have put together a laminated guide booklet on Titlow Beach,

> **For more information:**
> www.banditocharters.com
> www.naknekcharters.com
> www.portholedivecharters.com

which you'll find on display at TLSea Diving in Des Moines. Walt Amidon, manager of Underwater Sports on Federal Way, has for years been quoted in the newspapers on the underwater habitat around the Tacoma Narrows Bridge.

THE HOOD CANAL: DIVE A FJORD LATELY?

On a map the Hood Canal looks like a thin strip of blue in the shape of a curved fishhook with a broken eyelet. In 1792 when Captain Vancouver named it after Admiral Hood, he didn't know that 300 years later the word "canal" would generally refer to an artificial waterway less than 40 feet across and 20 feet deep. But the Hood Canal is actually the only true fjord in the lower 48 states; it has over 240

The south end of Sund Rock has its own small sandy beach and secluded trail.

miles of shoreline and at some points is 1.5 miles wide and large enough for orcas to crisscross in search of a dinner of harbor seals. It averages 500 feet of depth in the central channel, which gives visiting nuclear submarines and deepwater squids ample room to roam; the maximum depth is 600 feet in Dabob Bay.

The best time to dive in the Hood is as soon as possible. In the winter visibility can be as good as 40 feet and up to 100 feet in places. In the summertime near shore it can drop to 3 feet until you descend below 40 feet, and then it may open up to 10 or 20 feet, depending on the day and currents (mostly wind-generated) and how far north or south on the canal you are diving. During the summertime the surface water can be above 63°F, but 12 feet below the temperature may drop to 52° or less.

The entrance to the Hood Canal has a high sill, so it takes six months or more for old layers of water to flush out and freshly oxygenated salt water to circulate in. This lack of dissolved oxygen has had an impact on local sea creatures, especially during the past couple of decades of land development and fast-paced residential growth. Large concentrations of nitrogen from increased water runoff combined with poorly functioning septic systems and fertilizer usage may have in the past contributed to occasional fish die-offs, behavioral changes in sea creatures and more sporadic population densities and relocations of top predators such as octopuses, wolf-eels and seals.

Most often when you see something in the news about the Hood Canal, it is bad news about low dissolved oxygen levels (DOLs), fish kills or invasive species. However, to set the record straight, one of the worst low DOLs and resulting fish kill occurred over 100 years ago and is recorded in the canal's sediment. Sure, having a mandatory septic inspection every five to ten years and reducing the amount of fertilizer used on lawns and golf courses could reduce future low DOLs, but a very low level could still occur due to the shape of the fjord and the slow flushing action caused by the canal's high sill.

These days significantly low levels of oxygen are mostly restricted to the south end of the canal, usually by the bend at Potlatch State Park or below. And even when creatures in the south end of the canal are stressed by low DOLs, the saltwater areas north of the Hama Hama River have been studied and found to contain thriving creature populations. The bottom line is, therefore, that we can reduce the intensity of low DOLs, but they may always exist as they have done to some degree over the long history of the region, and that even in times of fish kills and creature distress, many areas of the Hood Canal will still be havens for sea creatures—provided we do our part in wildlife conservation. As for invasive species, scientific groups, dive clubs and local residents are doing what they can to reduce the number of invasive tunicate colonies and removing other invasive species as well. This will be an ongoing and long-term effort.

In the meantime, however, the major concern to most residents and tourist alike is the Navy's proposals for alternate expansion ranges in the Hood Canal. If it does expand the area of C-4 explosions, SEAL team assaults on oyster-laden beaches, sonar signal testing and torpedo testing ranges, the best boat dive sites in the Hood Canal could be declared off-limits at unpredictable times and for unscheduled durations. You couldn't even plan to go out to the fishing grounds, and the northern boat ways could be closed without any advance notice other than the arrival of a fast, gray boat loaded with M-16-armed men stopping short of your boat and requesting you to stop engines immediately. Expanding the Navy's range of operations could essentially sporadically close down tourism on or near the water and put "Closed" signs across the doors of many small local businesses. And even if the Navy is willing to compensate those who lose their livelihoods, it seems a high price for all of us to pay for homeland security. Hopefully, with a little public and community input, the Navy will decide not to expand its test ranges, and we can all keep diving so many remarkable dive sites in the Hood Canal.

Shore Dive Sites

Please keep in mind that anytime you do a shore dive in Mason or Jefferson County you must use a dive flag or risk receiving a misdemeanor citation from law enforcement, especially if you are diving near boats or if other risk factors are involved. Besides a court date and a fine, no diver wants to collect fishing gear on the seat of his pants.

Most of the well-known dive locations on the Hood Canal are next to private property. Hood Sport 'n Dive in downtown Hoodsport offers an exclusive shore access to the Sund Rock marine preserve. For about $15 plus tax you can drive down to their parking area next to the water's edge where part of the access fee has been used to provide an on-site, (new and improved) extra large, one-stall porta-potty-style convenience center; such a small amenity can be a real reputation, if not a life, saver.

The south wall of Sund Rock usually sports wolf-eels, octopuses, plumose anemones, shrimp and crabs between 40 and 60 feet. The deeper north wall has the remains of a 45-foot boat at 35 feet, and invertebrates including beds of sea whips down at 95 feet. Although I've seen giant Pacific octopuses out in the open on the north wall and by the den at 70 feet, the south wall is the must-dive for octopuses and wolf-eels.

This site can get busy at certain times of the year. On just one typical day there were two dive groups from Oregon—Mark Fisher, owner of Hydrosports Dive and Travel in Keizer, and Matt Jenkins, with a group from Salem Scuba and Travel. Single buddy teams and groups from all over the Northwest come here on a monthly basis to do check-out dives and have fun.

Octopus Hole, just a few minutes north of Sund Rock, is the second most popular shore dive site. To dive here you have to park and gear up on the shoulder of Highway 101 just south of Lilliwaup. You'll need to watch for cars and trucks as you make your way over a guardrail to a group of boulders that form steps down to the water's edge at high tide or to a narrow strip of beach at low tide. One of the last times I was up there, Jack Spencer of Sunset Sports in North Bend, Oregon, was briefing an advanced class of divers. The tide was low, giving him and the students plenty of beach space. This is a wall dive that, depending on the tides, can be between 20 and 45 feet deep. The small floating platform that was chained near the beginning of the wall broke away during a winter storm, so now the best way to find the wall is to dive and swim at a 45-degree angle from shore until you reach 40 feet, level off, then follow the substrate southward. To save air, you can also do a surface-swim straight out from the fallen tree that is pointing out into the water, then descend 40 feet. You'll either land right on the wall or a few feet north of it, depending on currents and tide level.

In the cracks of the three slightly separated south walls of

Hood Sport 'n Dive. Here, drysuit holes and leaks are repaired literally right on the spot.

Octopus Hole you'll find wolf-eels, rockfish and octopuses if they are not out collecting food. Between the first two walls at 40 feet, you'll find a flat, rock slab-covered octopus maternity den. Female octopuses are genetically programmed to die shortly after their eggs hatch, and for some reason each year just about the time the eggs hatch and the mother dies, the rest of the octopuses in the surrounding area move away. Then a few months later they return to the area, and a new mother will brood her eggs in the vacated nursery den. It's an interesting annual event and worthy of further study for a master's degree.

I first discovered Mike's Beach Resort (not to be confused with Mike's Diving Center) a few years ago when I was looking for new places to hold dive classes. Short swims, no boat traffic, practically no passing currents and access to awesome deep as well as shallow dive sites makes this resort a great place for a variety of dive classes and a great destination for divers of all experience levels. It lies next to a great arc of interspersed gravel- and oyster-laden shoreline. For $10 (or free for the resort's guests) you can walk down a ramp and step down the stairs or across beaches and oyster beds to dive a

At Octopus Hole, head straight out to where this fallen tree points, and you will find a wall at 45ft of depth.

wide range of habitats. Beginning divers can go out to 50 feet and see all the creatures they want. There's an eight-foot octopus out at the sunken barge. The three wolf-eels by the reef have become so accustomed to divers that they have been known to nudge a diver away from their vicinity if they believe it's time for him to move along. (It's nice to be a species that's tolerated by the locals.) Technical divers will find a wall dive on the north end starting at 150 feet. The south end of the resort at about 90 feet is a great location for advanced divers to see cloud sponges that are typically found up north in the San Juans or Canada. There are gardens of tall, narrow, white sea whips on display daily between 80 to 110 feet. Crabs and smaller invertebrates are everywhere and it will take several dives to see it all. On-site scientific studies have shown that even in times of low dissolved oxygen levels the sea life in this part of the fjord is continuously growing and multiplying.

Although visibility can get up to 100 feet in December and January, in the summertime you may have to descend some 20 to 40 feet before visibility opens up to 20 to 40 feet. Around the first of September, the temperature of the water on the surface may feel like 60° to 70°F and this makes the surface ideal for swimming and kayaking, but a mere 14 feet below the surface the water turns to a slightly cooler 51°. So even during the summer months a drysuit comes in handy here.

On our latest visit out to Mike's we went in search of cloud sponges. We started our journey down at the south end of the beach resort, but since the beach is so long, we actually had to drive down Highway 101 from the main resort area to this site. At the top of the road adjacent to the south dive site is a locked gate. With the access key they had given us, we backed down a steep gravel road, but I only recommend this maneuver with a four-wheel drive and dry surface conditions. Near the end of the road we parked, suited up, walked down a short embankment then strolled across a rather smooth rock and oyster shell-laden beach. Once in the water we set a course to where we thought the cloud sponges could be located and off we went below the waves.

Sure enough, in the first few feet we could hardly see each other, but down around 20 feet visibility opened up and we saw Dungeness crab 15 feet away from us running as fast as 10 legs would carry them. Let me just say that it was fortunate for them that crab season was out and camera season was in. We passed by lots of small fish as we followed the slope down to deeper water. At around 100 feet we realized that we had missed our mark, but we weren't disappointed because we found ourselves in a field of waist-high sea whips. Their long, narrow white stalks looked like a headless tulip field straight out of *Alice in Wonderland*. Rather than backtrack to where we thought the cloud sponges would be, we glided over the sea whip field for a few minutes then ascended the slope again. At 80 feet we found a large boulder with a good-sized opening around one side of its base with crab carapaces, broken claws and assorted shell remnants symmetrically scattered near it. The giant Pacific octopus residing in the den was evidently out for lunch at the moment, but from the size and amount of discarded crab shell remnants, I knew this one had to be big, so I made a mental note of the site to come back for a future photo opportunity.

Near shore we had a close encounter with about seven different species of shrimp and a starry flounder that refused to move until my camera practically touched its lips. As for sponges, we did find a patch of beautiful white sponges encrusted on some boulders, but we never did see the cloud sponges. Since it was our first dive at the south site, we just wanted to have fun exploring, and we knew that we would be coming back soon.

You can also dive at many local state parks. Potlatch State Park is the most popular of these sites due to its easy walk-in access, camping facilities right across the street and lack of boat traffic. A sand and gravel substrate mixed in with patches of mud provides a nice haven for Dungeness crabs so bring your shellfish license, net and crab measuring gauge. I've seen sand dollars wash up on shore here too, so I know there are some sand dollar beds out there somewhere. Keep in mind that the visibility can get really low on the south end of the park and that currents can actually make it hard to swim straight in to shore on the north end, but they do make for a nice leisurely drift dive.

Boat Dives

To see the greatest amount of life in the Hood Canal on a single dive, you really have to dive from a boat because there are underwater pinnacles, seamounts, ledges, and walls that are impossible to reach from shore, and the sea life seems to be more abundant around them. The south wall of Pulali Point is a fantastic wall dive between 40 and 120 feet deep with lots of small invertebrates. During our first dive briefing here with Don Coleman of Pacific Adventure Dive Charters, he said we would see plenty of wolf-eels and octopuses between 70 and 80 feet. Sure enough, right at 78 feet we found a couple of wolf-eels and a female octopus guarding her den full of eggs. If you look out away from this wall, you might glimpse a spiny dogfish. They are very skittish, but their small size makes them good photo subjects.

The Pinnacle is my favorite Hood Canal boat dive site. Don has dived this site over 400 times and claims that there has been something different to see here every time. Divers generally follow the anchor down to 38 feet and then descend the northeast side of the pinnacle where you can quickly run into the first of five-plus wolf-eels. The pinnacle is teeming with life and is an excellent location for naturalists and photographers. I especially like the glowing color of the vermilion rockfish. The Pinnacle goes down to 150 feet, but life begins on this seamount top at 28 feet underwater, and you can spend the better part of your dive around 70 feet and never make it around the entire pinnacle. This is one of my favorite spots for photographing wolf-eels south of Canada.

On one of my last dives aboard Don Coleman's new *Down Time,* a group from the Portland/Vancouver area had just completed two dives and had come back to the dock to exchange a few divers and switch Nitrox tanks for two more dives. Doing four dives in one day when you are from out of town has to be the most efficient way to get the most out of one trip. They had just returned from the Pinnacle and Rosey's Ravine where, after completing some thousand dives, Don had seen his first sixgill shark.

The first dive I made with this group was the west wall of Pulali Point. While my buddy Chris Hanson and I were peering into the cracks and crevices, an eight-foot wolf-eel returning from a nearby seafood buffet excursion swam right under Chris and disappeared behind some boulders. We also saw lots of little fish, but I couldn't believe how large the lingcod were growing here.

After a choice of soups and hot dogs, the group wanted to do another dive at the Pinnacle, and down at 80 feet Chris and I found our first pair of wolf-eels, making six wolf-eels on this dive. The shallowest one was a male at only 38 feet in depth. All I can say is that if you like Sund Rock and Octopus Hole, then you are going to love the boat dive sites.

Dive Charters

There is only one Coast Guard-approved, licensed and insured, year-round dive charter service in the Hood. Don and Diane Coleman, who sailed the world before they settled in this fjord, own and operate Pacific Adventure Dive Charters in Brinnon. In their spare time Don is busy as a recreational diver and a dive instructor, and he is always on the lookout for new dive sites. I believe Diane, in addition to her many other duties, is still the harbor master/manager of Pleasant Harbor Marina, close to mile marker 309 on Highway 101. Together they run a well-priced yet first-class dive charter operation and routinely visit eight well-known dive sites as well as scout out other undisclosed locations. Their new charter boat is a remodeled 38-foot Chris Craft Commander Sports Fisherman. With this larger boat they still limit themselves to taking out six divers at a time,

The market/deli at Pleasant Harbor Marina in Brinnon is the first stop after a great day of boat diving in the Hood Canal.

The new *Down Time* boat on the Hood Canal. A lot of care and consideration for divers' comfort and overall dive experience went into the design and remodelling of this vessel.

but the added space provides more comfort and room than their previous boat and allows them to bring along an extra divemaster to increase overall safety.

I was impressed by how the boat was laid out with a dry cabin and galley below so you can wear your drysuit or wetsuit all day on this boat if you like. On the main deck is a sheltered wet area for enjoying snacks or viewing the local scenery. There is also a covered area at the stern for gearing up and going overboard. A specially designed head with a unique curved wooden door gives a wet or dry diver plenty of room to maneuver while seeking privacy and immediate personal relief.

Both Don and Diane are licensed captains and they seamlessly switch duties and titles according to the needs of the moment. On the upper deck or flying bridge you can sit and talk to Don as he steers the boat, bask in the sun or watch for seals. If you are trying to avoid the sun, next to Diane's controls on the main deck cabin sits a flat screen monitor that constantly displays some 650 local underwater images. If you want to know more about any of

the creatures displayed, just ask or thumb through the collection of books they keep handy in the dry cabin.

After my first day of diving with them, I only had one complaint: they tried to feed us too much. Before the first dive Diane handed out water bottles and bite-sized chocolates. As we surfaced from our first dive they had hot dogs and hot soup ready to warm us up. After the second dive Diane pulled freshly baked cookies out of the oven and put them on display while we quickly unbuckled our gear. Needless to say, I was suddenly forced to shelve my South Beach Diet plan in favor of a more exotic offshore feeding frenzy.

Seeing fish and other sea creatures may be a hit or miss proposition, but diving with Pacific Adventure seems to be a hit every time, which perhaps explains why over 70 percent of their charter customers qualify as repeat descenders. Don and Diane make you feel so welcome that once you've met them, seen their dive operation and dived a few amazing underwater sites with them, it's hard not to want to keep your dive gear packed so you can join them again as soon as possible.

Dive Shops
Ron Ault and Don Kinney own Hood Sport 'n Dive. In addition to collecting a small fee for diving at Sund Rock and lending you the key to the site entrance, the staff at Hood Sport 'n Dive can tell you

Mike's Diving Center is close to Potlatch State Park.

all about the local dive hot spots. If you are using Nitrox, enriched air or tech diver gasses, this is the place to visit.

While an experimental diver in the Navy, Ron was the first diver down to 1,000 feet, a world record that required 10 days of decompression time. Don, the other owner, teaches IANTD/TDI/SDI/PSI and solo diver classes. What makes his classes unique is that you can complete a course over a single block of days, which comes in especially handy if long distances are involved. You can literally eat, sleep and breathe diving for days on end with no extra cost for housing, as Don's courses are on site and at the time of this writing are all-inclusive. The store hours vary according to the seasons, but Ron and Don have been known to open the shop just about any day and time as they go out of their way to accommodate divers who call ahead and make advance arrangements.

Mike and Shirley Smith have owned and operated Mike's Diving Center, located a mile north of Potlatch State Park, for 30 years and have owned the Octopus Hole for the past 18 years. But Mike and Shirley don't charge a fee for diving the Octopus Hole. Instead, a posted sign marks the spot and welcomes you. Along with providing air and diving supplies, they also rent out an eight-person guesthouse that is so popular that some time slots are booked up to a year in advance. Between dives you can hang out in its great room or play ping-pong in the recreation room. Shirley wants you to know that the local beaches and accommodations aren't always as busy on the weekends and holidays as the TV news media like to portray, so don't hesitate to come out to the Hood anytime of year, and stop in at the dive shop if you would like to know more about this popular dive site.

Where to Stay

Along the shores of the Hood Canal are scores of state parks and camping areas as well as Camp Parsons, the oldest continuously operating Boy Scout camp west of the Mississippi and the third oldest BSA camp nationwide. There are also numerous RV parks, motels and beach resorts with or without spas.

When it comes to the local resorts, the Alderbrook Resort and Spa in Union has to be the most luxurious resort, with its indoor swim facilities, nearby golf course, tennis courts and fine dining,

Mike's Beach Resort is a popular dive club, dive group, and amorous couples' destination year-round.

but Mike's Beach Resort just nine miles north of Lilliwaup with 2,000 feet of shoreline takes the cake for serious divers. Mike and Illiana Schultz own and operate this resort built for a total capacity of 150 divers plus RV and campsites, but they are just as good at accommodating smaller sized groups or even exclusive cabin parties who want to spend an intimate weekend in a private Jacuzzi. My wife and I prefer the beach cabins with their large windows overlooking the Hood Canal. At high tide you can see fish jumping, seals passing by and eagles flying overhead. At low tide you can see the oyster beds and tiny invertebrates exposed in small pools of salt water. Not only can this experience be rather romantic, but also and even more importantly great diving is only a few feet away.

The Glen Ayr Canal Resort has 700 feet of shoreline just across the street from its main facilities. The owners have recently installed a locker/drying room dedicated to divers. Their beaches do make a good training area, and the three toilets they parked down at the 50-foot level, which are now filled with sea creatures, stick out like a royal oasis in the sand. But the real reason to stay here has to be the great accommodations and close proximity to Octopus Hole, Sund Rock and downtown Hoodsport.

The Sunrise Motel is even closer to Hoodsport, but intermittent and sudden boat traffic may preclude prudent shore diving practices this close to downtown Hoodsport during the fishing season.

After visiting and diving this scenic fjord (erroneously called a canal) a few times, I enjoyed it so much that I moved to this area and for a time, a dive with a harbor seal was less than 25 minutes away from my keyboard and mouse pad. You may not be inspired enough by the natural beauty to pack up and move to the

> **For more information:**
> www.hoodsportndive.com
> www.mikesbeachresort.com
> www.pacadventure.com
> www.glenayr.com
> http://hood.hctc.com/~sunrise/
> Mike's Diving Center
> 206-877-9568

Hood Canal area, but I do know that at the very least you'll end up making repeat visits to this area. I meet a lot of out-of-state divers here in the Hood, perhaps because the next best fjord is either in Norway, Canada or the south island of New Zealand. Either way, any adventurous diver should not miss out on the natural scenic beauty and the creatures calling this body of water home.

Oregon State

THE OREGON COAST

The Oregon coast is one of the most scenic coastlines in the world. I'm not just saying this because I'm a fifth generation Oregonian, but because I had the opportunity to compare coastlines around the world during my previous occupation with Pan American World Airways. Sure, Australia, Brazil and Hawaii have waters you can actually swim in without a wetsuit and without becoming cold and numb, but for sheer breathtaking beauty and for witnessing the awesome raw power of Mother Nature crashing tons of salt water in the form of white frothy waves against cliffs, coves and exposed shorelines, it's hard to beat the Oregon coast. The roadsides around Depoe Bay and Bandon are just two of the more spectacular viewing areas.

I like to split the Oregon coast into two parts. In the northern salt waters of this state you are more likely to find harbor seals, northern abalone and sixgill sharks. In Oregon's southern waters

For local residents, breathtaking one-of-a-kind views of the Oregon coastline are a dime a dozen.

you're more likely to encounter colonies of California sea lions and red abalone. But whether you go north or south, you will find giant octopuses, wolf-eels, moonsnails, clams, rock and swimming scallops and perhaps even migrating gray whales. Lingcod, rockfish, dogfish and sea stars fill out the lineup of ubiquitous coastal suspects. Ultimately, 27 species of sharks, skates and rays top the list of predatory creatures swimming up and down the Oregon coastline.

Dive Sites

Walk-in shore diving off the coast of Oregon can be very physically demanding so think high slack tide any time you want to dive here. There are some beaches that divers routinely access, but most open-ocean diving in Oregon is done by boat. Year-round divers rely a great deal on the semi-sheltered confines of bays, jetties, docks and other rock-bordered, wave-reducing zones. The farthest north that I've personally witnessed divers walking into open ocean water is just south of Canon Beach at Oswald State Park. It's about a mile walk down the trail to Short Sands Beach or Shorties, as the surfers call it. Visibility can drop to less than three feet close to shore, and the waves and currents can really test one's strength and physical condition. I have to give those divers credit, though; in Washington State almost no one would attempt to cross the waves and go shore diving off the outer coastline. Up and down the Oregon coast the names of the best near-shore ocean dive sites end in rock or rocks: Three Arch, Castle, Falcon, Gull, Otter, Pyramid, Twin, Johnson, Grace and even Haystack at Cape Kawanda. What all these rocks and pinnacles have in common is an abundance of sea life clinging tenaciously to the adjacent substrate and rock walls. Most are shallow dive sites of less than 100 feet; in fact, it's interesting to note that some areas along the Oregon coast don't exceed more than 150 feet until you are some six miles out to sea, and these grounds are rich in salmon and other commercial marine life at specific times of the year. The long stretches of sandy beach harbor little more than sea stars, sand dollars, Dungeness crabs, mole crabs, jellies and other smaller invertebrates; it's always the rocks adjacent to the beaches that form the life-nurturing tide pools.

According to Dick Erickson, owner of Garibaldi Aqua Sports, Inc., the best place to shore dive on the northern coast of Oregon is at the Three Graces Rocks, which sit just to the right of Garibaldi on Tillamook Bay. The depth here is around 40 feet and visibility is between 10 and 30 feet. Octopuses, wolf-eels, crabs and rockfish are the main attractions. Diving off the jetty would be the second

Lewis's moonsnails have so much exposed flesh that you can barely see the exterior of their shells. BERNARD P. HANBY

best bet. At 45 feet you'll find lots of crabs and other invertebrates. The rest of Tillamook Bay is mostly sand. Dick has done a fair amount of boat diving near the old lighthouse and recovered items such as a brass porthole window and an old brass spotlight housing.

In southern Oregon most divers stick to the bays and jetty for shore dives. My father used to dive off Coos Bay, Charleston and Bandon, but I would never advise shore diving where an ex-Marine used to dive. He barely survived several combat missions including being blown off the top of a Sherman tank during the Korean War, and this gave him an unusual disregard for danger.

For year-round shore diving locations, Newport Bay has the rock-piled Fingers, Crab Dock and Wacoma Dock. Coos Bay has sandy areas that are great for catching crabs, and some of the smaller bays such as Waldport and Nehalem make good spots for gear reviews, increasing your navigation skills, looking for artifacts and just having a good time hanging out with some lost sole or flounder.

Dive Shops

Dick Erickson's Garibaldi Aqua Sports Inc. has been in the same location for 25 years, so he's seen lots of changes. He says that dive shops up north in Astoria have opened and closed again because divers all have to come down to Garibaldi to dive. Dick is also thinking of retiring sometime in the near future, so if you think you might be interested in owning a dive shop close to Tillamook Bay (just across the street and a short walk to the water), you may want to give him a call. At the time of this writing, Dick may have

The white, sloping lateral line is the most distinguishing feature of the Canary rockfish. BERNARD P. HANBY

These rocks are a couple of hundred footsteps south of Haystack Rock at Canon Beach, Oregon.

the only operating air-refill station and dive shop north of Coos Bay, which is several hours to the south.

If you want to enjoy southern Oregon's near-shore diving, it's best to sign up with a local dive shop such as Sunset Sports in North Bend. The charter boat season starts in May according to Jack Spencer, the manager at Sunset Sports. Two of his favorite boat dives are out of Tillamook Bay at Cape Lookout and Three Arch Rocks. Charter boats are also available out of Bandon and Newport.

I also talked with Chris Olsen of Newport Marina Store and Charter one sunny February day. He would have really loved to be out with a charter that day but the dive charter business in Oregon is very seasonal. It's the spring and summer months when everyone wants to dive off the coast, but he says there are fall and winter days that are just as good, if not better, when it comes to visibility. Newport Marina Store and Charter most frequently works with dive shops out of Corvallis, Eugene and Salem, but they will work with private clubs and groups too, provided they are accompanied by their own certified divemaster. The coves around Bandon and

For more information:
www.aquarium.org
Sunset Sports, North Bend
541-756-3483
Newport Marina
Store & Charter
1-877-867-4470

Depoe Bay look like great spots to check out diving from a boat too.

One place every diver visiting or living in Oregon should see is the Oregon Coast Aquarium just south of the bridge in Newport. It's got every creature you would see on a typical West Coast dive without the necessity of donning a mask and drysuit. You can also spend a week visiting all the parks and coastal tide pools to see migrating as well as sessile sea life. Oregon State Parks puts out a separate map for each of these endeavors as well as one for lighthouse touring enthusiasts. There's a lot to see above and below the coastal waters of Oregon, and for generations of my family it's been a tradition to explore this beautiful region. Whether you settle down here for 150-plus years as my family has or just visit for the weekend, you should have a memorable time and some great dives too.

Freshwater Dives

WARPLANES AND OTHER RELICS

Recently *Evening Magazine* on television featured a story called "What's under Lake Washington," a topic I had been researching just three weeks earlier. The TV crew showed salvage diver Bob Mester dropping side sonar equipment into the water and next we saw the outline of a wreck on the monitor. The voice-over explained that some 47 planes and more than 100 boats have been located on the bottom of the lake and that the fresh water keeps them in good condition. They showed the sunken 1918 ferryboat *Falcon* at 190 feet, then the remains of a plane scattered on and between layers of mud and silt. A tech diver, carrying two stage bottles in addition to the twin tanks on his back, spun a water-worn rubber wheel on exposed landing gear before the camera cut to 18 coal cars that had sunk in 200 feet of water near Mercer Island in 1875. In just a few minutes the film crew showed what must have taken thousands of hours to locate and hundreds of dives to photograph, explore and, in some cases, bring to the surface and place in museums.

It's absolutely amazing what ordinary people working with commonly available equipment have found in Lake Washington over the years. Sand Point Naval Station, formerly located along the northwestern shoreline on what is now Magnuson Park, was a busy training center during World War II, and sometimes new pilots and new model airplanes created the perfect mix for mid-air collisions and other accidents to occur. In other cases, perfectly good planes fell off barges while being shipped across the lake to Boeing Field in Renton or planes struck pilings while landing, flipped over and sank. Some of the warplanes discovered in the lake over the years include a fully armed PB4Y-2 Privateer four-engine bomber, a Lockheed PV2D Harpoon patrol bomber, two Curtiss SB2C Helldiver bombers, two Gruman F4F Wildcat fighters, a couple of Gruman TBF-1 Avenger torpedo bombers, several Corsair fighter planes, a 1940 Republic Seabee amphibious plane, a Vultee BT-13 Valiant basic trainer and one warplane that was as big as a 737—a PBM-5 Mariner patrol craft.

Mount Rainier vista (14,400 feet) taken at Seward Park on the shores of Lake Washington. ISTOCKPHOTO

Over the years the Navy as well as private salvage operators have recovered some of these planes, but the Navy considers all of its planes, sunk or otherwise, still its property. Apparently the Navy only considers its property abandoned in cases where private parties are trying to sue after a derelict has caused damage to civilian vessels or property. However, the Navy did lose one court battle concerning a Curtiss SB2C Helldiver bomber raised near Juanita Point from 150 feet of water. It had been used for military training exercises then discarded on purpose into the lake.

Of the other recovered warplanes, one of the Corsairs is now at the Seattle Museum of Flight, and the Seabee was recovered from a depth of 73 feet. The Navy tried to recover the PB4Y-2 Privateer bomber but stopped after the loss of its two inboard engines, then tried to raise the PBM-5 Mariner but discontinued that effort after snapping the plane into sections. However, a Navy crew did salvage the nose engine of a Gruman Avenger as well as a section of the aft fuselage where the ventral guns were located, the area presumably occupied by a missing crewman. This list makes it sound like the Navy is better at wrecking planes than it is at salvage operations but the truth is, the Navy doesn't go out of its way to advertise its positive salvage operations, such as how many functional 500-pound bombs and other classified or dangerous military items they have recovered from the depths of Lake Washington.

For the past couple of decades professional groups such as the Inner Space Exploration Team and the Submerged Cultural Resource Exploration Team (SCRET) (pronounced "secret") have been locating and video-recording the majority of these sites. SCRET also has an extensive web site that gives excellent views of the wrecks, the background on each artifact explored and a brief history of how each one came to rest at the bottom of Lake Washington

Fortunately, you don't need your own professional team or side sonar equipment to visit some of the unrecovered warplanes, but you will need technical dive training to visit such sites as the PB4Y-2 Privateer bomber at 150-plus feet or the PV2D Harpoon patrol bomber at 140 feet. Porthole Dive Charters routinely takes tech divers to these two sites as well as to other locations, some of which Porthole's Captain Mike Ferguson can't reveal to the general public because he is sworn to secrecy. Some of the tech diver groups he has taken out on Lake Washington include Fifth Dimension Scuba from Issaquah, Starfish Diving Inc. from Seattle, Adventures Down Under from Bellingham and a few groups of Oregon tech divers too.

Although the big PBM-5 Martin Mariner resting at 72 feet sounds like a great dive site, the plane sits upside down in 5 to 10 feet of mud and silt. The most you'll see is part of a prop sticking out of the silt, the bottom of the hull, a part of a wing pontoon and some of the exposed tail section. You can also peek inside gun mounts and open cargo doors and maybe spot some aviation-enthusiastic crayfish. One diver described this site as a one-thumb-down, 15-minute dive.

Once you've seen the warplanes, it will take you another couple of hundred dives to see the rest of the wrecks and artifacts at the bottom of Lake Washington. Mother Nature has also done her fair share of leaving mementos in the lake. For a brief period around 13,000 or 14,000 years ago the lake was part of salty Puget Sound, but it returned to a freshwater habitat just in geological time to endure four earthquakes that allowed shorelines full of trees to slide into the lake. The last landslide can be dated to between AD 894 and AD 897 and it swept 150-foot-high sections of southern Mercer Island a quarter of a mile down and under the surface of the lake. At other times in the past the surface level has fluctuated some 40 feet, although it was man who lowered the lake nine feet since 1916 to be level with Lake Union. What all this means is that below 30 feet near such places as Kennydale you can see forests of trees standing tall or remnants of ancient fish traps and Indian fire pits collecting silt.

Weather has also played a role in depositing artifacts on the substratum. Strong winds were to blame for the sinking of the barge that carried those 18 rail cars of coal to 200 feet. Some artifacts, such as 1870-era bottles, were just tossed into the lake by early settlers who lacked a convenient nearby recycling center. But a note of caution: it is illegal to remove any object that is over 30 years old from the lake as it is regarded as a historical artifact; one gentleman was prosecuted for removing some of the ancient sunken trees. The only things I've found in the lake to date are a few waterlogged cellphones, a drifting dollar bill, an empty wallet and a brand new Swiss Army knife. Perhaps you'll have better luck than I did.

For more information:
www.starfishdivinginc.com
www.fifthd.com
www.scret.org
www.portholedivecharters.com
www.adventuresdownunder.com
www.innerspaceexploration.org
www.museumofflight.org

Other Pacific Northwest lakes have also collected their share of artifacts. For example, a 1927 Chevrolet rests about 170 feet deep in Crescent Lake in Olympic National Park. The Submerged Resource Center team of the National Park Service found human remains near the wreck, which suggests that the car was driven by Russell and Blanche Warren, who disappeared while driving home on July 3, 1929. Solving mysteries like this is just one of the many adventures you can take part in under a lake's surface; I used to go up to the seven lakes near Smokey Point just to catch crayfish (crawdads) and retrieve fishing lures. By diving in lakes you might not end up on *Evening Magazine* or get interviewed by host John Curley, but you could discover that you have a deep passion for warplanes and other relics of the past.

Other Great Northwest Freshwater Dives

Sometimes when you go out to a restaurant and are faced by a menu of words you've never heard of before, the only way to taste a wide variety of items at one sitting is to try the house sample platter. In this case, I've collected a sampler of some of the best freshwater diving from Montana, Idaho, Oregon and Washington to whet the appetite and wet the dive gear of underwater gastronomical aficionados.

Starting with Montana, we'll dive right into Flathead Lake, the largest natural freshwater lake west of the Rockies. At 28 miles long and 15 miles wide, you could put the entire island of Cozumel right inside its boundaries, but at 2,967 feet in altitude I don't think it's ever going to happen. The largest island on the lake is named Wild Horse Island and as you've probably guessed, there are wild horses on it in addition to bighorn sheep and bald eagles, and you may find deer, moose or bear swimming to and from the island. Some parts of the lake are 380 feet deep, and milling around beneath the surface are some 25 species of freshwater fish, including one particular species called mackinaw, which grows to over three feet in length. And if you think fish half the length of your body are worth looking at, then keep a sharp eye out because, ever since 1889 when Captain James C. Kerr spotted what was later described as a 40- to 60-foot Mackinaw Ness Monster, people partying on the beach have been seeing strange things rippling through the water. There are several dive shops in the nearby town of Kalispell and they can all recommend their favorite entry points along the shoreline of Flathead Lake such as Blue Bay, Cedar Island, Paint Rock or Crystal Creek.

Lake Pend Oreille (pronounced "pondoray") in Idaho is our second stop on this journey. At 1,170 feet deep it's the fifth deepest lake in the nation. During World War II it was home to the second largest Navy base in the nation. There is no telling what the Navy left down at the bottom of this lake. Foundations of military structures including the brig can still be found at Ferragut State Park. For thousands of years this land was the summer hunting grounds of

Secluded corner of the beautiful Flathead Lake in northwestern Montana.
ISTOCKPHOTO

the Flathead (Salish) Indians and it's not uncommon to still find arrowheads on the ground.

With state permission some enterprising divers are reclaiming unique, mineral-stained pine logs that sank during the logging days of the early 1900s. Recreational divers have found a 100- to 380-year-old wooden canoe in just 40 feet of water. At the Trestle Creek recreational area divers have found old railroad tracks at 45 feet and two boxcars starting at 92 feet and dipping down past 112 to 125 feet. Diver Rick Inman and his buddies recently did a trimix technical dive in low visibility and, using a rope to do a sweeping survey of the area at 150 feet, came across a hand-operated railroad car, the type that sinks into quicksand in the movie *Blazing Saddles*. Because of its past history, this high-altitude lake has plenty to offer divers at all littoral levels. The best time to dive Pend Oreille Lake is early spring to late fall when silting and water runoff from the nearby mountains isn't an issue. Expect to see kids swimming in the 60°F-plus surface waters in the summer but plan to encounter 40° waters at depth.

The next stop takes us southeast to Clear Lake, Oregon. Thousands of years ago this area was a lava flood plain, but in time spring water filtered up through the ash and filled the basin. Add petrified stumps and logs and mix with a few imported trout and you have one of the most eerie dive sites on this planet. It's like floating above a 40°F liquid-filled alien world. The water is so clear that you may want to do a night dive here just to lie on your back while floating above the substrate and look up at the stars as they dance, twist and bend around your rising and expanding exhalation bubbles.

If you would like to camp or spend the night in a rustic cabin here, reserve your spot ahead of time. Also plan your dive excursion to this 918-foot-high site as close to summertime as possible so you don't get locked in or out due to snow. The closest dive shops are in Salem or Eugene although other last-minute food and supplies can be purchased in nearby Mill City.

While there are other great freshwater dive sites in Oregon, Washington, Idaho and Montana to explore, this short list should not only satisfy your dive adventure cravings but also entice you to try a few other popular locations along the way.

Warming Up to Cold-water Diving

Why dive cold waters? I expect this question from someone kicking sand on a tropical beach, but whenever it comes from a warm-water diver living in the Northwest it amazes me. Jacques-Yves Cousteau, myself and many other local diving enthusiasts have discovered that there are few places in the world that support such an awesomely abundant and delightfully diverse marine ecosystem—from large gray whales and giant octopuses right down to thumb-sized stubby squid.

It's well known that if you can dive Pacific Northwest waters, you can dive anywhere in the world, but what does it take to comfortably transition from diving the warm world to becoming a cold-water-acclimated Northwest diver? To start with, it's more than just renting or owning a 7-mm wetsuit, hood and thick gloves. It's more than drysuits filled with argon gas too. It's about keeping warm between dives by dipping your hands, gloves and hood in a five-gallon Thermos of hot water. It's about wind protection for your body and sheltered tank setup perimeters. It's about suntan lotion, lip balm, plenty of towels and chemically activated hand warmers. Oh yes, and hot liquids and food between dives plays well too.

Sure, local wetsuits are thicker and that leads to more volume that you'll have to adjust for underwater. You'll have to wear two to three times the amount of weight that you wore in the tropics, and this means you'll have to increase the attention you pay to your buoyancy at depth. But it's just a skill enhancement with a learning curve that gets faster and easier with continued practice. Short walks to shore in full gear and short swims also help you adjust to the extra weight. And as far as shore dives go, Sund Rock on the Hood Canal may have the shortest entry walk to reach the water while the Mukilteo T-dock and Seacrest Cove Two in west Seattle may be tied for the shortest swim distances before attaining reasonable depth.

Other things to consider before your first Northwest dive include buying at least one flashlight to peer between rocks to find giant Pacific octopuses and wolf-eels hiding in the crevices, and the bigger the light the more impressive the sights. Dive lights also come in handy on dark, deep dives inside some of the mighty artificial reef/

wrecks of British Columbia, for signaling to your buddy or finding your car keys after night dives.

Be sure to practise on land with a compass that actually has a lubber line and a rotating bezel before attempting cold-water diving, because plankton, currents and fog on the surface can be disorienting for even seasoned divers. Compass skills will also help you navigate the hundreds of sunken wrecks and artifacts around the Bruce Higgins Underwater Trails in Edmonds, Washington, the pillars of the KVI Towers in south Puget Sound or find your way back to the beach after playing with the seals around Whytecliff Park in West Vancouver, BC.

Most of us cold-water divers carry one or two dive knives and scissors either attached to the inside of a leg or in the chest region on a hose or buoyancy compensator. But if you take my advice and avoid diving through the thick local kelp beds, the only real time you will need a knife is to cut fishing line from lures and nebulous loose strings.

And finally, we all carry regular or Dive Alert Plus pneumatic whistles, signal sausages and mirrors on days when boats are more than two feet away and fog could roll in faster than you can heat up chicken noodle soup in the galley. Hey, we all saw a particularly flawed movie, and now all of us divers, worldwide, are extra careful not to find ourselves drifting unnoticed to or from the Bahamas.

As far as training goes, if you feel that your dive skills are rusty, take a dive/refresher course with a local dive professional. You'll receive hands-on assistance with choosing glove thickness, weights, masks, BCs and other gear, plus get in a local dive or two. Taking a full cold, open-water refresher course may be just the ticket to getting you comfortable with your new and improved dive skills. And an advanced diver course, in addition to enhancing your skills, could be your ticket to boat rides in the Hood Canal, off Quadra Island or Vancouver Island from Victoria, Nanaimo, Comox and right up to Port Hardy. Different dive agencies have different names for these excursions, but the diving associated with the trip is almost always great.

Whatever you do, don't put off diving the great Pacific Northwest another tidal exchange. Sure, I like diving the South Pacific and the Caribbean just like the next great white or tiger shark, but

I also love diving here in the Northwest just like the skittish little spiny dogfish or the rather elusive and seldom seen prehistoric six-gill shark. Our Emerald Seas have bodacious beauty and sexy sea life that are in a class of their own, and they make this area one of the top regions to dive in the world. Any harbor seal, dolphin or orca would tell you this too, but it's best if you discover for yourself how exciting cold-water adventures and local Northwest dive experiences can be.

INDEX

MARINE LIFE OF THE PACIFIC NORTHWEST

A Photographic Encyclopedia of Invertebrates, Seaweeds and Selected Fishes

by Andy Lamb & Bernard P. Hanby, photographs by Bernard P. Hanby

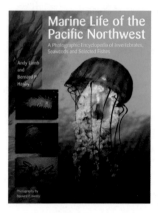

The most comprehensive collection of photographs of the Pacific Northwest marine life published!

With 1,700 superb color photographs of over 1,400 species, *Marine Life of the Pacific Northwest: A Photographic Encyclopedia of Invertebrates, Seaweeds and Selected Fishes* is the most comprehensive collection of photographs of Pacific Northwest marine life ever published. It is designed to allow the reader to recognize virtually any coastal organism that might be encountered from southern Alaska to southern Oregon—from sea lettuces and feather boa kelp through to the leopard ribbon worm, Pacific red octopus, spiny-thigh sea spider and gutless awning-clam. Each species is identified with photographs and includes a description with information on range, habitat, appearance and behaviour.

Andy Lamb and **Bernard Hanby** have spent most of their lifetimes studying and recording Pacific Northwest marine life and have completed over 4,000 scuba dives between them. Some of the species included in this volume have never been featured in print before. Color-coded for quick reference and including a glossary and full index, *Marine Life of the Pacific Northwest* is a must-have for scuba divers, biologists, beachcombers or anyone interested in marine life and beautiful underwater photography.

ISBN 13: 978-1-55017-361-1 · ISBN 10: 1-55017-361-8
Hardcover, 8.5 x 11 · 398 pp